Celebrity Circus

Books by Charles Higham

Theatre and Film

HOLLYWOOD IN THE FORTIES
(with Joel Greenberg)

THE CELLULOID MUSE:
Hollywood Directors Speak
(with Joel Greenberg)

THE FILMS OF ORSON WELLES

HOLLYWOOD AT SUNSET

HOLLYWOOD CAMERAMEN

ZIEGFELD

CECIL B. DEMILLE:
A Biography

THE ART OF THE AMERICAN FILM

AVA

KATE:
The Life of Katharine Hepburn

CHARLES LAUGHTON:
An Intimate Biography

THE ADVENTURES OF CONAN DOYLE:
The Life of the Creator of Sherlock Holmes

MARLENE:
The Life of Marlene Dietrich

CELEBRITY CIRCUS

Celebrity Circus

Charles Higham

DELACORTE PRESS/NEW YORK

Published by
Delacorte Press
1 Dag Hammarskjold Plaza
New York, N.Y. 10017

Manufactured in the United States of America

First printing

Designed by Giorgetta Bell McRee

LIBRARY OF CONGRESS CATALOGING IN PUBLICATION DATA

Higham, Charles, 1931–
Celebrity circus.

1. Moving-picture actors and actresses—United
States—Interviews. 2. Moving-picture producers
and directors—United States—Interviews. I. Title
PN1998.A2H49   791.43′028′0922 [B]   78–24451

ISBN 0–440–01210–4

For Seymour Peck
and Guy Flatley

Acknowledgments

I am grateful to the editors of *The New York Times, Los Angeles* magazine, *Action: the Director's Guild Magazine, TV Times* and *The Sydney Morning Herald,* in whose pages these articles originally appeared. I should also like to thank my successive editors at *The New York Times,* Seymour Peck and Guy Flatley, and Bill Honen for their advice and encouragement during the past nine years.

Contents

The Ringmasters

Celebrity Circus

Prologue: Interview with Another Self

Charles Higham's house stands high above Griffith Park, Los Angeles, overlooking rich clusters of eucalyptus and pine. Deer sniff the morning air, fog curls over the dragon scales of red roof tiles and coyotes howl in the hills. To the east, mountains glitter like agate against an ice-blue sky. To the west, the ugly beige sprawl of Los Angeles is excused by an ocean of early morning lights. It is just after dawn: the moon is filmy, a cataract-covered eye. A complacent gray Goodyear blimp dangles like a larva under fat clouds.

The house itself is a riot of contrasting art and artifacts: Haitian primitives commemorating church or river rituals glow with bright colors over Victorian couches and baroque French vases; Italian statues flank the fireplace, smiling across a plump brown Japanese cloisonné cat; closets glitter with English and German figurines and Bavarian glass; in a corner, Hollywood's idea of an Egyptian mummy case stands next to a handwoven Burmese house tapestry in red silk, embellished with elephants and temples and bells. The impression is of an eccentric private museum more probably to be found overlooking Regent's Park in 1899.

Not surprisingly, Higham himself seems somewhat nineteenth century in mood, a tall Victorian Englishman in his forties with graying dark hair and fair English skin talking in a subdued voice as his favorite work, Delius's Double Concerto, ripples delicately through the china and glassware of the living room. When not writing his "entertainments," or books about the stars, he is improbably engaged in writing poetry. He has published five books of verse in England. Poetry is his vocation, the writing of popular biographies his profession. He has written only one prose work in which his professional and vocational interests have met, as it were, on the margin: his biography of Sir Arthur Conan Doyle, published in 1976.

It is unlikely that anybody else in Los Angeles would be interviewed at six A.M. Higham is a day person in a city of night people. We take tea with lemon and honey and English ginger biscuits as we discuss Higham's career. How did he get started? "I was the only son of Sir Charles Higham, an eccentric and flamboyant English advertising tycoon and member of Parliament, who had a permanent table and a permanent river suite at the Savoy Hotel, a mansion in Surrey, called rather improperly The Mount, with five live-in servants and two gardeners, two Silver Ghost Rolls-Royces, and a haunted cottage called Wychanger, built on the site where witches were burned in the Middle Ages. Sir Charles was the most famous advertising man in England. He had a sign which ran two hundred feet along Piccadilly and read, 'SIR CHARLES HIGHAM ADVISES THE BRITISH PUBLIC TO BUY DUNLOP TIRES.' He also staged a Boston Tea Party in reverse by launching the famous Sir Thomas Lipton's tea campaign of the 1920s which persuaded millions of Americans to drink tea. He cannot be held responsible for the tea bag . . .

"I spent my childhood in silver, ermine-rugged Rollses and sumptuous Art Deco rooms, looking out at the English rain, or crossing the Atlantic in suites, coming down to the saloon for dinner in a white tuxedo at the age of seven to be joined at the table by an average of four internationally famous stars. I remember being partner at Bingo with Madeleine Carroll and Bing Crosby. It's scarcely any wonder that I was bitten with the movie bug from the beginning. I was so precocious that I began compiling crossword puzzles for *The Listener,* the organ of the British Broadcasting Corporation, at the age of sixteen. I was so tiresomely important that when I had my tonsils removed, I was operated on in an anteroom of the Savoy Hotel Grill by the leading British surgeon, Sir Geoffrey Colledge. The episode is in the history of the Savoy by Stanley Jackson.

"I had my own nanny, tutor, and valet. I never had to do anything except go down to meals the instant the gong rang and attend carefully to my lessons. Attempts to send me to school were disastrous. I struggled through five years of preparatory school but never passed an examination and lasted only one term at public school. I returned to private tutors, most of whom were cashiered army officers who smelled vaguely of briar tobacco and lost reputations and who all seemed to have either a glass eye or a leg in a cast. I remember one person called Captain Lancaster who wept so copiously while reading me an excerpt from *Lorna Doone* that his glass eye rolled out and became buried somewhere in a complex Persian rug. It took hours to find it."

After mingling in literary circles in London in the early 1950s, Higham fled the black and white of postwar England and an emotion-charged home for the Technicolor dust and sunlight of Australia. Turning his back on the family, he made his living writing hysterical "historical" feature articles for Rupert Murdoch's *Sydney Daily Mirror.* In these, he would have opening sentences which read rather like, "Four thousand maddened virgins fled the Sultan's palace in Isfahan on the blood-drenched night of February 7, 1432." Later, he became literary editor of the best known Australian weekly, *The Bulletin.*

What brought Higham to America? "I had been publishing literary essays and verse in Australia, Britain, and the United States during most of the 1960s. The University of California at Santa Cruz asked me to be Regent's Professor in 1969. This meant teaching poetry to a small class, giving seminars, and poetry readings.

"Most of the time, the class played Bob Dylan records and smoked pot. I sat back and read Wallace Stevens, seldom aloud. None of the papers reached above a B minus level.

Spelling and punctuation and American students were evidently strangers. It rained for three months without stopping in the redwood forests and my gingerbread 'Danish' campus house had an infestation of beetles. Worse, I had to deal with the other Regent's Professor, the celebrated critic and polemicist, Dwight Macdonald. Beside him, the rain and the beetles were pleasures.

"I was writing a book on Orson Welles for the University of California Press. For it I wanted to interview his favorite composer, Bernard Herrman. I particularly wanted to know the source of the libretto Herrman used for the fake opera in *Citizen Kane.* He refused to tell me. An irascible horror of a man, he had been banned from virtually every bookshop in the world because he would go in and demand books on a particular species of bird, and if it wasn't in stock, he would throw all the rest of the bird books to the floor.

"I told Herrman he would give me the source of the libretto because I had something he needed desperately. He laughed like a demon king in an old melodrama. There could, he said, be nothing I had in my possession which he could possibly want.

"I told him he was wrong. I owned the original penciled score of the fake opera itself, which he had lost in 1942 and had been seeking at vast expense ever since.

"He told me I was lying. I informed him with equal certainty that I was not. Finally, he agreed to a meeting in the lobby of my hotel. I said that I would give him a copy of the score in return for the source of the libretto. He had no alternative but to agree. He wanted the original, but I would not part with that—even for the score of an undiscovered opera by Wagner.

"We met in the lobby. He snatched the copy angrily from my hand as he snapped at me, 'The libretto came from an obscure play by Racine. I'm not going to tell you the name of it unless you give me the original.' I declined to do so. He disappeared into the night. I went to the public library. I discovered there were dozens of obscure plays by Racine. By the time I had plowed through the last one, the library closed.

The words of the libretto were not to be found. I had been double-crossed!

"Then, on an instinct, I went back to the library the next day. I found a Racine concordance, a guide to every single word and line in Racine. The libretto had been drawn from Racine's most famous play, *Phèdre.*"

Charles Higham sipped more tea. "Equipped with nothing more lethal than a notebook and a butterfly net I have dealt with similar people since. Welles himself proved to be a particularly dangerous rhinoceros. Because he was three times my weight, it took him three times longer get into his car to reach the people I interviewed and tell them not to see me. His volcanic rage pursued me for years.

"My book *The Films of Orson Welles* came out in 1970. Since it was published by a university press I had to do something special to launch it, and myself, on the American scene. I didn't want to go back to Australia, and my money was running out.

"I called Raymond Sokolov of *Newsweek*, who was on the verge of leaving for Europe. I had heard he had read and liked the book and so I suggested he stop packing and come into the office in New York to interview me! To my astonishment, he did so. The result was a page and a half in *Newsweek* devoted to me and the book.

"After the article appeared, Peter Bogdanovich, whose translation from white hope into white elephant in four short years in Hollywood had not yet taken place, was so incensed by it that he attacked me in *The New York Times.* I replied in a satirical interview with myself, and the result was that Seymour Peck, the brilliant and all-powerful editor of the *Times* Arts and Leisure section, took me on as a regular contributor.

"It was the beginning of the happiest professional association of my life. And Guy Flatley, his assistant, has remained a close friend."

What, I asked Mr. Higham, had been his main problem in the eight years he had lived in Hollywood? "The mispronunciation of my name. Invariably, it is rhymed with *Brigham* as in *Young.* So I have devised a poem for talk-show hosts and others whose mistake might be made public. It reads:

My name is not Higgam
But sounds just like Hyam.
You don't have to dig 'im,
As long as you buy 'im!

"Sometimes, it works."

What was it like, coming to Hollywood? "Less pleasant than it had seemed when I visited it. Then, when I was a foreign something-or-other, studio limousines would greet me at the door of my hotel and sweep me off to various exotic destinations. I remember interviewing David O. Selznick, Walt Disney, and Sam Goldwyn all on the same day.

"Suddenly, I had to conduct interviews without any means of transportation. I couldn't drive, and had a complete mechanical block at the time which prevented me from learning. I had to take buses, which in Los Angeles are the slowest and sleaziest in the world, and then walk several miles, often uphill, to interview stars for *The New York Times!*

"Not to be able to drive was to be a leper even though I happened to represent the most influential newspaper in the country!"

Had anyone proved impossible? "Yes. Many. Especially the late Miriam Hopkins. I was introduced to her as an author who had written a book on Cecil B. DeMille. She said, 'Why?' When we arrived at a dinner at University of Southern California in honor of the director Allan Dwan, a senior official approached her and said, 'Miss Hopkins I've admired you for a long, long, long time.' She said, 'Did you have to say a long, long, long time? Couldn't you just have said a long time? You're dull. You're stupid. Go away, fix yourself a drink, and don't come back!' "

How does Mr. Higham go about interviewing stars and directors?

"I try to enter the interview without preconceptions. I try to treat the celebrities as though I've known them all my life

—in a sense, I have—and this atmosphere of relaxation and informality makes them feel at ease. But one thing I always remember. If I ever let the conversation veer away from them to any other person or subject, their eyes will go blank and the interview will be over!

"I always use a tape recorder. The well-known writer Ernest Lehman said to me, looking at it contemptuously, 'That's a very cheap recorder.' I replied, 'Yes. I only use the expensive one for important people.' I like to use a small contraption which stays slightly out of the eyeline of the subject.

"Mae West was one who refused to tolerate the recorder, and after she discovered she was being taped had it carefully dismantled and placed in the entrance hall of her apartment until the interview was over. Her cries of 'No, no, *no!* I never do!' are still on the first two minutes of the tape, like the exclamation of a rape victim. Lucille Ball and Ralph Bakshi looked at the machine as though they were staring into the barrels of a shotgun. Paul Anka hugged it to his breast like a child. Roman Polanski insisted on recording the interview separately to make sure I was totally accurate."

In closing, I asked Charles Higham if he felt differently now after eight years of trekking through the Hollywood jungle. "I'm still as fond of movies as ever, and of the daffy, un-hinged, unsettling, but delightful people who make them. I enjoy interviewing enormously, enter each house as a new adventure, and am sufficiently naive to believe that each inter-view is going to come up roses. So far, I haven't been thrown out of anyone's house or received more than three rude phone calls (one from Roddy McDowall and two from the second Mrs. Errol Flynn). Isn't that surprising?" As he shows me out, Charles Higham looks very happy indeed.

Sawdust & Spangles

Katharine Hepburn

This article changed my life. When Guy Flatley of *The New York Times* called me and asked if I would be interested in interviewing Katharine Hepburn, I could only say, foolishly, "Would I ever!" I remember I was warned I must not be a minute early or late. I called for the time on the telephone. I corrected my car clock. I synchronized it with my watch. I arrived five minutes early and sat out the period, crossing to the front door and ringing the bell at the exact second of 1:30 P.M. The door flew open, and Miss Hepburn was there, looking at her watch. "You're punctual!" she snapped. I couldn't deny it. I wondered what would have happened if I had been a minute early or late. I wouldn't have written a best seller (the publisher of *Kate* commissioned the book without an outline after reading the article). I couldn't have bought my house. Ah, punctuality!

———————— ★ ————————

1973

Katharine Hepburn opens the front door herself. "You must come and look at my Christmas wreath," she says, as, together with her secretary, a gentle English lady called Phyllis, she ushers me into the living room of her West Hollywood cottage. She walks over to the sparkling winter fire, picks up the green wreath, and shows me its intricately woven leaves. "I made it myself. I'm as proud of it as anything I've done." She so often plays embittered, broken-down old women on the screen it's a relief to find her as alive with enthusiasm as a young girl, cheeks ruddy with sunburn, movements quick and precise, her figure almost as attractively skinny as it was when she played *The Philadelphia Story* more than thirty years ago.

Her living room has the leathery simplicity of an old sea captain's. Above the cheerful fire welcoming the visitor on a chilly, foggy California afternoon, stands a handsome model of an antique sailing ship, and on the walls sparkling landscapes of Cuba, exquisitely painted by Hepburn herself. She curls up contentedly as a cat in a big black chair, looking affectionately around the room as though seeing it for the first time: reflected flames flickering on brassware, wood rubbed to a fine polish.

At sixty-four, the star has the same agreeably shiny, well-worn look, an Alice-Sit-by-the-Fire with the fine lines of a Connecticut gentlewoman, cheekbones delicately chiseled, nose sharply patrician, jaw strong and determined, and a mind of piercing sharpness which can throw cold water on all pretentiousness. Only the smoky, blue-green eyes suggest the pain she obviously still feels six years after the death of her adored companion, Spencer Tracy.

She is still smarting, too, at the intrusive discussion of their relationship in Garson Kanin's book, *Tracy and Hepburn.* Indeed, she would not discuss the book at all, and it is well known in Hollywood that she and her close friend, director George Cukor, crossed the Kanins off their guest list when the memoir appeared. She prefers to begin by discussing Anthony Harvey's ABC-TV production of Tennessee Williams's *The Glass Menagerie* in which she plays the faded Southern belle Amanda Wingfield, with Sam Waterston and Michael Moriarty also in the cast.

"It's a great play. It says more about what a lack of money can do to human beings than any play I know. Tennessee put all his early suffering, his early frustration into it. Amanda is the most tenderly observed, the most accessible woman he ever created. And I understand her. Father was a Southerner

—a Virginian. Very few people know that. They think I'm 'pure' New England.

"I had aunts, cousins I could base the character on. It's true, I worked with a couple of Southern ladies on my accent. But I didn't need to brush up very much. I *remembered,* you see."

Phyllis serves tea from a handsome silver pot, and Hepburn, still curled up in the chair, indicates a table crowded with a festive array of cookies, cakes, and pies. I pick up a ginger snap. "And you must try my Thanksgiving mince pie. I baked it myself!" Hepburn proudly says as I mention how moving I found a scene in which Amanda recalls her life in the Deep South. "The dress I wore in that scene was the wedding dress I wore in the stage version of *The Philadelphia Story.*" And it still fitted perfectly? Hepburn throws back her head and roars with laughter, and Phyllis, startled, almost upsets her teacup. "That's a *lovely* compliment!" Hepburn says. "But, well, no"—her voice is pure Tracy Lord—"Not *exactly.* I simply said to the wardrobe lady, 'Let it out a little at the back!' "

She had, of course, seen Laurette Taylor as Amanda in the original stage production of *The Glass Menagerie?* "Yes, I saw Laurette several times in it. I first saw her act it in Chicago. I went backstage. She was hefty, and round, with very, very fine hair which was all done up in rags, and she had little pots around her, with colored makeup in them. She *fascinated* me. She and Spencer Tracy had the same quality—they never *drove* a part, they just sort of *let it happen.* I think they're the two best actors I've ever seen.

"The great thing about Laurette as Amanda was that you were never aware of her giving a performance. You never saw the wheels go round. Spencer did the same thing. They would totally absorb a part so that when they were called upon to do it, it just sort of 'happened.' If anything went wrong, they would just go along with it. In the first scene I ever played with Spencer in *Woman of the Year,* I knocked over a glass of water. He handed me his handkerchief and I thought, Oh, you old so-and-so, you're going to make me mop it up right in the middle of a scene! So I started to mop it and the water started to go down under the table and he just stood there watching me. He wasn't thrown at all."

Hepburn hands me sugar for my tea, and as I take it from her, we manage to drop the sugar bowl. Now Hepburn, Phyllis, and I are on all fours, looking for fugitive lumps. Hepburn jumps up, grinning, and her grin doesn't vanish even when I bring up the topic of Tony Richardson's American Film Theatre production of Edward Albee's *A Delicate Balance,* in which she plays a Connecticut matriarch. The play, about two intruders who disrupt a self-contained Connecticut household, had at first not attracted her.

"When Ely Landau suggested I do it, I said, 'Oh, no. What's all this about?' I'm a simple, nice person. I like to make Christmas wreaths, sweep floors. I don't understand all this complicated stuff. I'm rather like my sister who's a farmer and says that the most difficult thing she likes to attempt is carrying two pails of milk over a fence.

"My *God,* that's a depressing play! I played it in order to be able to understand what it was all about. It was only when I actually acted it out that I understood it. It's about self-protection. I think we are all *enormously* self-protective. I identified with these people who resented the intruders into their privacy, and I think that's what made me, after not wanting to do it at all, finally decide to go ahead. I'm a very private person. Here were these people, with their own set lives, miserable though they might be, and they wanted to keep their 'shell' intact. When two people came in and established a position in the household, they became threatening. The intruders expressed opinions. You don't want people to express opinions in your house, you only want your *own* opinion to be expressed. I think all of us banish people when they intrude—in any sense. Yes, I grasped the play finally. But it wasn't easy."

She also hadn't wanted to play *Coco,* the 1969 musical about Coco Chanel, which she had acted on Broadway. Was that because it was hard for someone who likes to live casually, who wears slacks, and has her hair done up in a bun on top of her head, to play a woman who was the very exemplar of high fashion? "Oh, my God, yes, but the problem was eased by the fact that Chanel was not fancy, that the essence of her style was simplicity. Exactly what I appreciate most. I was scared to death to meet her. I had worn the same clothes for forty years, literally, even the shoes. I thought, if I don't like her, and I have to play her, it will be an agony. Finally, Alan Lerner said, 'Don't be silly, you'll like her.'

"So we went to her apartment over her salon in Paris. I brought her a little African brass medallion. I didn't give it to her, I left it on a table with a note. It was hard to talk to her. She spoke only French and my French is very faltering. We had a delicious lunch and she—after a carefully delayed great entrance—was enchanting. Alan and I went to see her fashion show afterward, sitting on the stairs. Then she went back to her apartment and found the medallion. She was like a little girl, she was so tremendously pleased by discovering the gift. I liked her at once, she was amusing, tough in a good sense, and fun. She got to me."

There was, of course, that moment in *Coco* when Chanel descended the stairs, looked hard at the audience, and spoke the word, "Shit!" Wasn't this very difficult for Hepburn, who hadn't uttered a swear word in her life? "It's true I'm the most unvulgar person in the world. But it was my idea to have her say 'shit.' I didn't think there was any other way of expressing her total disgust. And you must remember she was alone. She didn't say it to anyone in the show. They didn't want me to use the word out here in Los Angeles. I wrote long letters insisting it be left in, even though I found it enormously offensive. We struggled to think of another word but it wasn't possible."

And then wasn't there an awful mishap during the run in which she was attacked by an intruder in her father's house? "Well, I don't really like to talk about that. It was when we opened in my hometown, Hartford, Connecticut, on tour. I was very nervous that night, because you know how your own people murder you when you go back home. After my last appearance there twenty years earlier, the local critics had said I was 'quite talentless.'

"I got home at two thirty in the morning, exhausted. A woman jumped out at me from a closet with a hammer. I recognized her at once: she was a trained nurse who had taken a job as my chauffeur. She claimed she was after her salary, that she'd never been paid. But she had. We struggled. She bit off the end of a finger."

Hepburn wiggles a whole finger at me. "We found it on the floor and the doctors put it back. I had to play a matinée the next day. My hand was bandaged for two months. The human bite is very dangerous. Miraculously, I never had the slightest infection. I went from one hand specialist to another all over this country. The pain! But thank God I didn't lose the finger. I could have been ill and wrecked the road tour. The show could have sunk."

Night has fallen now and Phyllis draws the curtains. Hepburn, who has scarcely moved during the conversation except to point out to me some new tidbit on the table, calls Phyllis to take the cups away. I ask Hepburn if she had her life to live over again, would she have done anything differently. "Well, I did have two great disappointments. Spencer wanted me to play both the good and the bad girls in *Dr. Jekyll and Mr. Hyde* and the studio wouldn't let him have his way. They thought he was crazy. He maintained that the good side of Jekyll would see the good girl, and the bad side would see the bad, but that they were really the same.

"Also, I would love to have played Shaw's *The Millionairess* on the screen, and Preston Sturges wrote the funniest script I ever read. But we couldn't get our version financed.

"Otherwise, no regrets. But if I hadn't been an actress, my life would have been almost exactly identical. I come from a settled New England background and I'm still much more at home in it than I am in Hollywood. Making pictures is like a 'trip' for me, fun, a child's adventure. When I was a little girl I used to adore the silent films, the big, big stars, Mary Pickford, Valentino, and when people asked me what I wanted to be when I grew up I said I wanted to be a movie star. Really! But when I became a star in the thirties I used to go back home as though nothing had happened and forget all about it. For much of my life I haven't worked in pictures at all. And my parents never came to Hollywood. I still go home and forget films.

"But the magic is still there. It's been there ever since I played my first role in a children's play, as Beast in *Beauty and the Beast* in Hartford, in a little Lord Fauntleroy suit and a beast's head. And it was wonderful to come to Hollywood when it was Hollywood, and live in a huge old mansion that once belonged to the silent director Fred Niblo, and say when Mary Pickford asked me to dinner, 'Oh, I never go out to dine!' "

How does she feel about Women's Lib? "I have been a very independent woman. I lived alone, I didn't marry, I assumed a masculine role, I earned my own living. I think that if a woman wants to be liberated completely, then she shouldn't expect a man to provide for her. If she marries, she can't really be 'lib.' She is bound to have to take care of her children— she can't just chain them up in a yard! And the animals have a pattern we can't ignore: the male goes out and fights, the female takes care of her young. I say to women, if you break that pattern—beware."

It is now intensely dark beyond the living room windows. Guests have arrived for dinner, and it is time to leave. In closing, I ask Hepburn to sum up her views, drawn from a lifetime of incomparable experience, on the art of acting.

"A lot of hogwash is talked about acting. It's not all that fancy! When Nijinsky visited Chaplin on a set, Charlie was about to have a custard pie in his face, and Nijinsky said, *'The nuances! The miraculous timing!'* And it's a lot of bunk. You laugh, you cry, you pick up a little bit, and then you're a working actor. It's a craft! You're out there desperately doing something you hope people will come and see. Nowadays directors, stars are constantly talking—pretentiously and a great deal more than they should—about their art. *Talk, talk, talk, talk, talk!* Spencer Tracy always said acting was 'Learn your lines and get on with it,' so does Larry Olivier, so does John Gielgud, all the great ones."

Katharine Hepburn rises, fixes a fresh bulb in a porch lamp to light me on my way, and guides me gently down some slippery, rain-damp steps to the street. "Life's what's important. Walking, houses, family. Birth and pain and joy—and then death. Acting's just waiting for a custard pie. That's all."

Mae West

I have seen Mae West several times since this piece was written. She gave an extraordinary one-woman performance at the Masquers Club in 1974, in which she reminisced about her life in song and story. She entertains beautifully. I recall a party at which she described a vaudeville tour, *circa* 1907, in which Sarah Bernhardt gave a condensed version of *L'Aiglon*. She was marvelous as the great black comedian Bert Williams, as The Divine Sarah, and as Eva Tanguay, the I Don't Care girl. She kept us entertained until well after midnight. One evening, an awkward little incident took place. Don Bachardy, the well-known artist, offered to draw Mae's picture. For an instant, she lost her composure. Then she handed him a photograph, taken many years ago, and said, "You can draw me from this."

That same evening, her companion Paul Novak brought in a large tray of glasses, each one filled to the brim with Scotch and soda. Nobody was asked what he or she would like to drink. I couldn't understand it. Next morning, I determined the reason. I remembered a tiny, seemingly insignificant detail. Miss West had reached for her glass and, in a Hitchcockian little scene, Paul Novak had shaken his head at her, saying, "No, no Mae! Not that one!" She had blanched and picked up another glass. The reason, I now hazarded, why everyone's drink had to be the same was that hers was a ginger ale. And she didn't want to seem to be different.

———————★———————

1969

"She's more available," the publicity man said on the telephone from Beverly Hills, "than she's ever been." It sounded encouraging, not to say inviting; and even now at an age between 70 and infinity, Mae West can still strike sparks in the mind. I had met her before, in 1965, when she was aloof, hard to reach, contactable only, in fact, by long-distance telephone from somewhere else. From Australia had seemed impressive enough, and later, when I booked the first call from a Hollywood telephone, the voice on the other end sighed like a dove: "Australia! Oh! How I admire those lifeguards!"

This time she was busy again, working on a television special devoted to her career, with Robert *(Sound of Music)* Wise at the helm, preparing a film to costar, hopefully, Peter O'Toole *(Sextet*)*, approving final proofs for an article in *Life* magazine. When I called her, she was bubbling with enthusiasm over all her different projects, with the odd Brooklyn drawl, dragging over the syllables, as heavy as ever with sexual ironies.

She lives—has lived for more than thirty-seven years—at the Ravenswood, an enormous pile of California gingerbread Gothic, looming above the groomed suburbs south of Hollywood Boulevard. In the entrance hall beyond the glass swinging doors, lush carpeting muffles footsteps, elevators sweep satined ladies down to dates with expensive "chauffeurs," a television screen flickers from hurricane-swept streets to the glum tombstone face of Nixon. Knowing Mae West's punctiliousness, I wait in a high-backed, vaguely "English" chair until the precise moment she has invited me. An odd-looking, emaciated woman walks past in gray-striped slacks, her face chalky white under a red straight wig. An Afghan hound lopes elegantly beside her. I notice the chain: it is made of solid gold.

Mae West's apartment is dramatically situated at the very end of a very long corridor. Someone is quarreling, perhaps

* Finally made (with Timothy Dalton instead) in 1977.

around a bend in the corridor, perhaps in an apartment: "That bust, that evil bust, has to go!" The words could have come from the script of *Rosemary's Baby,* and the solid door of the West retreat has a slightly sinister air, a tiny aperture opening about halfway up and a gray face peeping through the little iron grille. "Whom may I say is calling?" says a man's voice; I cannot make out the eyes.

I announce myself, and a series of bolts is undone, bringing back shades of Edgar Wallace and *The Door With Seven Locks.*

Suddenly I am confronted with a man who—I am not small —I could stand behind and not be seen. It is Paul Novak, weight lifter, former titleholder in the pectorals derby, and constant companion of Mae West for decades.

With a mournful grace, he shows me into the living room. I look around, determined to memorize the details. All white, the furnishings have the air of Louis XIV. The grand piano is covered with an ivory-colored shawl, and on it is a picture of Mae West herself in a silver frame. Enormous bowls of flowers, mainly artificial white plastic, erupt in every corner. A statue of the star, naked, glitters beyond a spray of imitation lilacs. Mirrors flank the walls, doubling the room so that the eye moves into infinite recesses. Carpets, walls, drapes, settee, chairs, all are white, with only pale reliefs in gold; one has the feeling of being inside an enormously expensive box of powder, battling for air.

I arrange the tape recorder tactfully in a shallow dish of plastic leaves. The star's entrance is delayed with inspired deliberateness, the guest with his back to the door, the Nancy Mitford clock ticking away terribly, not another sound. She could be anywhere in the apartment, or even out. Five minutes pass, then ten. Suddenly, after that, there is just the faintest disturbance of the air behind me, the almost imperceptible swishing of a skirt across a silky carpet.

Instinctively, still not absolutely certain she has arrived, I get up. Paul Novak cuts across my awareness of her by bringing forward a third presence: a creature cradled with lidless, unblinking eyes, shrewd as a banker's, in his arms. It uncoils like a lazy child, covered in fine hair, and the eyes look at me with liquid half-interest. "Meet our African woolly monkey," Mae West says, as I politely but gingerly squeeze a languid paw as thin as a leaf.

The monkey and his keeper withdraw, and Miss West motions me to sit down. She is dressed in a long white garment, richly ceremonial, which disappointingly covers her body from neck to ankle. Her hair is vaguely eighteenth century, a brassy gold, with ringlets framing a face tiny, precise, scarcely lined, and pretty as her monkey's. The eyes are smoky, blue, and impenetrable, conveying, like the hands that pluck at the dress, an extraordinary toughness and resilience. She has boxed time and death to the floor of the ring, and the referee has stopped counting. No more bells are clanging for her, and if she does finally go, the lucky ones can always go up and see her some time.

She is genial at first, until I turn on the tape-recorder switch. A small but determined hand crawls through the plastic leaves after the thin black snake of the microphone wire. "What's that?" "A tape recorder." "Oh, no, no, no, I never do!" "Why not?" *"Because I don't, that's why!"* She leaves the room abruptly, and her companion comes in, picks up the recorder, and deposits it somewhere out of sight. A moment later he returns and silently and disapprovingly hands me several pieces of paper and a pencil. Then Miss West also reappears, and graciously permits the interview.

I begin by asking her about the furnishings of her home. "I came out here in the early thirties," she says. "And just moved right in. Well, the studio just wouldn't let me live in *a simple style!* So you know what they did? They hired their art director, their top man at Paramount, Hans Dreier, to do the whole apartment out the way a star should be accustomed to! So they took the Louis the Fourteenth stuff they had around and moved it all in. And I haven't changed it, except when the carpets wore out, ever since, dear." Suddenly I realize where I have seen those furnishings before: in Rudolph Valentino's silent version of *Monsieur Beaucaire* . . . they had been in his bedroom.

She talks about the whole of her life from her birth in

Brooklyn on August 17, 1893, to Battling Jack West, a fist-happy Anglo-Irishman. She acquired an image at the age of four, when she made her mother buy a blond, blue-eyed doll with a lilac dress—and acquired, too, a lifelong passion for lilac. On the stage from moppet level, she stormed through vaudeville beginnings to a smash hit in 1911 in *A la Broadway and Hello, Paris,* wriggled to bluenoses' shocked dismay, and yet preserved a strict health code: "I hated drinking, heavy drinking, even then, dear, and I wouldn't stand anything obscene in conversation."

For her, sex was something good, clean, and wholesome, and above all, fun; "I have done openly," she always said, "what comes naturally." In the twenties, she launched a career as a writer, devising her act herself. She created a show called *SEX*—the capitals were obligatory—and only eighty-five people came, scared away by the title, but after word of mouth got around, the crowds outside made it look like the Fourth of July.

"No one would advertise the show, dear," Mae West says. "There was ta-boo on that word, SEX! So I sent boys all over town with stickers! If you stopped for a minute when one walked by, why, you got a sticker stuck clean across your back . . . with SEX printed on it! And it ran three hundred and seventy-five performances!

"Then I wrote *THE DRAG!* It was even more daring than *SEX.* It was about homosexuality. I showed forty men dressed up as women. It was about a love affair between two men. . . . Can you imagine the shock it caused then? They banned it for New York! Now I'm just about to publish it for the first time. As a novel! It's still a social problem and it's even more topical today. It will be a hit, I know it will, dear. . . .

"They put me on trial for *SEX.* When they asked the officer in court to say what he was complaining about, they asked him if he had seen my navel. He said, 'No, but I saw something in the middle that moved from east to west!' Can you imagine the laughter?

"But they put me in jail anyway. I wanted to wear silk underwear but some old hag told me it wasn't Saks Fifth

Avenue. Luckily, the warden let me wear it. I went from the Tombs Prison—oh, that place, dear, the *food!*—to Welfare Island, and that wasn't so bad."

In Hollywood in 1932, Mae West went straight to the Ravenswood and stayed there. She hated her first script—*Night After Night*—and threatened to go home. "It was terrible, but they let me rewrite it, my way." Later, she wrote that the studios "were giant factories turning out the same length of scented tripe." She changed all that. "I saved Paramount . . . they were up to here in hock. By the time I was through, they were way ahead. I *saved* them, dear.

"They let me do my stage show *Diamond Lil* and *She Done Him Wrong.* It changed the whole world's fashions. I wore floppy hats and the world wore them. Skirts got longer and longer. More people saw me than saw Napoleon. I was a legend. But you know the best thing? I brought my family out to Hollywood, and that was great.

"I had a burning ambition, dear, to tame lions. So I got hold of a lion-taming story, and I rewrote it as *I'm No Angel.* I played the lion tamer. I cracked a whip. Those lions loved me. I felt such a thrill when they did what I wanted! And around the time we were planning these pictures I saw a young guy in the studio—oh, so handsome, so big! He hadn't done anything, I hired him, and his name was Cary Grant.

"They called me the Statue of Libido. I made more and more hits. I met Marlene Dietrich; she was near me at the studio and she'd bake me nice cakes. The one time I hated making pictures was when I did *My Little Chickadee,* with W. C. Fields. He drank too much. I was disgusted. I said I wouldn't go on with him. And later on he claimed he wrote the picture with me, when he only did one scene. I didn't like being with him.

"Soon after that I began to think about leaving the movies. I had everything I wanted. I was sated. I began to get interested in spirituality.

"I grew interested in the question of survival. I discovered that for me the Church could only supply a little of the answer. I found this wonderful man called the Reverend Jack

Kelly of Buffalo. He prophesied things when he was blind-folded, to people in his audience. He saw Pearl Harbor ahead of time.

"Soon I had evidence from Kelly and others of the here-after. Today, I frequently consult with Dr. Ireland, a foremost spiritualist leader. I go to séances often. You see, dear, even though I have praised the flesh and the enjoyment of the body, I have never drunk or smoked, I have kept myself healthy all my life, and that includes enjoying sex, of course. I believe that the spirit lives after the flesh has gone, and that we must look after *its* welfare, too.

"And I have so many troubles. But I won't lose my temper, not ever. There is this woman who just called me the other day. She has been writing me for years; she is supposed to be a fan of mine. Finally I arrange for her to come here, and she gets some photographs, stuff like that. Then she goes back to her hometown and claims to be a relative of mine, that I'm her own blood. Can you believe that? Do you see, she could claim some of my money that way, when I'm gone. Gone *on*, that is. I remember a priest came to me one day, and I said, 'Father, why don't you come up and see me sometime?' "

She is tired now; the interview is over. As I leave, the small courageous figure in the ivory dress, the long ringlets, turns and turns, gazing in a mirror, like that tiny fragile doll she had bought at the age of four, and made the store assistant climb to the very top of a tall ladder to bring down. She could still charm anybody off any ladder. The bodyguard undoes the Door with Seven Locks. And there, just inside it on the carpet in a corner, carefully dismantled with the microphone several inches away, is my tape recorder.

Jerry Lewis

Getting to see Jerry Lewis was quite a hassle. I hate airplanes. But I was a new contributor to *The New York Times* and didn't dare refuse to make the air journey to Reno to interview him. It was a horrendously bumpy flight through the mountains, and to make matters worse, the pilot insisted on banking the plane almost sideways so that the passengers could get a good view of Crater Lake. I kept my eyes closed the whole time.

Arriving badly shaken at my destination, I was surprised to find myself met for the first and so far the only time in my life by the star's own car. I was driven to Harrah's through the garish streets of Boom Town. The hotel was monstrous with vulgar color and noise.

When I reached the entrance to the suite, I was greeted by electronically operated gates. Guards hovered about. I might as well have been visiting Howard Hughes. When I arrived in the suite itself, I was astonished to find Jerry Lewis dressed like a child, in a tight period boy's suit, with shorts and long white socks. He spoke in an extremely subdued, respectful voice; even though I was some seven years his junior, I might have been his father. Then, in the middle of the conversation, the phone rang and he went to answer it. It was easy to hear his voice through the half-open door. He was screaming in anger. His wife shrugged apologetically. Throughout the interview, she had been knitting nonstop. A long line of thread led to a ball of wool which lay halfway across the floor. But she never took her eyes off him for an instant. It was as though she were one of the Fates in a Scandinavian fairy tale, weaving his destiny's web.

He returned from the telephone call and resumed talking in his subdued, considerate tone, right in the middle of a sentence. "And what," he went on, "do you think of the aesthetics of comedy?"

––––––– ★ –––––––

1972

"We're dealing with a disease, a *cancer!* That man almost stopped me from finishing my picture! I almost had a heart attack. Maybe I'd have survived. Just. But if that picture had been left incomplete, it would have very nearly killed me."

A furious Jerry Lewis is referring to producer Nat Wachsberger, for whom he directed *The Day the Clown Cried* in Sweden.* It's Lewis's first dramatic movie and in it he plays a clown in Nazi Germany. He quarreled bitterly with Wachsberger during the production, and the producer even called the shooting to a halt at one stage. Lewis, forced to complete the picture with his own money, is now preparing a suit, charging that Wachsberger never paid anybody and indeed failed to appear at all during the shooting. Wachsberger, on the other hand, is suing Lewis for breach of contract.

"The suffering, the hell I went through with Wachsberger had one advantage," says Lewis. "I put all the pain on the screen. If it had been my first picture, the suffering would have destroyed me. But I have had the experience to know how to *use* suffering. I think it's given a new depth to my playing of the clown, Helmut, whose agony is the center of the picture."

Lewis is talking in a hotel suite high above the stifling, neon-lit squalor of Reno, where he is winding up a nightclub engagement. On the nightclub stage, he is tux-clad and

* As of 1978, the picture remains unreleased.

tough, making *Portnoy's Complaint* jokes about toilets and masturbation. But now he is surprisingly subdued, with a modest, considerate, almost scholarly air. It seems clear from his sober manner and the tragic tone of the new film that Lewis—long worshiped by the French critics, but consistently chopped up at home—is looking for a new, serious image as an actor, as well as a director.

"Helmut, the clown, had once been internationally famous," Lewis continues. "But because of his egotistical thinking, his callous attitude, he destroys his own career. He makes a public statement maligning the state and he is put in a labor farm. Behind a fence are forty children—all Jews. The Germans use Helmut to perform for the children—to keep them quiet.

"I spent a year and a half preparing this picture: I read everything ever written on the period. We know Hitler killed six million Jews. But what I hadn't known was that seventy-seven percent of those Jews were under fifteen years old. Why? In the picture, the clown says to the Nazi commandant, 'Why must the children die?' And the commandant replies, 'Adults can be changed. They understand fear, they understand compromise. But children remember!'

"I'm shocked to be saying this, but as a child I never went to a circus. It cost too much. The one time I tried to sneak into a tent someone hit me with a two-by-four plank. It almost broke my back. The trauma of that was so terrible I was twenty-five before I tried to see a circus again. When I did, I fell in love with it. The greatest thing I can remember in my whole career was the Ringling Brothers & Barnum and Bailey clowns asking me to appear with them at the Shrine Auditorium in Los Angeles in 1965. I played in front of twenty-five thousand people and not one of them knew who I was. To this day nobody knows I did that.

"When I left the auditorium, I pulled off the wig and took off the makeup and I burst into tears. Oh, did I cry! I experienced a shocking revelation—that when a clown is through with a performance, he's nothing, nobody. The people had laughed and wept and applauded. But if I wasn't

Jerry Lewis, I could have walked through them afterward and they wouldn't have known who the hell I was. I trembled so much when I thought about it that I couldn't sleep that night. Next day, I went to a typewriter and wrote a twelve-page screen treatment, 'Two-Faced Clown.' One day I'll make it. When I'm ready."

From the beginning of his life in Newark, New Jersey, forty-six years ago, Lewis has been a natural clown. Virtually born in a trunk, he was already making himself up at the age of five. During school vacations, his father, a singer, and his mother, a pianist, featured him in their Borscht Circuit act. Aside from that, he seldom saw his parents. "The bar mitzvah on the Saturday before mine had a thousand people, with cake and wine. Mine had me, the rabbi, and my grandmother."

Lewis's extreme loneliness as an only child made him yearn for a family of his own. When he was eighteen, he met Patti Palmer, a singer with big bands, including Jimmy Dorsey's. Ten days later they got married, and they now have six sons: Gary, a rock singer; Ron, an adopted boy; Scott, Chris, Anthony, and Joseph. "When I was young, I wasn't disciplined at all. I've raised my boys the old-fashioned way, with spankings, sending them upstairs if they misbehave at parties, the works. I believe discipline is the proof of love. We're very close.

"Patti and I are as locked together as two people can be. After our firstborn, Patti had been told she couldn't have any more children. It was horrible that Gary would be an only child. Patti wouldn't believe the doctors and she had herself cut open several times. She proved the doctors were wrong. Finally, when she was pregnant with Scott, I went up to a hundred ninety pounds and got morning sickness. Is it any wonder that Scott is my favorite?"

After marrying Patti, Lewis continued plugging away as a solo act until he teamed up with Dean Martin in Atlantic City. They threw away the old two-milkmen, two-mailmen format of most comedy duos, and achieved a funny contrast between Lewis's monkeyish ineptitude and Martin's sleepy, sexy charm. The team became overwhelmingly successful. Producer Hal B. Wallis, then at Paramount, saw them, signed them to a long-term contract, and they churned out a string of madcap movies, including *My Friend Irma, At War With the Army,* and *Artists and Models.* Martin more or less went through the motions, but Lewis was constantly running around behind the cameras, finding out how to make pictures.

"Finally I knew it was time. I went out on my own. Besides, I was angry with Wallis. He's a great picture maker. But in terms of humanity, of dealing with people, no."

Lewis sighs deeply at the mention of Dean Martin. "I decided to end the partnership when I found I could look him in the eye on the stage and didn't like him. I haven't seen him in years. Ours was a love relationship and the relationship ended. I still love him as a performer. If anyone criticized him in my presence, I'd kill them. But see him personally? No."

After the rift with Wallis, Paramount's studio boss, Y. Frank Freeman, gave Lewis absolute carte blanche as producer-director-writer-star of a series of movies, the best of which were *The Nutty Professor* and *Ladies' Man.* The pictures made millions, despite often brutal domestic reviews. But when Freeman became seriously ill, "The green shades moved in. They promised to send a print of one of my pictures to a boys' home. The day it was due for delivery, they changed their minds. I walked out of Paramount and I never went back."

In recent years, Lewis's pictures have not fared so well at the box office. But that blow has been softened by very successful personal appearances, particularly a memorable one at the Olympia in Paris. "I heard that Chaplin was up there in the spotlight booth, night after night, watching me. He didn't want to be in the audience, for fear of unsettling me. Thank God, I didn't know he was there or I'd have frozen. He's the greatest. I would say he's influenced me, and so has Harpo. Groucho I hated. I always thought he was the original dirty old man, totally insensitive. But Harpo! He humanized the Marx Brothers."

Lewis's television career—except for his famous muscular dystrophy marathons and his appearances as a substitute for Johnny Carson—had been shaky, hadn't it? "Yes, and do you know why? I knew I was going to be part of twenty hours of trash that would never be seen again. Psychologically, I couldn't put very much into it. The temporary nature of television destroyed me. Essentially, I always have in mind that my great-great-great grandchildren will see me in my pictures, that I have to be impeccable for them. There is no way they can ever see me on television.* Thank God! And I hated the endless hypocrisy and lying, the crap, the stopwatch. My funny bone has no time for statistics. I couldn't bear the clock dictating when I would start and finish a joke. And the censorship—network censors are stupid, anticreative men. What those stupid morons don't understand is that if you're given freedom you don't abuse it.

"I ran into trouble on a network show I did. The southern network affiliates said, 'You don't need to let everybody know you're a Jew, do you?' And they also said, 'You don't have to have niggers on, do you?' 'Well,' I told them, 'yes, I do.' I went ahead and had a black on every one of the thirteen shows after that. So I lost a thirty-eight-million-dollar contract. One reason my lawyers have ulcers is that I've taken such stands.

"Television has been one of the most destructive forces in our society. Ask me about violence, and I'll tell you television has caused it. I maintain that if a man sees a killing on the news it may trigger off a sick mind. Sirhan Sirhan would never have carried a gun had he not seen the way Jack Ruby shot Lee Harvey Oswald in a crowded corridor. I don't want to suppress news. But if I were in control, I would suppress visualizing the news. Patti has done a heroic job of keeping the kids away from that.

"And television has made everything commonplace. When Cary Grant used to walk down a street in New York, the city was on fire with excitement. Nowadays, it wouldn't mean a thing. You've got to have dreams. Television destroys dreams, it makes everything real."

Lewis pauses for a moment before changing the subject from television to movies. "In *The Day the Clown Cried*, I've

* Mr. Lewis seems to have forgotten tapes.

tried to show by example how selfish we are all becoming, and that we must get back to being kind to each other. I've shown it through the central figure of the clown. Here is this selfish, thoughtless man, who has lived all of his life making people laugh, but who is at heart a cold egotist. These children in the prison camp, he says to himself, who are they? Why should he descend to entertain them? But as he looks into their eyes, he sees the love they have for him, and he becomes a human being. Their love overwhelms him. Now he is theirs.

"I was terrified of directing the last scene. I had been a hundred and thirteen days on the picture with only three hours of sleep a night. I had been without my family. I was exhausted, beaten. When I thought of doing that scene, I was paralyzed; I couldn't think or move. I stood there in my clown's costume, with the cameras ready. Suddenly the children were all around me, unasked, undirected, and they clung to my arms and legs, they looked up at me so trustingly. I felt love pouring out of me. I thought, 'This is what my whole life has been leading to.' I thought what the clown thought. I forgot about trying to direct. I had the cameras turn and I began to walk, with the children clinging to me, singing, into the gas ovens. And the door closed behind us."

Dinah Shore

Dinah Shore's press agent forbade me to ask her about her affair with Burt Reynolds, which was then at its peak. I remembered that everyone in Hollywood is conscientiously late for everything. I decided to arrive at her home ten minutes early. She would probably be in her living room at the moment of the interview, while the press agent would definitely be late.

Correct. She walked in the room at precisely three o'clock. Knowing I had no time to waste, I complimented her on her medallion which, since she wore it rather ostentatiously, was probably a gift from Reynolds. She laughed and showed it to me. I had everything I needed before the press agent arrived.

———— ★ ————

1972

These days, Dinah Shore proudly wears a gold medallion bearing the words: "For Big D. In God We Trust. Burt." The effects of her celebrated affair with Burt Reynolds have obviously been beneficial: She looks marvelous, not much different from the way she did when, in bangs and a snood, padded shoulders, swinging pleated skirts, and ankle-strap shoes, she sang "Yes, My Darling Daughter" and "I Can't Give You Anything But Love, Baby" to zoot-suited dudes or ponytailed bobby soxers all through the Fabulous Forties.

Her hair is as honey-blond, her voice as honey-sweet as they always were. Strolling into the large, cool living room of her Beverly Hills home, wearing a rainbow-striped sweater and white bell-bottoms, she doesn't look a day over thirty-five. She has survived as a youthful star and as an extremely attractive human being when most of her contemporaries have retired, died, or become mummified. It's by no means difficult to see what the Man who made the Nude Centerfold sees in this creamy dish.

Patting a melancholy female basset hound called Grock, Dinah talks about her new romance over afternoon tea and sandwiches in that lilting Tennessee accent which hasn't left her in all of her fifty-five years. "We met on my show. When people ask how we got together, I laugh and say, 'We are computer mated.' I had seen Burt before, of course, on the Merv Griffin show and other talk shows, and I had been attracted to him at once, even though we hadn't actually met.

"When he came on the show I liked him still more. First of all, and obviously, he was a dreamboat. Second, I was pleased to see he had a genuine sense of fun. After that we met again and finally we began to go steady. I think what binds us together is that we both have a fear and dislike of quarrels. He's Aquarius, I'm Pisces, which means that we just have to live our lives harmoniously; everything else is intolerable. We laugh together, which relaxes me. If he'd been the type of man who likes powerful confrontations, strong discussions, endless arguments, we couldn't possibly have gotten along.

"I'm basically shy and withdrawn and I can't stand any open displays of strong emotion. I also don't like exhibitionism. It's totally against my nature. When Burt told me about the nude centerfold, I was mildly shocked. I thought it was a very bad idea. Bad for his image, worse for mine. I said, 'No, no, no, don't do it. It's a crazy idea.' He said, 'It's a first, I think it'll work.' I told him, 'No, I don't want it! and he insisted, 'It's going to be funny.'

"Well, he went ahead and did it anyway. You can say I was overridden. I waited for the proofs, feeling pretty darn awful.

The day he brought them home, I was afraid to look at them. Then when I finally saw them I had to laugh. I just fell over! I realized the whole thing wasn't at all distasteful; it was simply the biggest put-on of all time.

"We still laugh every time we think about it. But the repercussions really are endless. Earth-shaking. We never thought it would have that much importance. The other day some friends came back from Tijuana and they brought us a copy of the centerfold in the form of a painting on velvet. It was six feet long and horribly life-size. Crazy!

"Actually I feel it's helped, not so much because of the publicity, but because it's all so very amusing, and because the image we both want for him is as a funny man. He's marvelous in *Deliverance,* in which he does some strong, heavy acting, but what I really want is for him to get a chance in a comedy."

Dinah, whose top-rated daily television talk show, *Dinah's Place,* is noted for its air of casual good fun, learned a need for lightness early in her childhood in Winchester, Tennessee. "I was stricken with polio when I was eighteen months old. I had to learn to walk twice over. My relatives always kept whispering about me at home, so I never was allowed to forget that something really terrible had happened to me. My inferiority complex stayed with me most of my life. My parents took me everywhere to make sure there wouldn't be too much permanent damage. Every doctor had a different theory. One would say, 'Cut that tendon,' another would say, 'Pull this, push that,' It was early in the Sister Kenny treatment period, and I had to have hot packs, constant massage. It went on until I was twelve; I can remember ten years of screaming with pain day after day as they stretched the muscles.

"I got pushed into athletics. My mother was a great sportswoman and I think it was a terrible shock to her when I got sick. If it killed her, she was going to turn me into an athlete, too. It almost killed me struggling through tennis and golf, but gradually I got stronger. I resented it at the time but now I'm deeply grateful to her. There isn't a mark left, and today I'm crazy about tennis. Of course I was left with the fear, would the polio transmit to my children? Thank goodness the doctors said it would not.

"That early experience made me shy and ambitious at the same time. I wanted to run faster than anyone else, and jump higher. I knew I had to do something to prove myself. I wanted to act, but there weren't any Tennessee Williamses around in those days and it wasn't easy for a girl with a Southern accent to get work. Luckily, I could sing. Every Southern belle learns to sing, just as she learns piano and needlework. It's a wonder I didn't learn to play the harp!

"My father wasn't happy about my wanting to be a singer. When he found I was really serious, he cut off all my charge accounts and my allowance. He thought that by making my life impossibly difficult he would discourage me. I would stay at home, and get married, have children, and keep my mouth shut. To tell you the honest-to-God truth I don't know whatever gave me the nerve to go into New York and try to work. I sold my camera, my radio, everything I owned so I could spend two weeks in New York and try to find a way through. I decided to change my real name—Frances—right off. I hated it. When I went for my first audition at radio station WNEW, I sang 'Dinah.' That did it. The disk jockeys called me Dinah after that, and I guess it stuck."

Uncompromisingly plain in those days, but with an irresistible energy and charm, Dinah went from success to success, including the radio jazz show, *The Chamber Music Society of Lower Basin Street,* and the Eddie Cantor program. There followed a succession of hit records, her "Yes, My Darling Daughter" selling a million on the famous old Bluebird label, followed by the almost equally successful "Blues in the Night," "Shoo Fly Pie," and "Doin' What Comes Natur'lly."

She became a jukebox darling, a GI favorite, and a Hollywood leading lady. She was at her best in a velvet skirt and fishnet stockings singing Harold Arlen's songs in *Up in Arms,* opposite Danny Kaye. She was also in *Thank Your Lucky Stars, Belle of the Yukon, Till the Clouds Roll By,* and *Aaron Slick From Punkin Crick.* To adapt the words of an *Up in Arms* song, she did not go around in a wonderful glow in the movies. "I hated them. Making them was so boring. You sat around interminably. And I never thought I was photogenic, I thought I looked horrible on the Technicolor screen.

"I was terrified during that whole period. To this day, if I hear some of those recordings and see those movies my knees start knocking. I knew I couldn't read music properly. Somehow I got by. I knew what the songs were saying, and by understanding the lyrics I managed to kind of breathe their meaning in the audience's ear."

She shudders when she hears from friends that they have seen one of her pictures again. "Now those monumental successes are played at three o'clock in the morning. I've become an insomniac's nightmare! Anyone who stays up to those ungodly hours to see *Aaron Slick From Punkin Crick* deserves what he gets."

Dinah's forties romance and marriage to George Montgomery reads like a movie scenario of the period. While performing on the Atlantic City Steel Pier with Eddie Cantor in 1941, she acquired a king-size crush on Montgomery, whom she went to see in *The Cowboy and the Blonde* with Mary Beth Hughes fifteen times. She still had the crush two years later. "In 1943, I was playing the Hollywood Canteen. I asked the people there, 'Who all will be here tonight?' And when they said, 'George Montgomery,' I flipped. I cried out. He was eating a sandwich in his military uniform, looking just dreamy. I told him, 'I'm a fan.' He said, 'I'm a fan too.' We laughed. Not long after that we got married.

"We were married eighteen years. We had a lovely daughter, Missy, who's busy being beautiful these days and doing some research on our show. We adopted a son, John David, who is doing well at Grove School in Madison, Connecticut. He plays guitar. Neither of them seems very ambitious. I guess it's hard on second-generation children, and I wouldn't want them to be under any pressure. We'll see.

"My marriage with George folded in 1962. Part of the problem was that he traveled a great deal, making movies overseas. But the real problem was that we were too bright with each other all the time. We couldn't tell each other our troubles.

The whole world had an image of us and so did we, a beautiful Technicolor image. We never quarreled; he never knew what deeply troubled me and I never knew what deeply troubled him. If you don't share your private distress and sadness, there is something fundamentally wrong with the relationship. In the end, we just drifted apart."

A second marriage, with Palm Springs contractor Morris Smith, who shared her passion for tennis, collapsed in 1964 after barely a year. She can't bear to discuss it today.

Meanwhile, Dinah had moved effortlessly from the forties to the fifties, collecting several Emmys and emerging as America's most likable square in the Ike and Mamie era. Her *Dinah Shore Show* on NBC, sponsored by Chevrolet, advanced her career to the point where she became a national figure. She loved doing it, enormously preferring the speed of television to the slow drag of movies. But it was her return to TV in 1970 with *Dinah's Place*, weekdays at ten on NBC, that really has been the most satisfying experience of her career. "I like the informal flavor. And I get a chance to sing. We do the entire week of shows in two days. We even tape an extra show just in case I want a long weekend vacation. That way I'm carried on a wave of enthusiasm from guest to guest, and that way I have some time to recover and get in some tennis.

"The only really tough part of the show is laying out the recipes. People keep saying we aren't as good as *The Galloping Gourmet,* or Julia Child shows. But we only have six minutes for the cooking segment of our thirty-minute show, while Graham Kerr and Julia have a full half hour. People think of us as a cooking show and I don't like to dispel that notion because it's enhanced my myth, but it really isn't a cooking show at all. In fact the cooking is quite simply an obstacle course.

"What we are is a 'Do' show. Almost everyone who comes on has something they want to do. Ethel Kennedy played the piano. Joanne Woodward did some beautiful needlepoint. Cliff Robertson made a linguine. Burt Lancaster did a perfect Italian spaghetti sauce."

Dinah generally likes to avoid very serious discussions of

religion or politics in her show, though these subjects are certainly touched on. "I do have very strong political views. I'm a Democrat, and I'm certainly rooting for McGovern. I think it's time a president stopped treating us like children and it's time Congress acquired more power of its own. They say McGovern's thinking is fuzzy, that he wanders and changes his direction. But I believe he can give us the freedom we have been lacking and that he will gave us credit for being adults."

One subject she has constantly dealt with on the show is Women's Lib. "I have mixed feelings about it myself. As you can see, I was always an emancipated woman, and I certainly think Germaine Greer and Gloria Steinem are doing a marvelous job.

"But as a wife and mother I've always thought that having a man go out and fight for you is a bargain I wouldn't want to renounce. Women seem to think they've got the wrong end of the deal, when in fact they've got the best end. Of course, when a woman works she should be paid the same because food and clothing cost the same for her. But if she threatens a man's job, then she's depriving a family of a breadwinner. Some of the Women's Lib ladies we've had on the show have shocked me. They weren't human, something from another planet, the enemy.

"I deplore that. It's always been a man's world and it probably always will be. I don't want to change that. All of my career, on the radio, in recording studios, in films, and on television, men have made the decisions for me, and they've usually been the right ones. It's been the same in my private life. I owe everything, my success and the degree of happiness I've achieved, to men. Why, as a woman, should I be ashamed to say that? Now a very special man, Burt, is making the decisions. I say to myself, Dinah, you're very lucky. Could anything be finah?"

Robert Blake

I liked Robert Blake immediately. But as the interview went on, I
began to like him rather less. He seemed aggressively opinionated,
and with theatrical skill he placed me well below his eye level. He
perched on a high stool; I almost lay on a couch. It worked . . .
while the interview went on. It was only when I left that I realized
the skill of the maneuver. Blake directed many of his own *Baretta*
series episodes. But not ostensibly. Now I could see how.

———————★———————

1976

On the *Baretta* set Robert Blake, small and nuggety, with a
wrestler's body in tight-fitting blue sweat shirt and jeans, is
berating the director and the crew.

"This speech I have to say—it's shit! It runs forever! The
sixth take, and every take the speech gets worse. *Writers! No
wonder I have to redo every line!*"

Somebody yells: "O.K., quiet, roll it! Action!" The scene
begins. Baretta is shouting at a crook who has tried to frame
him on a robbery charge: "Who put ten grand in my place so
you could find it and point the finger at me? Who, who?"

Blake plays the scene with fierce intensity and commitment,
making the stale lines spring startlingly to life. He's a tough,
slogging actor in the John Garfield mold.

He played Garfield as a boy in the 1940s movie, *Humoresque.* Blake strides out to his trailer, parked on a drab studio side street. With him is his wife, mother of their two children, a pretty former actress whose professional name was Sandra Kerry. She is said to be a tower of strength.

"Sandra is an incredible woman," says Curtis Harrington, a director who has handled two *Baretta* episodes.

"She was a very good actress indeed, and now she's proven to be a magnificent wife, who has seen Robert through career crises and breakdowns, which would have crushed most women."

Perched on a high chair, Blake munches multilayered sandwiches, swigs beer from an outsize tankard, and plunges into the question of what has made *Baretta* a top-rated show.

"I had been doing a lot of appearances on the Johnny Carson show," he said. "One time I showed a belt with a nude man and woman wrestling on the clasp, and Johnny had to fight to keep that show on the air.

"On the Dick Cavett show I told the critic John Simon what I thought of him. He wants to be famous so he tears everyone to pieces. I asked him what qualified him to be a critic. He started talking about working in a repertory theater in Rumania. . . .

"Anyway, those controversial Johnny Carson shows got me a TV audience. At the end of 1973, ABC had ten cancellations and needed a midseason replacement. Universal offered them me and a new show format, guaranteeing thirteen episodes.

"ABC grabbed the show, but Universal really had no idea what the series was going to be about.

"Ten of us here put our heads together. I came up with the character of an Italian detective who comes from the slums, just as I did.

"I wanted him to be a tough guy, but with a heart, the kind of guy John Garfield used to play. My wife provided the various running characters who crop up from show to show. One of our directors, Bernie Kowalski, came up with the idea of the bird—a cockatoo—who's Baretta's constant companion."

Why a bird? "Because when I invented the character, I gave

him a background of having been in the merchant marine. I asked the set decorators to show me pictures of various locations he'd have gone to, and one of a bird, the kind sailors like to keep in their cabins.

"Kowalski said, 'Let's have the bird appear,' and I told him O.K.

"At first, we thought we'd have a stuffed bird. But I said, 'No, it won't work. The audience will smell it's phony.'

"We auditioned birds. Ray Berwick, the famous trainer who did Hitchcock's *The Birds,* came up with some, and Lalah—called Fred in the series—won. He was a goddamned genius of an actor. He'd been entertaining tourists on the tour of Berwick's bird-farm.

"Trouble is, Lalah is a brilliant, high-strung bird and he'll peck you all the time. He'll get mad at you if you don't play a scene right."

Gradually, Blake has built up the Baretta character: "He's enviable and lovable. He's uncorruptible. He makes love to four women before breakfast.

"He had a wonderful father and mother. He could have been bad but he turned out to be good. He's an ideal of everything I wanted to be when I was a street kid, and couldn't be."

Blake's life as a child was far different from Baretta's. Born James Gubitosi of Italian stock about forty years ago in Nutley, a depressing New Jersey industrial town, where the sky was filled with smoke and the pollution poisoned the flowers, Blake was the son of parents so poor that the family existed on the edge of starvation.

His mother worked as a domestic, his father was a bum. "I wanted a father who gave me advice, and I didn't have one. So I invented for Baretta a father who gives him advice."

The family went west to Hollywood, and Blake, aged four, got a job as an actor. He despised himself, earning money on a round-the-clock grind when he should have been at school, playing games, and going fishing like other kids.

"I led an abnormal life," Blake said, "and I wasn't even earning money for my future. My family took everything. A lot of other kid actors of the time, among them Scotty Beckett and Bobby Driscoll, turned into deadbeats and died young.

"A few pulled through, but not many. I was miserable doing Our Gang, and Little Beaver in the Red Ryder movies. When I got too old for these I worked as a stunt boy, getting my limbs broken for a hundred and fifty dollars an hour. Hollywood—ugh! It was a meat factory. Finally, I got so far down I was an extra. I got into drugs, starting with pot and graduating to heroin.

"Finally I got some work as an actor, in *PT 109*, and in *This Property Is Condemned.* I heard they were looking for someone to play Perry, one of the killers in *In Cold Blood*, Truman Capote's story about a real-life pair of murderers."

Blake bombarded the producer-director-writer, Richard Brooks, with a barrage of photographs, résumés, and other details. He was completely ruled out at first, but Brooks gradually came around to seeing that this short, dark, fierce actor could be perfectly contrasted with the skinny, neurotic Scott Wilson playing the other murderer.

Blake said: "I had hopes that picture would make me a star. It bombed. The critics liked me, but I didn't even get nominated. All the upbeat pictures, the comedies, got nominated that year—Dustin Hoffman in *The Graduate.* Schlock like that.

"*In Cold Blood* was black and white. It was serious; it bombed. I was a basket case after that. I went into psychiatry, I had a breakdown. I had worked for nothing on the picture. I was flat broke. I went on drugs again. Somehow I pulled back.

"I put all my hopes on a picture about Indians, *Tell Them Willie Boy Was Here.* It bombed, too. The director had done a great John Garfield picture, *Force of Evil*, but now it was twenty years later and he'd been blacklisted. The spirit had gone.

"I tried again, *Electra Glide in Blue*, about a maverick cop, was destroyed. Finished. I was on the suicide trail.

"Other stars who'd come up with me, Hoffman, Nicholson, were big time. I was garbage at the box office. People didn't know my name from nothing. I hated the guts of Hollywood.

But I came back into the ring. I talked to Universal. We started doing *Baretta.*

"This week Baretta is third in the nation after *Bionic Woman* and *All in the Family. Bionic Woman!*" Blake groans, clenching his head in his fists.

"I try to draw Baretta from my own experience. I lived in the city as a kid, hung around poolrooms. I was intrigued by gangsters, and I draw from that knowledge in putting this show together.

"I'm trying to make Baretta into a human being. I fall asleep with all that detective bull you see on the tube. I try to find something Baretta cares about which will make it easier to act him.

"We did one show about selling guns to kids—I feel very strongly against that practice in our country.

"I'm also proud of a show we did which attacked the idea of young kids leaving home too early in life. What we said was: 'Even if your parents are junk, you should stick with them until you're really ready to go out into life, because the world out there is hell, and you've got to be really tough to face it.'

" 'If you run away from home, you're going to be running away from life as well.' Television is the most powerful propaganda tool in the history of the world. Hitler in his lifetime never got the exposure *Baretta* gets in one night.

"If you combine the Bible and every piece of literature in the world, you still wouldn't find the equal of the power of one night of television.

"But the trouble is, so much of it's dead. It's a depressingly accurate reflection of most of the people involved with it.

"The rot starts in Washington, with the senators who are supposed to be the watchdogs of our moral standards. The networks are run by deadheads, the sponsors are deadheads, the writers and actors—they're numb all down the line.

"It's an impotent medium, and American culture as a whole is emotionally impotent, sterile, dead. That's reflected in the fact that sexual impotence and frigidity are on the rise.

"People are politically exhausted, by assassinations, Vietnam, the collapse of the left wing, the collapse of flower power, and President Ford.

"TV once was great—we had the *Richard Boone Repertory Theatre, Playhouse 90,* wonderful live shows bringing the best of American theater. Look at it now! Then we had more heart, more soul.

"We're living in a dead culture. Only a dead culture could produce stuff like *The Six Million Dollar Man* and *Bionic Woman,* series about people-as-machines!

"In *Baretta* I'm trying to change things around, make my own rules, kick America's corpse, and say, 'Get up.'

"If I can make the corpse twitch a little, put ideas in its dead head, then I'll have achieved something.

"Can I do it?" Robert Blake strides out of his trailer and back to the set. "Goddammit if I'm not going to try."

Tom Ewell

Years ago, I saw Tom Ewell and Bert Lahr in *Waiting for Godot.* I never saw such terrific performances. Ewell was brilliant too in a 1950s comedy entitled *The Girl Can't Help It,* directed by the late and unjustly forgotten Frank Tashlin. This rueful comedian would probably have been one of the greatest of circus clowns. Today, he is sadly neglected. Won't someone write a Broadway vehicle for him?

---★---

1977

His face is a friendly ruin. His eyes are somber, his cheeks deeply lined. His hair is lank.

He once told Katharine Hepburn he was going to do a play based on the life of Sinclair ("Red") Lewis, author of *Babbitt* and *Main Street.* "Oh, you'd be perfect!" Miss Hepburn exclaimed. "Red was the ugliest man I ever met!"

Gloomy and picturesquely ugly he may well be, but sad sack comedian Tom Ewell, whom Robert Blake begged for and won as his *Baretta* costar, is one of the most gifted comedians alive.

I shall never forget him in *The Girl Can't Help It,* gazing with a mixture of desire and dismay at Jayne Mansfield's enormous breasts; or in *The Seven Year Itch,* guiltily awash in a late middle-aged love affair with Marilyn Monroe; or on stage in New York in *Waiting for Godot,* in a performance which the critic Walter Kerr accurately called one of the greatest of the past twenty years.

Ewell credits Katharine Hepburn with having brought him to Hollywood—after years of struggle and a stint in the U.S. Navy in World War II—for the comedy *Adam's Rib,* in which he costarred with her and Spencer Tracy. He played the henpecked husband of Judy Holliday.

Ewell said, "Hepburn called me personally in New York and said, 'Look, if you do this film, I'll do everything I can to be your press agent.' She kept her promise!

"She was wonderful with Judy Holliday. She worked like a dog to throw the emphasis on her with extra lines and close-ups. No other star ever did that.

"I use to visit Kate in John Barrymore's old house high up in Beverly Hills. She had a grand piano with a shawl over it, enormous wicker furniture, everything the way it had been when he lived there in the twenties. I loved her.

"You ask me what meant most to me in my career? *Waiting for Godot,* of course. There's a story built into that. I decided to do it in Miami, with Bert Lahr. It was just after the war, when it was fast becoming one of the classic plays of a generation.

"A friend of mine had opened a theater in Miami. I didn't understand a word of the play, but I had to do it. Disaster! One of the actors was a drunken dancer who wouldn't attend rehearsals. Another went into an oxygen tank and only turned up for dress rehearsal. We rehearsed in a boathouse.

"Bert and I fought. He wanted to play Godot for laughs. Here was this grim play about tramps and the futility of all existence and the theater owner, who hadn't read it, announced it was Tom Ewell and Bert Lahr in a French farce, *Waiting for Godot!*

"It was crazy. Tickets were fifty dollars apiece. There was

a huge contingent of Broadway types, millionaires, stars, John Jacob Astor, the governor of Florida, Joan Fontaine, Red Buttons, everyone, a packed house of a thousand people. A filet mignon dinner, champagne, the works.

"Well, we started in. I spoke a four-letter word. The play was full of them. As I spoke it a slow rumbling sound ran through the theater. People started to leave. They'd get their friends to leave with them. Eventually only my mother and my uncle were left in the theater!

"*Life* magazine took a picture of the opening. It showed an empty house! When I went back to New York and did the play again, twenty years later, it was a hit!"

I asked Ewell about Marilyn Monroe, with whom he appeared in *The Seven Year Itch.* "Marilyn didn't think she was any good. She suffered from a tremendous inferiority complex. It was very difficult for her to show up on a set. More difficult for her than for anyone I've ever worked with.

"She wanted so desperately to be good that she found it hard to do even the smallest scene. She used to vomit before she went on before the camera. Perry Como is the only other actor I've known who did that. He did it before he went on in front of an audience at a concert."

Ewell paused, and began to attack a toasted cheese sandwich. "Jayne Mansfield was quite different. She was devoted entirely to her own publicity. We appeared together in *The Girl Can't Help It* for the director Frank Tashlin, who had a marvelous cartoonist's eye.

"The studio was trying to create another Marilyn. I'll never forget the first day Jayne and I met, which was also the first day of shooting.

"Jayne was wearing a dress which was too tight to walk in. Mickey Hargitay, who was married to her, had to carry her on to the set over his head like a suitcase! She was stiff as a board! He deposited her on the sound stage and she stood up like a shop window dummy! I'll never forget it.

"She'd be looking over my shoulder in the middle of a scene. I assumed she was looking at Mickey. There was love in her eyes. Well, I snuck a glance around, and she was gazing into a full-length mirror! I couldn't believe it!

"She watched herself throughout the shooting, watched herself acting. I had to have the director take the mirror away. I couldn't stand working that way.

"I liked Jayne. She was sweet, devoted to her family and to animals. And yet, the stunts! At one time she had part of a set catch fire and had herself carried out of it! The studio police and fire department went crazy!

"When I asked if I could go to her wedding, she said, 'Tom, I've only got fifty seats at the church and I have forty-eight press coming!' The press never had a better friend."

If *The Seven Year Itch, Waiting for Godot* and *The Girl Can't Help It* were Tom Ewell's greatest triumphs, what had been his greatest disappointment? "Unquestionably, *Gatsby.* I'd been hired to appear in the movie of *The Great Gatsby* with Robert Redford. The director, Jack Clayton, called me and told me, 'I have a wonderful cameo for you to play. It will be the funniest drunk who has ever been seen on the screen.'

"I read the script and it had four wonderful scenes. I called him and told him I'd love to do it. I worked on it all summer at Rhode Island and in England. I really thought, well, here's a chance to see how good I am.

"Christmas Eve I received a cable. The cable was from Jack Clayton, and said, 'It breaks my heart to have to tell you that we're going to cut you out of the picture.'

"*Gatsby* had run too long, and I wasn't a central character, just a subsidiary recurrent figure in the story. And then the cable went on: 'We will have to leave you in for one brief appearance in a cemetery. Can we remove your name from the credits?'

"It was horrible. On Christmas Eve! I cabled back: 'Do anything you want. And if you like, you can say I just happened to be in the cemetery that day when the scene was being shot and I was photographed by accident.'" Tom Ewell's face looks sour. "It was tough. A great, great part— of a guy who went to all Gatsby's parties but never actually met him, and then was the only one out of his whole giddy social set who went to the funeral."

It was only one of a series of disasters which hit Tom Ewell in the 1970s. He was in a play which folded because the leading lady had lost her husband with a heart attack and she found she could not act just that kind of role in the play itself.

His ill-fated TV series, *The Tom Ewell Show,* barely struggled through a season, chiefly because the writers wrote the wrong kind of routines for him.

In the years of his unhappy professional decline, Ewell retired to lick his wounds in his hometown, Owensboro, Kentucky, where his mother still lives. He traveled about, living in New York, Scottsdale, Arizona, New England, California, with his wife and son. Rootless and probably not too happy, he accepted the job in *Baretta* from Robert Blake, who personally approached him. Why did he do it? "I needed the work. And I admire Robert and his wife very much."

Did he like *Baretta?* Ewell tensed. "If I didn't like the series I wouldn't be fool enough to sit here and say so, now would I? I never see the show so I don't know how it turns out.

"I'd rather not discuss it. Let's just say I found Robert Blake to be as creative a man as I've ever met. And leave it at that.

"Blake is the only one who wanted me for the show. The Tower, as they laughingly refer to it [the MCA-Universal Executive Building], didn't want me, nor did the network. They did everything in the world they could do to prevent me from being in it. But Robert wanted me. They refused to even call me for an interview. He called me."

It must have taken a great deal of guts not to slip back into alcoholism, which plagued Ewell for most of the 1930s and 1940s and which he even suffered from in the U.S. Navy in the North Atlantic.

Ewell said: "The reason I started drinking is for me and my psychiatrist. I won't discuss it. My family were farmers in the bourbon state, Kentucky, and they all drank. I was known more or less affectionately as the town drunk.

"I got out of drinking because I knew I was killing myself

and I decided to get out and live. A psychiatrist made me join Alcoholics Anonymous. I did.

"I used to give speeches on behalf on AA. I'm in my thirty-first year as a member. I gave up making speeches about the first or second year of membership. I realized I was being used as a star, so I decided to retire to the sidelines and work underground.

"If someone in California having a major drinking problem came to New York, I was able to see that somebody met them and took care of them. Many of the star names were very big. One of the big stars tried to commit suicide and I saved his life. It's part of our code that we never mention names and that we work without using our names."

Has there been a ray of light anywhere? "My wife is a wonderful woman. And my son, Tate, is making good. This year, at last, he put it all together.

"He wanted to be a lawyer for a while because law is in the family. Then he tried political science. This year he discovered journalism. He's gotten a job working in the office of the governor of Wisconsin while he goes to college. He's eager to get a job in Oregon writing about environmental problems.

"I'm not just heaving a sigh of relief. I'm bursting with pride!" And for the first time in a two-hour lunch, Sad Sack Tom Ewell smiled.

Julie Andrews

Most sophisticated people seem to find Julie Andrews too caries-producing for their taste. I always felt she had a cool firmness, a steely precision that relieved the marshmallow softness of most of her vehicles. I find her best on a stage: she seems more obviously in command, less overpoweringly brisk, more human and accessible. She's capable of encompassing a range of songs: sometimes it's too wide a range (she has a deplorable weakness for Paul Williams), but generally it shows a striking versatility. All right, I confess it. I'm a fan.

Getting to this interview was especially horrendous. I had to fight traffic all the way from West Hollywood to Century City on a suffocating day, get bumped from two parking lots, and finally walk almost a mile from the nearest available one through a maze of anonymous, 1984ish buildings to the office where the interview was to take place. Sweating and out of breath, I reached my destination at the appointed time only to find Miss Andrews wasn't there! She kept me waiting for almost an hour and then ran in cheerfully as though nothing had happened. I was still calm and pleased. I *said* I was a fan.

———————— ★ ————————

1977

Not since Luise Rainer went from winning two Oscars to oblivion in three short years, has any motion-picture star risen so fast or fallen so far. In the tormented 1960s, Miss Andrews's pleasant escapist musicals *Mary Poppins* and *The Sound of Music* earned enormous sums of money at the box office, but the fatal succession of *Star!, Darling Lili,* and *The Tamarind Seed* wiped her out as a superstar. Now she has begun to fight her way back to the top as a solo performer, with successful performances at the London Palladium, and at Caesar's Palace in Las Vegas, where she played for a whopping $250,000 a week.

In a world where purity has become a dirty word, Julie Andrews has remained defiantly wholesome: as brisk and fresh and bright as Mary Poppins ever was. She has never provided copy for the gossip columns. After an unhappy divorce, she has been serenely married to the writer-director Blake Edwards for almost a decade. The couple live in a romantic Swiss chalet at Gstaad with a brood of teenagers and children, including three from their previous marriages and two Vietnamese orphans—a family situation worthy of *The Sound of Music.*

Dressed in a crisp, cool shirt and pants, she sits in an office in Century City. She still has the narrow Modigliani face and the teenage figure she had twenty years ago; in fact, her appearance has changed very little since her Broadway triumph as Eliza Doolittle in *My Fair Lady,* back in 1956.

A better actress than she has been given credit for—she was particularly effective in a demanding dramatic role in Paddy Chayefsky's *The Americanization of Emily*—she has survived a blitz of criticism from the press. For example a *Newsweek* reviewer wrote that she played the love scenes in her last picture, the underrated *The Tamarind Seed,* like a competent dietician. One is curious to know how she weathered the bad reviews, not to mention the public's obvious disapproval of her decision to play a bitter, drunken Gertrude Lawrence in *Star!* and an enemy spy in *Darling Lili.*

"I pulled through largely because I believed in those pictures and disagreed with the critical and popular estimate of them, and because I had my family. Blake was marvelous. And I always preferred being at home in Gstaad to working. It's a dream house. The most beautiful view in the world. The best time is being there. We can close the doors against the world and hole up and hide. In Gstaad, I have always felt there is nothing that can harm me. Ever."

Still, there must have been some reason for the disastrous box-office showing of her most recent films. "I think *Star!* failed because the public wasn't very happy with seeing me in drunken scenes. I wanted to be completely honest in portraying Gertrude Lawrence. I wanted to show that at times she was almost silly. It was very hard for me to play drunk scenes. I had to force myself to do it. It took an awfully long time to work up to it; I even thought about taking a drink or even a drug, but if I did that, I couldn't have played it at all, could I? Finally I got the key: I found that drunken people lose oxygen: when they exhale they almost collapse. The diaphragm just goes. I used that, and I *think it worked.*

"The public couldn't accept me as a spy in *Darling Lili,* and that disappointed me awfully. The opening scene was the most difficult thing I have had to do; it was shot in a darkened theater, and it was done in one enormous take. They kept moving cables around and pulling curtains away, and it was a nightmare. There were 360-degree turns of the camera all around me. And we had to do it twice! Once in Dublin in a theater, and then, because the stage was too bumpy, in a studio! And then the film was not successful. Very sad."

Unquestionably, she has been a victim of type-casting. "I can't knock *The Sound of Music* and *Mary Poppins,* because they gave such an awful lot of pleasure to such an awful lot of people. But that kind of exposure does put one into the greatest danger. I won an Oscar for *Mary Poppins* and then went on and made the most successful musical up to that time. Now I can see that I was too quickly bracketed in one category, and I couldn't escape from it."

Since she is quite comfortably fixed, why did she decide to

come out of semiretirement and start again on the concert stage? "Actually, it wasn't *my* idea at all. Caesar's Palace had never stopped trying to get me for Las Vegas and I'd always refused. Finally, they made me a tremendous offer I couldn't say no to. Blake talked me into going ahead. And right after that, I was offered the London Palladium. But I'd have been perfectly content to have stayed at home in Switzerland."

Comebacks are not easily come by. "It's been very difficult. Agony. It's misery preparing, trying to get it perfect. It's very hard for me to relax, to let any rough edges show. I get very tense in rehearsal. I clown around an awful lot, but underneath the pressure's building. When it's time for the performance, I'm *petrified.* I go through *agonies* of stage fright. Especially if there's a song I'm not a hundred percent comfortable with. I did a Paul Williams song in London I wasn't quite right for. It was lovely, but I dreaded going on with it. If the opening song doesn't completely connect with what I'm feeling that night, I become *awfully* anxious."

How was Las Vegas? "Not enjoyable. The work that went into it was tremendous. It involved two performances a night, the second at one A.M.! There were large production numbers, and it was like being hurled out of a cannon from the moment I got onstage! The first three days were *hell;* on the first night, I was awake all night long because I was so geared up. And I couldn't sleep in the day, either. It was horrible."

There is always the pressure, too, of learning new songs. "Yes. I have to be very careful about singing contemporary songs. I'm told I have clear diction and unless the lyrics are very interesting, it sounds quite wrong. So many modern songs are merely repetitive. I can't sing oh-wo-wo-wo, now can I? It's *absurd.* Lovely when other people do it, but when I do it, it's just awful. I don't mind rock, actually—I get such a dose of it from my children that I have to like it."

Miss Andrews is a "technical" singer, one who is thrown completely by the slightest error in an orchestra. "I'm not a natural singer, it's just sheer, slogging hard work for me. I am filled with envy for natural singers, for people who can just get up and sing cold. I can't. I sound like a rusty engine when I try to. It takes six weeks of solid practicing before I'm ready to even let a *soul* hear me. I've gone on training all my life with a wonderful lady called Madame Stiles Allen, who used to be a fine dramatic singer in opera and oratorio."

Miss Andrews breaks off to look at the color sketches of her costumes for a new show, and instantly, firmly, decides on the precise shade of green she wants. Her manner is still charming, but there is also a hint of the ruthless conviction of the superstar. Relaxing again, she shows me a picture of her adopted Vietnamese children—two adorable, chubby faces peering out of the black and white snapshots. "Blake and I weren't having any success having kids of our own together," she says, "and we wanted children very badly. André and Mia Farrow Previn suggested we should adopt two orphans; they have three. Emma, my fourteen-year-old daughter with Tony Walton, took some persuading, but she finally said, 'All right, Mummy. As long as you don't ask me to baby-sit.' Now she's the biggest mother to the babies of us all."

One of Miss Andrews's greatest pleasures has been writing two children's books, *Mandy* and *The Last of the Really Great Whangdoodles.* She wrote *Mandy* shortly after her marriage to Blake Edwards. "We were doing *Darling Lili* in Paris. Life was chaos. To film and to be mother and manager of a household in a foreign country was a nightmare—I was losing the battle daily. Finally, I said, 'O.K., we're going to have some rules around here. Let's play a game. Anybody who fails to pick up laundry in the morning or brush teeth or clean is going to have to pay a forefeit.' Jenny—Blake's daughter—very wisely said, 'O.K., but you've got to play the game too.' I asked her, 'What am I going to do?' And she said, 'Stop swearing so much!' I lost in ten minutes flat! Had to pay a forefeit! 'What's my forefeit?' I asked Jenny. She said, 'Write me a story!' So I came up with the idea of *Mandy,* about a little girl who lives in the city orphanage and discovers the country."

But what about Julie Andrews, the movie star? Will there be films in her future? "Absolutely, *definitely!* I want to do a remake of an old picture called *Rachel and the Stranger* with Blake, about the romance of two very simple people on the

Canadian lakes. I have also written a script with Blake of *Whangdoodle,* which I won't appear in, but I think Blake will do very soon. Henry Mancini and Leslie Bricusse have done some of the most *gorgeous* songs. Most of all, I want to do a picture Blake has written and will direct called *S.O.B.* It's a wild comedy about a woman who won an Oscar for *Peter Pan* years ago and then did utterly different parts and is now trying to find her way back."

Julie Andrews laughs. "Wouldn't that be loverly?"

Joan Blondell

Of all the stars I have interviewed, I have liked Joan Blondell the best. She is unique in my experience in being an actress who is devoid of ego, self-congratulation and self-pity, and would not dream of quoting a favorable review of herself. She is down to earth and human and real. This is almost unheard of in Saran-wrapped Hollywood.

I was late for the interview for the only time in my life. I had locked my keys in my car. I called her to tell her. Most stars would have berated me. She said, "I've done it four times this year. Happens to me all the time. Don't worry, honey."

As a result, I didn't. And she was probably lying. I love her always.

———————★———————

1972

"I looked for the old dressing rooms at Warners, where Kay Francis and Eddie Robinson, Bette Davis and Ann Dvorak lived and breathed, and there was nothing left. I try, I really try not to gaze too far into the past. But then it all floods in, the grips and the gaffers from the old days step by and take me in a big bear hug and they say, 'Oh, Joanie, it's good to have you back.' And I feel so tender I could cry."

It's Joan Blondell talking, over Bloody Marys and eggs Benedict at 2:00 P.M., in the kind of Los Angeles restaurant—all sporting prints and imitation mahogany paneling and bright red leather—Mildred Pierce opened up when she finally threw in her waitress's apron for Zachary Scott's Monty Beragon. Joan has been working at her old studio, where she played 'em blond, bright and brash in pictures like *The Public Enemy* and *Bullets or Ballots* a zillion light years ago. This time around, she is a star of *Banyon,* an NBC-TV series. It's about a Sam Spade–like detective played by Robert Forster in Humphrey Bogart's actual suits, set in the period of Joan's Warners heyday—1937. ("The other day they played Edward VIII's abdication speech for a scene. Last time I heard that was when they stopped shooting for it on *The King and the Chorus Girl!*")

The lady is still as honey-blond, as cuddly and jolly and down-to-earth as she always was, huge, Kewpie-doll, china blue eyes wide with excitement or brimming with tears at memories of the Good Old Days, digging into her food like a child, throatily drawling as she talks with an open, unsophisticated warmth about babies and dogs and trips abroad and growing up in vaudeville. The plump figure tucked neatly into the blue trouser suit, the bright pink cheeks, the line of rapid talk: this is one star whose off-screen image doesn't disappoint at all.

She is enjoying *Banyon* hugely, and her part in it, the Aline MacMahon–like head of a stenographic school. She very much welcomes the fact that the hats and marcel bobs and shoes are perfect to the last detail. She should know. In fact, so much of the wardrobe has been taken out of dusty Warners closets she may well wind up wearing things she wore way back when. "I keep getting memories. Not of all those pictures when I played stenographers and nurses and girl reporters and gang molls, but of what someone long dead said to me in front of stage twenty-seven, and who I played mixed doubles with on the tennis court at the back. I look up, and hear a voice, and see a face, and there's no one there."

She sips her Bloody Mary, forty years fall away, and suddenly she's a bright young broad, slugging it out so the Warners shareholders can reap better dividends, right up and along there with Bette and Humphrey and Jimmy and Kay and Aline. "We worked twice as hard in those days. We started work at five in the morning, which meant getting up at four. Makeup, all that junk, then whammo on the nose, straight over to the set at eight, knowing all your lines. We'd work clean through Saturday night. They'd bring in sandwiches like straw for the horses and we'd finally make it into bed on Sunday morning as the sun hit the pillows." Her voice grows raucous with pleasure, "Damn good thing we were young!"

Yeah, she says, all those pictures kind of run together in her memory, from *Sinners' Holiday,* the 1930 movie in which she and James Cagney made their debuts, all the way to *Stay Away, Joe* in 1968 with Elvis Presley (whom she adored). "I remember one picture because a baby was teething, another one because a kid had measles." All she could remember thinking, those years at Warners, was how she could get home to cook dinner for her successive husbands: cameraman George Barnes and Dick Powell. She doesn't like to talk about those marriages or her later one to Mike Todd. "Let's just say George was a great cinematographer, Dick was a wonderful singer and dancer, and Mike was a fine promoter who could talk anybody into anything. That's the way people remember them and"—a touch of bitter sadness in the voice—"I wouldn't want to change their images for a minute. They're all dead and gone now, anyway."

She much prefers to talk about her kids—in fact, she says, they're all that matters: her son Norman Scott Powell, a TV producer, and her daughter, Ellen Powell, a veterinarian. She is desperately proud of both of them. And her grandchildren.

Visits with the family mean far more to her than movie buffs rushing up to tell her how they adored her croaking "Remember My Forgotten Man" under the lamppost in *Gold Diggers of 1933.* Yet like it or not, she symbolizes, in that sequence, the thirties, just as Crawford in broad-shouldered mink on a fog-cloaked wharf in *Mildred Pierce* moodily symbolizes the forties.

Working in pictures for Joanie wasn't a matter of pushing an ambition for greatness: she never had the drive of a Stanwyck or a Davis. She simply wanted to do a good job, like a lady riveter, then kiss good-bye to it all and drive off from Burbank, like a bat out of hell.

Like Bette, she rebelled against all the inferior roles she was handed; unlike Bette she opted out of Warners altogether and fled to Columbia, where Harry Cohn, for once, behaved like a gentleman, and 20th Century-Fox, where she played the warm, fleshy, blowsy carny queen, Zeena, in *Nightmare Alley.* She was good, too, as Aunt Cissy in *A Tree Grows in Brooklyn,* directed by Elia Kazan. "Thank God censorship has improved since then. They cut the best scene I ever played, and the best piece of acting I have ever done.

"Aunt Cissy is a very quiet woman loved by everybody in the family. She takes the colorful tins the contraceptives are placed in—they have girls' faces on them and names like Agnes or Betsy—and gives them to the children to play with.

"One day she accidentally leaves a rubber in a tin. The little boy asks me about it, and in the most beautiful writing the author, Betty Smith, did, Cissy tries to explain to the children what the rubber is, not by talking about the actual thing, but about love and life itself. It was very simply done, and all of us players hugged each other spontaneously at the end of the scene. It was marvelous and the Legion of Decency made us take it out. Wasn't that stupid?"

Joan Blondell—amid a great deal of rubbish—went on to make a few rather good films: *The Blue Veil, Will Success Spoil Rock Hunter?, Angel Baby,* and a pleasant TV series, *Here Come the Brides,* based on *Seven Brides for Seven Brothers.* She enjoyed *Here Come the Brides,* but she hadn't enjoyed at all her recent Off-Broadway stage appearance as the mother in Paul Zindel's *The Effect of Gamma Rays on Man-in-the-Moon Marigolds.* "I'll tell you how that got started. I had two little pug dogs, one for nineteen years, the other for seventeen. They went everywhere with me. The children had grown up, I didn't have a husband any longer, and everyone has to have something close, to love. They were all I had in the world. I loved those pug dogs with all my heart. I had a pretty home for the three of us here high up in the mountains, and then suddenly, the eldest dog, Birtie, died. She almost pleaded to die. I saw her look up at me as she lay in my arms, then she closed her eyes, and that was it, forever. The other little one didn't last much longer.

"I felt an overpowering weakness. I couldn't stand that house, or the car, or anything. I could see my dogs' eyes everywhere, their sounds, the little trick we had of lying all curled up together, and suddenly it had gone. So I sold my house, my car, and everything that could possibly remind me of them. I called my agent and I said, 'Can you find me something play wise that would take me to New York for three months to get over this agony?' He offered me *Gamma Rays*. I did not like it, I did not understand it. But at least it was an escape. And I had nothing else to hang on to.

"I didn't understand the mother role I had to play. I didn't *understand* a woman that closed herself off from the world and ruined a couple of darling young girls, and killed a *rabbit,* for heaven's sake. But it was the only job that I could get for three months. I thought when I read it, maybe they can change things in the writing for me, to make it more *understandable.* They didn't. I tried to do it. It was very, very painful to do every night. I walked the floor of my small apartment all day long; I was so exhausted when I got to the theater I hardly knew what was going on. Twenty-four hours a day I was trapped inside that terrible woman, fighting to get out. I said to the producer, 'Can't we say she's insane?' But the author did not want that written in. Thank God, I was out of the play for a while with, of all crazy things, the *mumps;* I was never so grateful for anything in my life. Maybe I got it from kissing too many dogs in the street. People sent me kid things, teddy bears, dolls, it was wonderful! And Arthur Godfrey sent me a message saying, 'Be grateful you're not a man!'

"Well, at least that particular nightmare ended. I was out of the play and the three months were up. Thank God. Then the most wonderful thing on earth happened. I should begin by telling you that, like most Americans, I have about ten words in my pocket, Just ten. I have never, to say the least, *been to school at Harvard!* I was born in a trunk in vaudeville. I worked all my life, I never took time out to get educated. But many years ago, I thought I would write a story my children would like.

"After a few months of writing, I would put it away and years would pass before I found it again. I'd take it out and read it and put it back. Then maybe I'd write some more. Well, my secretary called a literary agent in New York and told her about it. The agent, Gloria Safier, called me. I told her the manuscript was in a trunk and I'd lost the key. She kept after me and finally I sent it. She called me at three o'clock one morning and she said, 'I have cried and I have laughed and I'm going to run with it!' She sold it in two days to Delacorte. And it has become the Literary Guild selection of the month for October! Little me! Joan Blondell!"

Suddenly, her laugh is like the sun breaking through. The tears for the lost past, for her lost dogs and her lost marriages, have vanished, and the eyes are as blue as the sky, more eager than ever.

Eggs Benedict polished off, she walks out into the scorching San Fernando Valley afternoon, and I drive her to her hotel. ("No more houses for me.") Before she gets out, she says, warm and motherly and sweet as Aunt Cissy ever was, "Be very careful now, driving home." She clutches my arm, smiles her Kewpie-doll smile, and is gone.

Kirk Douglas

This was one of my first Hollywood interviews, and the only one I've ever conducted at breakfast. When not working, most stars seem barely visible before one thirty in the afternoon.

I spent the interview in a state of alarm. I was unnerved by the violent squawks of a tropical bird in a cage behind Mr. Douglas's head. I was also afraid that his emphatic fist-blows on a glass breakfast table would shatter it, causing us to be cut to pieces and the breakfast to spill over the floor.

I met Mr. Douglas again several years later. We were on a talk show conducted by Mrs. Bing Crosby in San Francisco. Mrs. Crosby said to me that in my book on Katharine Hepburn I had described Kate as the weaker partner in the relationship with Spencer Tracy. I denied this and said that the opposite was true. Mrs. Crosby grew cold. She said, "Mr. Higham, I read every word of your book." I replied, "And I *wrote* every word of it."

Kirk Douglas approved my remark. I could be his friend anytime.

———————————★———————————

1970

The line of the mouth is unyielding, turned down sharply at the corners. The jaw juts sharply, punctured at the exact center by a dimple you could put your finger in. The eyes are cool, glittering like mica. The wrestler's body seems tensed to strike or grapple. Against the loud cries of a tropical bird in a bamboo cage, flanked with razor-sharp leaves, his voice has a high insistence.

Kirk Douglas's screen personality suggests a driving strength and force—whether as boxer *(Champion)*, musician *(Young Man With a Horn)*, reporter *(Ace in the Hole)*, policeman *(Detective Story)*, artist *(Lust for Life)* or martinet army chief *(Seven Days in May)*. It wasn't surprising, then, having a late breakfast with him at his house in Beverly Hills, to find that this electric, vivid man is a dynamo away from the screen.

In a bad time in Hollywood, he has typically come up with an original way of financing a picture: his next feature, *A Gunfight,* will be paid for by an Apache Indian tribe, the first time this has happened in screen history. It isn't that the film has anything to do with Indians either; it's simply that groups of this kind, ethnic and otherwise, seem interested in supporting the movie industry. The time may not be too far off when a movie about the Eskimos can be backed by a Congolese pygmy clan.

Douglas has just finished a new picture, *There Was a Crooked Man,* a Western directed by Joseph L. Mankiewicz, famous for his *All About Eve.* It is Douglas's fiftieth production, a fact that makes him more than painfully conscious of his age. But he doesn't look anything like his fifty-three years, and he works out vigorously every day to keep a figure most men of thirty would envy.

The only son of seven children of a Russian immigrant, Douglas was born in Amsterdam, New York, in December 1916. "We were, to put it mildly, a very humble family," he said. "In fact, why mince matters? We often went hungry. I can remember times when I had a hole in my stomach the size of the Mammoth Cave.

"Since I was the only boy I was the 'ham in the sandwich'—that's to say, I kept the others fed. I just don't know how the heck I did it. I used to sell soda pop and candy to the mill hands. Maybe I might make enough in a day to buy some cornflakes and milk. Lunch was one egg beaten up with water, fried and cut into halves to make sandwiches. Sometimes if I had a nickel I might get around to buying some milk.

"We usually ate boiled soup bones and stale bread." Kirk Douglas plowed into a dish of bacon and eggs with sterling silver knife and fork. "I got a job as a bookkeeper. . . . From then on, my life was just like a B movie. Rags to riches with a hell of a struggle in between. I fought my way up, I admit it. If I hadn't, I'd still be shoveling dirt down there at the bottom of the ladder where everything's black. . . ."

Evidently, Douglas's experiences had taught him the vibrant realism of his portraits of struggle. How had he gotten his first break?

"I acted at college—St. Lawrence University in Canton, New York—wrestled and won the International Collegiate Wrestling Championship, and went into acting—sort of drifted in via waiting tables in a restaurant and playing a singing telegraph messenger in a Broadway play that's now mercifully forgotten.

"After the Army in World War Two, I did some more stage. Luckily, Lauren Bacall caught me in one show and recommended me to a Hollywood producer. The rest is history."

Was it true that he went to remarkable lengths to ensure the authenticity of his playing? "Well, someone once said that my chest heaved and my jaw jutted before a scene ever started. But I guess, yes, I have tried to live each part.

"I remember a funny thing happened on my boxing picture, *Champion*. A dresser who worked with me on that one was such a miserable character he never had a good word to say for anyone. I was amazed when at the first tests he said to me, 'I think you're going to be just great in this picture.' I stood back about three feet. Then came the punch line. He added: 'You're playing just about the lowest, meanest rat in the world. You're so ideally cast—you'll make a perfect bastard in the movie.' "

Douglas laughed. "When I played *Champion*—my first big

hit, in the late 1940s—I hadn't boxed a round in my life. I had three left hands. But I trained and trained with an ex-pro till I was battered senseless. Suddenly I got the killer instinct. I lashed back, and knocked the poor guy cold!

"For *The Story of Three Loves,* with Leslie Caron, I was a trapeze artist. I learned to conquer my fear and didn't use a stand-in; I trained with a real troupe. . . . I'll never forget the first time I reached for that swinging bar and thought, Suppose I miss it? My palms sweat when I think about it.

"I juggled till I was dizzy for *The Juggler.* When I had to be a journalist for a picture, I got a friend of mine on a California newspaper to take me on. I remember asking someone how you got a by-line. They told me, 'You'll have to work a hell of a long time before you get that.' The first day I worked there I got a by-line. The guy came back and said, 'I got it all wrong. All you need to get a by-line is to be a movie star!' "

For *Lust for Life,* Douglas's version of the career of Vincent van Gogh, he even learned to paint. "I won't make the grand master league," he said. "But there was a scene in which I was painting a country scene and a whole lot of crows fly down around me, and I sketched them in. Well, we won't count the number of crows I painted before I got them right. I guess around five hundred. Finally I succeeded. I guess they looked O.K., but I hope no art critics in the audience passed out cold."

Douglas is furious with critics who say that Hollywood is dead and stars are finished. "I'd like to know where all the pictures are still being made, and where the studios are—Hollywood, that's where. And more and more of our people are coming back from Europe because the climate and facilities are second to none.

"Stars are here to stay. Just because nobody ever hears of Alan Ladd or Veronica Lake anymore doesn't mean there aren't going to be stars.

"Isn't Dustin Hoffman a star? Isn't Mia Farrow? And Jane Fonda? And *Peter* Fonda, for that matter? This antistar thing is just the frustration worked off their tracks by a bunch of

New York critics who've got nothing to do with life out here at all. We're gutsy, we're working hard in this hot sun, and we're still making the best pictures. And anyone who says we aren't can go lie down and die."

Gene Kelly

I had always wanted to interview Gene Kelly. His engaging dance routines lighted up my childhood: the fabulous "Alter Ego" dance in *Cover Girl* was a particular pleasure. I found him as lively and charming as I had expected and living in a beautifully spacious, airy house. A house to dance in.

His appearance in *That's Entertainment!* showed that, though his waist might have thickened a little and he had taken to wearing a toupée, his charm was undimmed. I have only one quarrel with his keenest admirers. He was never as great as Fred Astaire.

1970

At the 20th Century-Fox commissary, jammed with stars and directors, the dishes are named after the company's recent pictures: too nervous to eat a Pretty Poison soup, a Boston Strangler sandwich, a Beneath the Planet of the Apes salad or a Valley of the Dolls Revisited omelet, I settle for a presumably harmless Dr. Doolittle steak, when across the aisle I note a face familiar from a score of great musicals: Gene Kelly.

Gene Kelly. The name conjures up school holidays during World War II, evoking through clouds of nostalgia the heyday of Technicolor, when with Rita Hayworth and Judy Garland

and (later) Leslie Caron, Kelly created the modern dance as millions know it on screen.

"He's just directed *Hello, Dolly!*" says the actor Ray Walston, who is at my table. I'm not surprised: it seems only logical that the biggest screen musical of them all should have been entrusted to the greatest film musical star of them all.

He wasn't, they said, seeing anybody; he was too deeply involved in the mammoth job of editing *Dolly* in the cutting rooms. But I was lucky: he had had a sudden bout of flu and was looking for a chance to relax over a drink. He wanted to talk, and I wanted to talk to him: after all, *Cover Girl, Anchors Aweigh, On the Town,* and *Singin' in the Rain* were, together with *An American in Paris,* among the best musical films Hollywood has ever done.

Dolly, with its $20 million budget and its gigantic parade scene, the most spectacular of all dance sequences, will have the informal realism and charm Kelly has made his trademark.* "From the very first," he tells me at his house in Beverly Hills, "I was determined to upset the tradition of Fred Astaire, white-tie-and-tails dancing.

"After all, they provided escape for the people in the Depression, but I wanted to bring dance to the people. Make it echo their natural rhythms, the movement of American bodies, the way we express our feelings dramatically, in an outgoing way.

"I got rid of the white tie and tails and replaced that artificial garb with sweat shirts, jeans, and loafers. When the audience went to a movie house to see one of my pictures, they saw themselves up there, dancing. At fun fairs, in parks, on streets, on the beaches . . . even on ships' decks. The way we live."

Following a smash hit on Broadway with *Pal Joey,* which in 1939–40 made Kelly a Broadway star, John Martin, critic of *The New York Times,* encouraged him to develop his naturalistic dance techniques.

David O. Selznick, producer of *Gone With the Wind,* hired

---

* A false prediction, alas. The picture was a dud.

him for the screen, of all things as a priest in *The Keys of the Kingdom,* a story of a missionary in China. The picture wasn't made until years later, and with Gregory Peck in the lead, but Kelly was snapped up by M-G-M, home of the musical, where Judy Garland had just had a smash hit in *The Wizard of Oz.*

"I found nobody at Metro was interested in choreography really," Kelly said. "They'd just stage a musical sequence the way it was done in a theater. I did *For Me and My Gal* with Judy Garland, and it was very fresh and free. Judy Garland in those days was a very relaxed, marvelous person. She was a 'pure' screen actress: she pitched her voice and her gestures very low, because she knew—which I didn't—that the sound track and camera pick up everything, and if you play at stage volume, it looks and sounds awful.

"We had a ball. Judy and I worked out the dances so that they looked the way people would dance who weren't professionals, yet they were, of course—had to be—of the highest professional standard. It was very exciting."

In *Anchors Aweigh,* about three sailors on the loose during shore leave, Kelly brought his style, insouciant, lilting, delightful, to its peak. He said that the origins of the picture lay in a whole tradition of ballets about sailors, ballets like *Les Matelots* and other works of Massine, and the Russian *The Red Poppy.*

"The sailor in modern ballet—we used him again in *On the Town*—was as much a cliché as the swan in the classic works, but the sailor's uniform was the only one we had at the time that adapted itself to dance ideally.

"It showed line and form and style while an army uniform would have cramped you; you couldn't raise your arms properly, you couldn't use expressive gestures."

As a result of this technique, Kelly released a whole new style of informal dancing on the world. The studios, hidebound as ever, fought him, and he had to struggle, in his famous picture, *Cover Girl,* with Rita Hayworth, to introduce a scene in which, with Rita and Phil Silvers, he danced along a street, using dustbin lids, a milkman, and various steps as props. In another scene, he even danced with his own alter ego image, reflected in various shop windows, in one of the greatest dance episodes in film history.

"People," the studio kept telling me, "don't go down a street singing and dancing. I said to them, "Remember Jeanette MacDonald and Nelson Eddy? People don't sing "Rose Marie" at each other across a lake on a canoe, either, do they?' Finally they saw it my way."

Kelly misses what he calls "the golden girls of the forties": Rita Hayworth, June Allyson, Judy Garland, Lana Turner. "What an aura they had! Screen leading ladies don't have it now. I was in the Navy for two years in World War II and all the guys would ask me about them. I had played with them all in movies."

In *An American in Paris,* Kelly worked with Ira Gershwin, Alan Jay Lerner, and Vincente (father of Liza) Minnelli on the story of an artist in the French capital, a film which cleaned up a fortune.

"We went to see Rouault because we wanted to use some of his paintings as the background to a ballet. I was terrified that the great artist would be upset at the idea of his works in a Hollywood musical. He was old and crippled with arthritis, in a wheelchair, and when we showed him the sketches, I thought he'd shake his head. Instead, he was delighted. And he loved the picture; he made us run it for him again and again."

As a result of the success of the picture, Kelly created ballets for the Paris stage. "Even de Gaulle was nice to me. He gave me the Légion d'Honneur!"

In *On the Town,* based on Leonard Bernstein's celebrated ballet, Kelly and Frank Sinatra danced all over New York without faking shots, doing their own stunts, breaking with tradition by shooting the whole picture on the skyscrapers, in the subways, and through the crowded thoroughfares of the city. "We hid the camera in a station wagon so the crowds wouldn't see us, and were so convincing as sailors not many people noticed us. I kept a stopwatch in my hand to check the rhythm of the dancing. Of course some people must have thought, Who are these crazy dancing sailors? But other people just walked by. . . . And we even shot on the roof of Radio City Music Hall, dancing on the very edge of the parapets, with hundreds of feet drops below us. . . ."

His purpose in this film, and in his other classics like *Invitation to the Dance,* was to bring dance to the world by the only means possible: the motion-picture screen. "In Malaya or the backwoods of Borneo you could use a little sixteen-millimeter projector and see what modern dance is."

I ask Gene Kelly about *Hello, Dolly!* the lavish picture on which Fox shot the bankroll.

"We had a very big sequence in it which exemplified my ideals of the dance: a whole mass of people gathering to greet Dolly, and a wild crowd dancing along the streets of New York," he says. "We have made the picture in a leisurely, quiet style, in keeping with its period setting. I want the audience to 'smell' the 1880s. I've measured it to the pace of living then.

"A world without smog, without dark skies. A better world. Barbra Streisand could dance just a little when we started. Now, after I worked my feet off, she can dance some more! They'd told me she'd had terrible clashes with William Wyler when she made *Funny Girl,* but she was marvelous with me. I think nerves got the better of her at first. She was terrified the way she'd come out on the screen. The Oscar gave her confidence.

"She is, above all, a tremendous worker. Today you usually get people who want to work just a couple of hours, and then leave the set because they're tired. But she'd go on and on until most people would drop. All the other people who had played the part—including Ginger Rogers and Carol Channing—were, well, troupers, veterans—to be strictly nice, 'approaching middle age.' But Barbra met the challenge very well. Of course, when you talk about her being difficult, other female stars being difficult, you have to remember what an awful life they live.

"Yes, awful, not glamorous, because they have to be glamorous all the time. They can't just relax and flop around like most people; they're in a goldfish bowl, and if they show one line or crease the world eats them alive. I'm glad I ain't a girl! Now wait a minute! That might be a title for a new song. . . ."

Lucille Ball

After this piece appeared Lucille Ball wrote me a bitter note on baby blue stationery with her name spelled out in red at the top, each letter printed through with tiny stars. "How could one so young," was her gist, "be so cruel?" All I had done was leave the tape recorder on, warning her of its presence. I replied to her in a brief poem which ran:

> If you would keep your house in order
> Don't talk into a tape recorder.

I did not receive a reply, in verse *or* prose.

1973

Tension on the *Mame* set at Warners: it is close to noon, and, since 9:00 A.M., director Gene Saks and choreographer Onna White have been driving Lucille Ball through her paces. Wearing a red Santa Claus cap, she mouths the words to her prerecorded, throaty singing of "Need a Little Christmas Now," following Mame's ruin in the Wall Street crash. And right in the middle of a take, the cap falls off. Un-Mameishly, the star stalks off angrily for a grim consultation with her milliner, known jocularly as the mad hatter. In a little while, she is back again, still fuming. Lighting up a cigarette, she grins starkly and clutches my arm. "I don't inhale," she whispers, almost inaudibly. "I daren't. Last night my esophagus gave out. It's always giving out. I turned blue. That's the way I'm going to die, with my esophagus going. I'm going to stifle, and I know it."

A few minutes later, still voiceless, she is croaking instructions to everyone. Grim, concentrated, she reminds one that making a musical is very much like riveting or mixing cement. Like a lady wrestler, she charges into each scene, nostrils flaring, ready to tackle anyone who crosses her. Then, as soon as the cameras turn, she sparkles like a young girl, kicks up a still shapely leg, charmingly crinkles her clown's face, and —this time—hangs on to her cap. She finishes the scene in a Santa Claus mask, arms flung wide, mouth bigger than Martha Raye's, wanting to scream but instead grinning from ear to ear until Gene Saks calls, "Cut!" Then, frowning deeply, she collapses into a chair.

Making a musical at the age of sixty-one is, for Lucy, an enormous test of courage and endurance—and would have been even if she hadn't had a skiing accident a year ago in which she broke her right leg. With Onna White, she worked for months on end for ninety minutes every morning, doing stretching and bending exercises which would have taxed a young ballerina. She still limps, but the moment the whistle blows, the limp disappears, she flashes into a dance routine, and there isn't a sign of discomfort on her face.

"I miss those exercises every day, now that they're over," she says. "I like all discipline. Up to *Mame* my only exercise had been never sitting down for two seconds, running around constantly. For *Mame* I had to learn not only to walk again, but to dance again. I hadn't danced in a movie for thirty years or more. Now I'm up at five every day. No social life, nothing. Jesus! Making movies! It's like you're running backward."

A few days later, we talk again in the leafy, very feminine living room of Lucy's sprawling white mansion in Beverly Hills. Wearing brown hot pants and drinking Pouilly-Fuissé on the rocks, she carries on almost without a break.

"I'm grateful to be doing. I was in the hospital five times; it took weeks of bed rest and a whole year to get over that accident. I did twenty-four shows of *Here's Lucy* in a cast. I wouldn't have massages and I wouldn't lie in bed one second longer than I had to. I suffer from claustrophobia. Dreadfully. I can't even stand to relax. If I do, I doze off. I wake up screaming DAAAA! Like that. I feel my arms are tied down by some guy. Tight and stifling! And the plaster cast! Forget it! At first they had me right up to the waist in it. Well, I took the heaviest thing I could find, which was the handle used to raise and lower the hospital bed, and I broke the damn cast all the way down to the calf. Three times in a row. Finally, they gave me what I wanted: a cast I could move in a little. I still screamed! But I kinda got used to it. Then I'd fall asleep and wake up and still be encased! I'd pound at the cast and cry out like a maniac, and they'd come running in.

"It was hell. Jesus! The antibiotics, the drugs! I thought I'd stifle. It's a miracle what Onna White did with me, training me for the part. Of course, things still happen to me. See this hand? With four broken nails? Hey! One just went on the floor! They get brittle when I work. Of course, I've had accidents all my life. I'm a Leo, so my extremities are apt to *snap like matchsticks*.

"When I was a child, I had rheumatic arthritis in both legs. I could hardly walk. Then, when I was just starting out as an actress in New York, I was driving a Model T through Central Park and it skidded. I was thrown out and I sat in a snowdrift all night. Nobody knew I was there. I caught pneumonia and, as a result, I was paralyzed. For two years I had no money— maybe eighty-two dollars to my name—so I became a guinea pig in a new clinic and took horse serum. It worked, and I walked.

"Ever since, it's been arms legs arms legs arms legs. When I was making *Fancy Pants* with Bob Hope, a horse stepped on one toe and Bruce Cabot in cowboy boots stepped on another. I was a slave to foot specialists for seven years. I was bitten by an alligator when I did *Roman Scandals* back in the 1930s. Lucky his teeth were out or I wouldn't be here to tell the tale. I've been bitten by two chimps. I was even bitten by *a bear,* on one of the *Lucy* shows.

"One of my worst accidents was when I was gored by the head of *a bull.* Just the head. Lucy was supposed to have taken up bullfighting but they decided it was too dangerous for me to go in a Mexican bullring. They put the bull's head on the front of a camera and ran it down a very long track at me. The damn thing jumped the track and came right at me with four guys behind it. Thank God Jerry Thorpe, the director, hit me and knocked me down, or I'd have been killed instantly. As it was, I still got gored. Oh God, *the blood!*

"But the worst was when my nose caught fire doing *Lucy.* It was done up as a clown's and Bill Holden lit a cigarette too close to me. The nose burst into flames. I screamed and dunked the nose in a cup of coffee. My hair smoldered a little before they hosed it. I went on with the scene and they put it in the show!"

Along with the physical ordeals, there had been the emotional ones. *I Love Lucy* was launched in 1951 chiefly to patch up her miserable marriage to Desi Arnaz, who had been traveling with his band since World War II. But the success the series brought, making them virtually Mr. and Mrs. America, smashed the marriage for good. They fought constantly for years, on and off the set, even after she converted to Catholicism for his sake. Her first child, Lucie, was born just after the series began, but she had her second, Desi, Jr., virtually on camera in 1953, with 85 percent of television owners watching her pregnancy. The marriage collapsed in 1960 ("Desi, Senior, drank too much, and he couldn't stand success," she says grimly). Luckily, her second marriage, to ex-comedian Gary Morton, who is now production chief of *Here's Lucy,* has worked out. But there was, during the 1960s and the early 1970s, the long agony over Desi, Jr.

"He had a Catholic education. His grades were bad and he suffered. His prekindergarten was the start. He was unhappy, even though the nuns spoiled and pampered him rotten. So I took him out of there. Then he went to a Catholic boys' school. That didn't work out either. We all went to New York when I did a Broadway musical called *Wildcat.* When we got back to California Desi wanted to go to military academy. They held him on weekend detentions for eight hours a day —he had to sit bolt upright the whole time. He was having nightmares at night. He couldn't sleep. I said, 'What's the matter with you?' And he said, 'They gave me detentions for tying a shoelace during drill when I was supposed to be at attention.' I said, 'Oh, come on!' And he told me that thirteen-year-old 'generals' were giving these bullying orders. I took him out of school again.

"He went to Beverly Hills High. My God, he'd come home hungry, tired! The poor waif! So I took him out of that school too. He went to Loyola University, where one of the teachers made a dirty crack about me. They had a fight. So I took him out of there, and he went on the TV show for a year and a half. He didn't take to it like Lucie because he didn't understand comedy the way she does. He was asleep on the sidelines when we'd call him and I was ready to smack him. When he said he wanted to do dramatic things, I said, 'Oh, really?' But he got out and worked. Unfortunately, I knew *Red Sky at Morning* wouldn't make a cent and it didn't. It was dull. I have hopes for *Marco,* in which he plays Marco Polo to Zero Mostel's Kubla Khan.

"Lucie lives on a budget, she works for scale on my show. Desi will never have any money. It all goes. Yes, sir. I adore his new fiancée, Liza Minnelli. I hope it lasts. I don't care if they never get married. They don't have time to settle down in a house. And they have seven dogs to take care of between them. They say, 'Can we leave them with you?' And I say, 'One cotton-picking minute! Once in a while, I'll take your dogs, and the puppies. But every time a dog drops a litter, you can't dump them on me. We've got five dogs already!' I don't think Liza will ever settle down. She doesn't know what settling down is. She's never had a home. I felt like a mother to her before my children were born, and I know her.

"Liza took on all the responsibility long before Judy died. She helped Lorna Luft go out on her own. And now she has the responsibility of her half brother, Joey Luft, who's a poor little guy and very lonely. She's too generous. She kills herself working and throws thousands here, thousands there. She told me she's trying to settle her mother's residue of financial problems. I said, 'Fine! But make sure she really owed them!' They took her for over a million and a quarter more than her mother's debt. Just for beginners. I got her an attorney and he is advising her, and I try to be a mother to her.

"I'm glad Desi, Junior, found her. Especially after that ghastly thing with Patty Duke when they had an illegitimate child. I was so put upon; I couldn't believe what was happening. There were a hundred stories in a hundred magazines, and they all made me sick. It was 'They did, they didn't, she didn't, she wouldn't, she didn't, I never did, he never did, they wouldn't, they won't, they did too much, they won't do anything.' It was the silliest bunch of crap I've ever read. I let it go on; I didn't sue anybody.

"Patty Duke was twelve years old when I first knew her. She was a bright young thing I loved. After she got married, she used to come over to the house. Then she left her husband. Next thing I knew, she was going with my son. I thought, Well, she's a little old for him, but so what? I thought nothing of it. He was going with other girls, she was going out with other guys. All of a sudden, there was *a baby.* Patty disappeared for months on end. Then she came here with the baby. Lucie and I welcomed her into our home. But I had my doubts if the baby was Desi's at all. I said to him, 'You feel responsible? Boy, you're all of sixteen and a half, you want to spend the rest of your life with this *person?* Are you really the father?' But he wanted the baby to be his; it made him feel very manly. I said, 'You have six more years of school; you haven't even started college,' and he said, 'I want the responsibility. I'm a man now.' I shrugged. And then Miss Duke just evaporated. It was all over."

Lucie Arnaz was, she said, not a problem at all, and she had welcomed her marriage to actor and filmmaker Philip Vandervort in 1971. She is sad that the marriage did not work out. Lucie has recently been dating female impersonator Jim Bailey.

Lucille Ball was head of the giant Desilu Corporation all those years; she had been greatly relieved to finally sell it to Charles Bluhdorn of Gulf and Western for $17 million. And —of all people—this basically conservative woman was accused of being a Communist by the House Un-American Activities Committee in 1953. "They cleared me, and my stupidity was my savior. I had no idea what they were talking about. They called me into one of those closed hearings. I didn't even have an answer for most of the questions. I kept saying, 'What is all this about meetings and people and propositions and signings?' It didn't make sense! I've forgotten most of what happened. I've developed a mental block."

Today, she is no longer a practicing Catholic, and the only church she attends is Norman Vincent Peale's. She is against President Nixon, hated the war in Vietnam, and is horrified by what she feels is a "false peace" which won't last. "How can we be anything but cynical? You can't believe in anything. There was a time when you could believe in a president. Who can believe in Nixon?

"Let's talk about something happier. Let's talk about *Mame.*" She limps to answer the telephone, limps back, and lights up another cigarette. "Once I got into it and started working with Onna White I began to enjoy it—as much as I can enjoy picture-making. Oh, God, those *hours!* But it's been a happy company. At least after our director, Gene Saks, who had never made a musical, got used to everything and learned how to get along with Onna White, whom I think he resented at first. Of course, that's all a lie about my wanting to put Bea Arthur out of the movie.

"I chose Bea before I had a director or anything. I had seen Bea as Vera Charles in Angela Lansbury's company and she was the greatest Vera Charles in the world. We wrapped the whole production schedule around Bea Arthur.

"One reason I'm making *Mame* is that I hate violent movies. O *God!* I see ten minutes and then I have to go home. *A Clockwork Orange*—horrible.

"I hope that in *Mame* we'll glorify a little something called hope and faith and love. The only thing that worries me about it is will anybody want to go and see it?* The queues are for sex and violence. I don't see young people wanting to see it. Older people have given up movies. Will they come out to see me when they can see me at home? I don't know."

Even as she growls her good-bye, Lucy's mind is working. "Tomorrow I have to ride in a hunt scene, sidesaddle. With my luck, I'll get thrown. And I have to catch the fox, turn it over on its back, and tickle its belly." She whips off her sunglasses, blue eyes very wide. "Just leave me with this thought: when I turn the fox over, how can I stop the damn thing from scratching me half to death?"

* She was right to worry.

Katharine Hepburn (ABC TELEVISION NETWORK)

Mae West (METROPOLITAN PHOTO SERVICE)

Jerry Lewis

Dinah Shore (JOHN R. HAMILTON/GLOBE PHOTOS)

Robert Blake
(ABC TELEVISION NETWORK)

Tom Ewell
(COPYRIGHT © 1971
JACK MITCHELL)

Julie Andrews

Joan Blondell
(JACK MITCHELL)

Kirk Douglas (NBC-TV)

Gene Kelly (JACK MITCHELL)

Lucille Ball with Robert Preston (WARNER BROS. INC.)

Paul Anka

John Cassavetes and Gena Rowlands (TONY ESPARZA)

Mary Miles Minter at 18

Robert Wagner (CBS-TV)

Robert Young (BRUCE MCBROOM, ABC TELEVISION NETWORK)

David Steinberg (TONY ESPARZA)

Mercedes McCambridge (TONY ESPARZA)

Paul Newman (BRUCE MCBROOM, ABC TELEVISION NETWORK)

Mary Pickford in *Little Annie Rooney* (UNITED ARTISTS CORPORATION)

Tiny Tim (FRED A. SABINE, NBC-TV)

Edward G. Robinson, 1972 (TONY ESPARZA)

Paul Anka

This interview touches me for two reasons. It's very remote in terms of space because it took place when I was living in Australia: it helped me cut my teeth as a journalist. I was very nervous, but Anka was marvelous to me. The interview is also remote in terms of time—1969 seems as far away as 1269. Remember when Anka campaigned for Muskie for President?

———————★———————

1969

"I was in Puerto Rico. Signing records in a store. Suddenly, there were kids everywhere. Thousands of kids. They broke through a wall! The police, well, feared for my safety. You know what they did? They put me in a coffin! Well, not an actual coffin, but a box that looked just like one. They carried me bodily up the back way to the roof. The crowd was coming after me. A helicopter flew in. I was transferred, still boxed, to the helicopter. It took off. We landed on a beach. That kind of ordeal, I like."

It wasn't the only likable ordeal—that episode of the early 1960s—for Paul Anka, who has written hundreds of hit songs, made several million dollars, and won at least twenty-four gold records representing sales of one million copies a disc.

His "Diana" is right up there with "White Christmas" as one of the top handful of best-selling records of all time; even he has probably lost count of the millions it has sold. The Canadian Film Board made a film about him *(Lonely Boy)*, he is constantly in demand at Las Vegas . . . why go on? And he is so obviously unaffected by his fame, so openly, untemperamentally a nice guy, that this solid-gold twenty-eight-year-old man would reduce the toughest cynic to writing in publicity release prose if he weren't very careful.

The fact is, actually, that Anka is a good deal more serious and complex than his image hints at, with strong political concerns.

His childhood in Ottawa (his parents were Syrian immigrants) was far less complicated than that of most stars. He started writing as a subteenybopper (stories as well as songs), won an amateur contest, and at fifteen stormed into Los Angeles with the multisyllabic "Blauwildebeestefontein"— named, of all things, after a town in John Buchan's novel *Prester John*, and composed overnight.

He flunked out, the record failed to sell, and he worked as a theater usher to save his fare back to Ottawa. Undeterred, he got hold of $100 and arrived in New York, walked into the first agency in the Manhattan telephone book, ABC-Paramount, sat down, picked out his song "Diana" on the piano, and was signed at once. A year or two and 8,500,000 sales of "Diana" later, he was intentionally famous. At seventeen.

What was the secret of his sudden appeal? "I guess I was the first kid to come along who not only sang his own songs, but wrote them as well. The difference was that I felt what I was singing because I had made it up myself. The early sixties was the first time that teenagers weren't content to hear songs just belted out which were made up by older experts, but wanted their own music, saying what they felt.

"In that way, I came up with the Beatles. Bob Dylan, who also came up around the time I did, composed songs that spoke for a generation. It was the beginning of a whole movement in music, in which the people, in effect, wrote their own songs. And I've always been 'true to the colors,' you might say."

Ideas pop up for songs at all times; he has often composed as many as six in one night. They jump into his head complete (there's a tape recorder and pencil beside his bed). Many famous singers have adapted his work to their own styles. "I guess I'm one of those publicists' dreams. You sit there and try to dream up a movie script, and there I am. Offers came in from all over the world. I played Europe, Australia, Japan, Puerto Rico.

"I always felt I wanted to appeal to older people as well, so I did an album called *My Heart Sings,* and I play nightclubs, and ABC-TV's *Cool Time.*

"I was in Algiers during the rebellion against France. I sang, and was going home when the crowd got really wild. There was a curfew, and they were angry about that; their mood was uncertain; I had a group of soldiers with me, with machine guns. I had to work my way to a jeep inch by inch . . . and the worst part was the army guys had broken up the show themselves to get people home by nine P.M. It wasn't too comfortable.

"I made movies. For Darryl F. Zanuck's story of the Normandy landings, *The Longest Day,* I did the title song. He cast me in the picture as well, as one of the GIs storming the beachheads. That was a tough one. I had to take a crash course in military training. Finally, I was up there scaling a cliff! I guess it looked all right on screen."

From an office in Manhattan, Anka ran a massive music business, Paul Anka Productions, the Spanka Music Corporation, and the Flanka Music Corporation, rode wildly through New York in a black Lincoln convertible, and went on to boom after boom in the pop business.

"My songs tend to tell a story, and that's a trend now. An autobiography, or fragments of autobiography. When the audience hears it, it identifies. I stopped writing for years because I felt my songs were getting 'commercial,' that I was prostituting myself. Today I have started again, and my songs again say what I feel.

"As you grow you get more pressures and these make you more vital. I feel we're all in grave danger in the Northern Hemisphere, and in spite of everything I've gotten out of life, I'm worried. But I have lived, and if you don't, if you just work as a star, you're mad."

Paul Anka's face darkened, and a new personality began to emerge, different from the boyish, cheerful hero of the charts I had been conscious of up to then. "You always pay for everything you get. People think, 'Paul Anka equals everything's perfect.' But take my mother. After I made my first hits, I brought her to New York, and that was wonderful. But she was a diabetic. And suddenly I realized she was dying. I sent her to every doctor. But I knew she was going. But a whole year I lived with that knowledge. She was thirty-seven years old when she went. I paid my dues, too, you see. I learned that part of life was losing, and that knowledge changed my music. Now I tell the truth in my songs. Nothing sweet, just the truth.

"Take my marriage. I don't believe my wife and I could be happy in some old-fashioned, false, love-loyalty situation. We have to be free, tough, and realistic. I travel alone. My wife and I go our own way." (He is married to Anne de Zogheb, daughter of a French-Egyptian count.)

He felt that life was getting harder, more dangerous. "Today, young people at last know 'where it's at.' When I was young, they didn't have the grim knowledge and power they have today. In our country, sixty-five percent of the country is under twenty-five. My generation were puppies in their teens. Not now.

"The youth movement, which I endorse to the hilt, knows our country is full of deadwood in power. The deadwood has to go. With violence, if need be. The politicians are baffled by the demands the kids are making, because they're too steeped in corruption and antiquated laws to know how to change.

"And every time the kids have gone out to make noise, they've gotten what they wanted. They sat still through my early years and got nothing but promises. They live in fear of the bomb and in fear of China. I know, because I'm with them every hour, every day. And they live in hatred of the government we have.

"Religion is dead for them. I still believe in God, but at twenty-eight I'm an older generation man. God means nothing to them.

"What they want isn't an afterlife. It's a chance to change this one. They want to vote. Why the hell, they say, can't we have one? We can serve in Vietnam, can't we? We want a vote at eighteen."

Paul Anka leaned forward fiercely in his chair. "If I'm going to end someone's life, they say, why can't I decide what guy is going to send me to kill? Their parents have no answers."

Unlike black power, though, there seemed no coherent, politically powerful and coordinated youth power. "The trouble is the black power people have a specific line of argument and the kids haven't: the black point is, 'We're suffering, we haven't been given, and we want.' We know the black cause.

"The young people have several isolated complaints that haven't fully melted into a political movement or force. We have no leader—nor do the blacks, as it happens, after Martin Luther King—but we need one more badly. We will get one, though; it just needs a match to set off the spark. And we will, we must, get the vote.

"There is only one man to represent us in the Presidency. That's Edmund Muskie, the man for 1972. He already has the young in the palm of his hand, and rightly so. I keep trying to find out from the hundreds of people I know whom student power can trust in politics. It's Muskie. You have the Kennedys, of course, who had a powerful sex image for the women, but most of their fans didn't understand political issues. Muskie is more real. But even when he's in power we won't relax. Because ahead of us there is still the nuclear weapon. And death."

John Cassavetes and Gena Rowlands

I must say that the only thing wrong with Gena Rowlands's career is that she chose the wrong director for a husband. Or husband for a director. Whichever way you look at it.

Mr. Cassavetes said during the interview that I was the most intelligent person who had ever interviewed him. He didn't say that after he read the interview. His comments, to one of the nicest press agents in the business, were, I suspect, in words of one syllable. I still think he's a damn good actor!

———————★———————

1975

The lady may not be a tramp, but she's certainly a slob. Her hair is a hopeless blond tangle. Her eyes are as bright with terror as those of a trapped bird. Her shapeless minidress is several years out of date. She is apt to make meaningless gestures, signaling with her thumb like a drunken hitchhiker and then winking, mischievously. She hops and chatters and runs.

Gena Rowlands's all-stops-out performance as Mabel Longhetti, emotionally disturbed housewife, in *A Woman Under the Influence* is being talked about. And so is the direction of her husband, John Cassavetes.

Opinions of Miss Rowlands's performance range from adulation (Rex Reed) to skepticism (Pauline Kael, who thinks that even though Miss Rowlands may be a great actress, she does everything to such excess in this film that she ends up by canceling out her own effectiveness). Cassavetes, too, is a controversial figure. Most critics seem either to love or hate his freewheeling, seemingly improvised, sometimes painfully repetitive approach.

The story of *A Woman Under the Influence* could not be characterized as romantic escapism. Yet the movie seems to be earning back its money—perhaps because audiences in these days of economic depression and intensified neuroses tend to identify with its troubled characters and situations. Nick Longhetti (Peter Falk) is a baffled hardhat, in love with his daffy, overemphatic wife, but at the same time, thoroughly embarrassed by her oddball behavior. Macho, he can't understand why his marriage has gone so sour—how his once charming child-wife has, in her late thirties, developed into an alarmingly unstable woman. Blind to the depth of her suffering, he tries to force her into normal behavior patterns, but only succeeds in pushing her over the edge into madness. Later, when she is released from a mental institution, he is even more dismayed: now, efficiently brainwashed, she possesses as much personality as a stick of celery. We last see her mechanically cleaning up her dining room, and Nick is as lost to her reality as ever.

It is a painful movie, with its lacerating portrait of a woman trying to please her husband and children, trying to achieve the kind of domestic happiness she sees on television, and discovering that the only Women's Lib possible for her is liberation into insanity. Miss Rowlands and Cassavetes were so determined to tell this story without compromise that they broke with the conventional studio distribution system, and— together with Peter Falk—financed and distributed the film themselves. Cassavetes had been dissatisfied with the methods employed by the studios in the promotion and distribution of his previous films. He had felt that they were inadequately publicized and frequently dumped into inappropriate theaters. He was upset by what he considered Universal's mishandling of his last film, *Minnie and Moscowitz.* So this time around, he wanted to do everything himself, from the first draft of the script to the booking of the theaters.

"I just couldn't trust any studio to handle the picture correctly," says Cassavetes with considerable passion. "I wanted no interference up front, in the writing, producing, and directing, and I wanted no interference in promoting and selling it. If anyone had interfered with my vision, I would probably have gone mad."

Happily, John and Gena's marriage is quite unlike that of Nick and Mabel's in *A Woman Under the Influence.* Compulsive workaholics, they are locked together in their relationship, and not even the most feverish Hollywood gossip has ever hinted at infidelity. Although they quarrel healthily—and frequently—they are very much bound up in their home, an informal house high in the Hollywood Hills, and in their children, Nicholas, fifteen, Alexandra, nine, and Zoë, four. And they are eager to be thought of as individuals, which is why they don't like to be interviewed together. I saw them a week apart.

First, I met Cassavetes. He has a striking physical presence: his pale, ascetic face, fierce dark eyes, and tense, muscular body suggest a man in the grip of an obsession. I began by asking him how he achieved the realism of *Influence.*

"In other pictures I had made—*Faces, Shadows, Husbands*—I used a great deal of improvisation to get a realistic effect. But too many extraneous elements crept in. This time I scripted the entire picture, from beginning to end, and then directed it in chronological sequence, just as it would have been lived. I used long, long takes so that the actors could develop emotional scenes without interruption.

"I knew as soon as I'd finished the script that I couldn't tolerate any interference from a studio or even from an independent financial backer. So I mortgaged my house to raise half of the million-dollar budget I needed, and Peter Falk provided the other half out of his earnings from *Columbo* on television. Everyone worked on deferred salaries. My mother played Peter Falk's mother and Gena's mother played her mother. One of my kids—Alexandra—played a neighborhood kid. Other relatives and friends helped out by acting or by working on the crew. It was an intensely cooperative effort. Now we're all slaving away on the distribution, going around talking to exhibitors, selling to independents, everything. I've been on the road myself, for weeks and weeks.

"Making the picture was tough. First, the weeks of wrestling to get the script right. I knew hardhat workers like Nick, and Gena knew women like Mabel, and although I wrote everything myself, we would discuss lines and situations with Peter Falk, to get his opinion, to see if he thought they were really true, really honest. Then our art director found us a perfect Nick-and-Mabel house and we started in. We sat around the house and again talked out every scene until it seemed right, seemed right in this particular environment.

"Once we began shooting, it was hell. The emotional strain was so great that we never went out, socially, for thirteen weeks. No movies, no parties, no home entertaining, nothing. At night we'd collapse, make coffee, then start talking about the work. Yesterday's work, last week's, last month's, next week's, next month's. We'd wake up in the night, and talk some more. It was that kind of total commitment. Sometimes the tension on the set was so great we could taste it. We'd quarrel, and somebody would say, 'No, that scene isn't true, it isn't honest, let's do it again.' One time, I remember, we lived it all so completely that I suddenly became Nick to Gena's Mabel. She looked at me with those big, glaring, beautiful eyes of hers and said to Peter, 'Will you hold him while I hit him?' "

Gena is so extraordinarily convincing as Mabel that one can't help expecting her to be that tense bundle of nerves offscreen, too. Though an occasional nervous smile may suddenly remind one of the vulnerable Mabel Longhetti, the main feeling experienced upon meeting her for the first time is one of shock—shock at what a gorgeous woman she is.

Delighted by the real woman, I manage to ask Gena how on earth she ever got under the skin of the mixed-up Mabel.

"First of all," she says, "I went out and found the kind of clothes Mabel would wear. Cheap clothes, the kind you can still find hanging in some shops. I bought everything off the rack because if they'd been made by a dressmaker, someone would have noticed. We never cheat.

"I wore Mabel's clothes and mussed my hair the way hers would be mussed. Also, I knew many girls who had had breakdowns. I drew little touches from each of them and a lot from myself. I don't mean I'm really going mad. But I'm a little crazy, we all are, and sometimes I let things go. It was a question of taking that small, wild, desperate feeling we all get sometimes and raising it to the highest pitch.

"John told me to go 'all out' in my playing, because Mabel is someone without inhibitions. She's freer than 'normal' people, she doesn't have restrictions on what she may do, she's trying to please, she's trying to be human and open in a mechanical society, and she's trying to be perfect, to be totally pleasing to her husband in every way, and it destroys her. I believe women do try to please their men in our society, so completely that they either lose their identity as women or go overboard and break down emotionally. I wanted to sum up the whole national way of life for women.

"Of course, when you lose your inhibitions as an actress as well as play someone who's uninhibited it's very dangerous. The air is very thin and rarefied out there on the end of a limb. But, as an actress, you have to be prepared to take risks—life-or-death risks."

It's fine to take risks as an actress, but doesn't Gena sometimes regret the loss of the glamour-girl image she enjoyed back in the 1950s, before she married John? "No, no. That kind of career is so artificial, and short-lived. Look what happened to Marilyn Monroe. Right this minute, I'm aware that people think of me as Mabel." Gena Rowlands smiles her beautiful, guarded smile. "And it doesn't bother me at all."

Mary Miles Minter

Eight years after this previously unpublished interview, Mary Miles Minter is still around. Recently, a friend of mine went by the house to see if there was any sign of life. He saw a disturbance at an upper window. A hand drew back a curtain, a pale face peeped out for an instant, and then withdrew. The drapes closed. There wasn't another inkling of occupancy. It was like a scene from Capote's *Other Voices, Other Rooms*. The plump, beleaguered figure in the darkened room, the memories still attacking her like savage moths, and, probably, the smell of camphor in the air. . . .

---★---

1970

"Would you," the bookstore man said, "be interested in interviewing Mary Miles Minter about a possible life story?" Would I? I would. She had figured in the greatest murder case in Hollywood's history.

Fifty years before the phone call, Mary Miles Minter had been a pink, soft, cuddly adult baby, a movie star adored by millions across the world. She appeared ringleted in gauzy photographs, framed in motifs of violets. James Montgomery Flagg painted her. Even at age twenty, she gazed innocently out of the screen, cast as a child. She was Mary Pickford's nearest rival in the schmaltz stakes.

Then, overnight, the meringue dream crumbled. On February 1, 1922, William Desmond Taylor, a jodhpured and putteed English expatriate director loved by both Mary and the comedienne Mabel Normand, was found shot in the back in his bungalow court apartment. Columns screamed. Smelling salts were fetched. Mabel Normand's love letters were found in Taylor's riding boots, but somebody claimed to have picked up Mary Miles Minter's initialed step-ins from his living room floor. Both ladies were through.

For five decades, with grave doubt hanging over Mary's formidable mother, Mrs. Shelby, Mary, her mother, and grandmother lived in their house at the beach, hiding their secrets, like the figures in a Lorca play. Mrs. Shelby died; the grandmother died. Mabel Normand, who was known to keep cocaine in her hair curlers, was dead by 1930. The mystery of Taylor's death remained unsolved. Mary Miles Minter lived on.

Would I see her? I could hardly wait.

Her voice on the telephone was high, sharp, commanding. She still had a Broadway British accent, pure Charles Frohman, circa 1911. Before her movie career she had been the stage Shirley Temple of her day, and Frohman, the great producer, had hung a green ribbon around her neck with a medallion on it. She was talking to me sixty years later in that same high, almost Oxonian tone.

She asked me down for the day. She was living in a former bishop's house in Santa Monica. It was built in the form of a cross.

She was a long time answering the door. The bell pealed hollowly, and no one came. I had time to listen to the buzz of wasps, the growl of a lawn mower, and the slow slurp of the Pacific on beige dirty sand.

At last the door opened. It was Baby Jane. She was enormous, dressed in a curious creation of timeless patterned cotton, with motifs of giant marigolds. Bright spots of rouge blazed from each cheek. Her eyes were a glassy periwinkle blue, secretive and expressionless. Her lips were painted in a cupid bow, straight out of a 1914 valentine. Her hips could have been sat on by two large children.

She ushered me into the living room where a maid was puffing up cushions. Every inch of the room was crowded with knickknacks; bookshelves towered about us. She showed me briefly the famous violet-colored stationery with purple butterflies on the letterhead, which she had used to write to William Desmond Taylor.

She seemed petrified of the tape recorder, looking at it as though it were a small black bomb. She had not given an interview in half a century. She was afraid of what she might say.

I had come to talk about the murder but for two hours she discussed nothing except the life of a gentlewoman in the Deep South at the beginning of the century, her infancy and schooling, her career on the stage. Then, at last, she got down to brass tacks.

She began by attacking Adela Rogers St. Johns, who had written in her memoirs that Mary Miles Minter's mother was guilty of the murder of Taylor. "I'm beginning to feel that the St. Johns woman may be guilty of having committed one of the great journalistic crimes of the century. She has pilloried a very good woman, a very innocent woman, who was not particularly well-liked, straight as a die, who had not the slightest occasion to be killing Mr. Taylor. She knew her daughter, inside out; she knew I was not having an affair with Mr. Taylor.

"It would have been quite a trick for me to have slipped out of the house to see Taylor at night without my mother knowing it. The house was so constructed that she would have seen my car leave from almost any window. And I never had money to go anywhere on my own. To this day, I don't handle money. I don't go shopping, I loathe it. I send my maid, Emmy, to get whatever I want."

Emmy came in, carrying a heavy tea tray. Sipping the brew, still looking uneasily at the recorder, Miss Minter continued: "It was absurd to suggest that I would have bought the step-ins that were supposed to have been found in the living room.

My mother always bought them. It would no more have occurred to her to have had my step-ins embroidered than to have flown to the moon. This woman Adela Rogers St. Johns is covering up the fact that her father planted the step-ins himself. Had them made himself. With my initials on them.

"There is no mystery about my mother's whereabouts on the fatal night. She was in her other house across town. There were decorators working on it, and she had to let them in, so she decided to stay there. On the murder night she was playing bridge with her tax consultant, Margery Burger, an actor named Carl Stockdale, and a man attached to the district attorney's department."

I asked Miss Minter if she would reconstruct for me the events of the night on which the murder took place. "I believe Mr. Taylor was killed by a boy who ran away following a robbery of a gas station down the street. The gas station was at the foot of Alvarado near Sixth. I understand that the owner happened to be there. Three youths attempted to hold him up. He shot a revolver at them and they scattered.

"He ran after them. I believe one of the boys fled into his apartment and shot Mr. Taylor with no motive whatsoever except that he had been surprised. It was an accident. He had seen Taylor standing outside the apartment saying good night to Mabel Normand and giving her a book to read. Leaving the door ajar. The boy could have got in through the front or the back without being noticed."

Miss Minter showed me a surprisingly detailed chart of the bungalow court, indicating how ingress may have been obtained. She had total recall of every detail of the rooms. She was at great pains to declare that she had never been upstairs, where the bedroom was. She launched into a discussion of the fact that many people had claimed they had seen Mrs. Shelby disguised as a man leaving the apartment, when the light from a streetlamp fell on her face. Miss Minter imperiously swept this idea like a crumb off a table. "I'm sure I don't know where *that* idea came from!" she said.

She conjured up a vivid picture of Taylor returning to the apartment after saying good night to Mabel Normand, sitting at his desk with his back to the dining room, while the refugee boy hid in the shadows, unable to get out without being seen. The boy, she suggested, had tried to crawl behind him to the door. Taylor heard him, tried to get up, and the boy panicked and shot him. The bullet had entered at an angle from the base of the spine; it must, she figured, have been fired from the floor.

"Henry Peavey, the black manservant, found the body in the morning, in a pool of blood, and went screaming into the courtyard. Mrs. Douglas MacLean, who lived in the court, said she saw a slight figure in boy's clothing closing the back door and slipping out of the apartment. That seems to me to fit with my theory."

I asked Miss Minter how she heard about Taylor's death. "Mother brought the news to me. I was dressing when she came pounding up the stairs to my room. I felt guilty, because I didn't have my dress on, and Mother was always impatient if I wasn't ready for her. So I closed the door. She yanked it open and she said, 'Taylor was found murdered in bed. Where were you last night?' I couldn't tell you what I said. I don't know. All I know is I went to pick up the car keys. I had to get into my car and go. I could see from the window that my car was blocked in the driveway.

"My mother was blocking the doorway. I found myself staring at her jugular vein. I said to her, 'You'll have to get away from the door.' She said, 'Where are you going?' I said, 'To him, of course! Get away from the door!' And I know that at a certain point she *got* away from the door.

"I went on downstairs and found my grandmother sitting in my car. My mother moved her car and Grandmother and I went in a great rush to Mr. Taylor's apartment.

"When I got there, it was full of police. Boxes of books were being carried out. 'Where is he?' I asked. 'Where is he?' They told me he was at Oberhauser and Oberhauser Mortuary at Tenth and Hill. I was so unaware of myself that I had gone a few feet and I turned around and did the most idiotic thing you can possibly imagine. He always wore a little silver ring on his left pinkie finger with a cabochon sapphire in it. I hadn't a shred of his except a card or a little note or two, and I felt I had to have something of him.

"I asked someone there, 'Did he leave a will?' hoping that he had left that ring to me. Now I ask you. Of all the idiotic things for me to have done. It's a miracle that that innocent question of mine wasn't blown up into something horrible in the minds of the police. Thank God, nothing happened.

"At last I found the mortuary. It was on a steep hill. There seemed to be a thousand steps up to it. Grandmother came along with me up the steps. She was a proud woman who would never wear flat-heeled shoes. She was trying to get up those steps. One of the Oberhausers and a white uniformed nurse came down the steps to get us. I said for some reason, 'I'm coming to give blood. Let's get in there where I can lie down on the table and you can pump the blood out of me into him.' He said, 'I can't do that.' I said, 'You don't understand. This is my man. I have the right. I claim this man. He belongs to *me!*' He said, 'I must tell you that there are circumstances involving this fatal injury.' I said, 'Fatal? He isn't dead. He couldn't be! When people are not dead, if you just take the right action they'll come back.'

"I cannot tell you how I pleaded and begged him and insisted on seeing Mr. Taylor. I was becoming hysterical.

"Finally he said, 'This is what I will do. If you promise to tell no one about this and come alone you can come tomorrow at noon and see the body. I promise you that for a brief time you will be with him.' I came back the next day. He ushered me into the room and Mr. Taylor was lying on a slab. His wonderful features reminded me of the figures on the tombs of the fallen warriors of yore. He was under a gray silk cover drawn up to his neck. Mr. Oberhauser said, 'I've allowed the upper portion to be undressed so that you could see him.'

"There was a bullet hole slightly to the back of his neck. It had gone up through the back. Finally Mr. Oberhauser made me understand that my man was dead. I had with me some roses. Red roses. I'm not very tall. I'm not even five feet two. I wanted to get up to him. To kiss him on the lips. And I couldn't lean over far enough. But as I touched him he was cold with an incredible coldness. Have you ever touched a departed person? That *deadly* cold! It convinced me as nothing else could that no life could return to this man. I stood beside him, holding on tight to his left arm, sobbing wildly. 'Who could have done this to him?' I asked. 'They crucified Jesus. Now they've crucified Mr. Taylor.'

"I left that place where he lay and went to Mabel Normand's house. The papers had said that she was the last person to see him alive. As I approached I noticed some police ahead of me. They stopped me, asking what I wanted. I told them. I got to the door, and some more policemen jumped up and told me I couldn't see her. She came to the head of the stairs asking, 'Who is it?' I called out my name. She told me to come up to her bedroom. I asked her what she knew about Mr. Taylor's death and she replied, 'My God, Mary, who could have anything against Bill?' I said, 'I haven't seen him for quite some time.' She said, 'I know. I know. Do you know why he was so fond of me? Because he told me I was the only one he could do it with.' She said, 'Mary, I've been keeping the secret for months and months. He worshiped the ground you walked on. He wanted to do the right thing by you. He feared that you would love him all the days of your life and that he loved you, too. He would never hurt you.' I said, 'The only way he could have hurt me was not to have become my husband. I wouldn't have cared if I'd had to wait to the end of my life. Mabel, I don't know what your views are about marriage, but I love the idea of a wedding, a wedding gown, a church, the majesty of it—that's the sort of wedding I want. I believe that you can only marry once. Regardless of canon law. You marry when you meet and you love and you know that you are loved. I say that in that instant you marry. You give yourself with everything you've got and you can no more take it back than you can become some other person.' She said, 'I know you were never lovers. He would have told me if you were.'

"We tried to think who might have killed him. We couldn't.

"The district attorney was out of town and had left an assistant in charge, a Mr. Nolan. My attorney took me down to Mr. Nolan who asked me what I was doing on the night of the murder. I said I was reading a book by Stephen Leacock named *Cruise of the Kawa*. My sister was with me—I can still see her sitting under a big mahogany lamp with a pink shade reading a magazine. The cook, Belle Simpson, was there also. They accepted my alibi. My mother's was accepted. Two years went by.

"A new district attorney, Mr. Asa Keys, came to my New York apartment in 1924. He was a big man, with a red face and a gruff haw-haw voice. He started to question me. He said if I answered his questions he would tell me who the guilty person was.

"He stood me against the mantel with light from all sides beating on my face and he asked me when I had last seen Taylor. I answered on December 23, 1921, when I brought him a Christmas present. He said, 'Stand right here. If you lie to me, that's the end of you.' I said, 'How dare you say that I would lie to you! What have I got to lie to you about?' Then he said, 'I have some checking up to do. Will you stay in this apartment and not attempt to reach anyone outside? I'll see to it that food is sent in.' I asked him, 'How long will I be pent up here?' He said, 'I don't know. But have I your word that you will not attempt to leave this place?' He promised to get back to me as soon as he could. I said I would do anything if he would promise to tell me the identity of the murderer. Three days or four days went by. He came back and said, 'Little lady, I'm the district attorney of Los Angeles and I probably shouldn't be telling you this. But you have the sweetest little million-dollar lawsuit against the County of Los Angeles that anyone could drop into your lap. Every damn word you told me was true.' I said, 'Did you think it wasn't? Mr. Keys, you don't think I did it, that I am the murderess? Do you mean to say that I'm the only suspect you have? That you really don't know anything? That you really don't have anyone at all, only me?' I wept.

"I told him, 'All I want is to know the murderer. I would ask nothing more than to be left alone in the room with him.' And do you know I still feel like that today? I would ask no greater release than to be allowed to get at him. I wouldn't need a weapon. I have not very strong hands as you can see. This one is maimed badly. But I'm sure I would find the strength. To hurt him." Mary Miles Minter was close to tears. "Yes. I would strike him. I would take justice into my hands. For what he did to Mr. Taylor. For what he did to the world."

Robert Wagner

I seized an excuse to interview Robert Wagner because I wanted to hear his story of an extraordinary mishap aboard a teleferique. Like so many people who suffer from acrophobia, I have a morbid interest in tales of disasters in high places. His account, as will be seen, was particularly harrowing. He has also conducted a dangerous high-wire act in sustaining his television series *Switch*. It has often been threatened with cancellation, and was only recently saved by a mass protest from the readers of the *National Enquirer*. Nuff said.

---- ★ ----

1977

At forty-seven, Robert Wagner is in a condition many men of thirty-seven would envy. He is tanned, trim, and a star of celebrity tennis matches (including successful bouts with Rod Laver, Fred Stolle, John Newcombe, and Ken Rosewall). He is remarried to the very attractive Natalie Wood (eleven years after their divorce and marriages to other people). He has an elegant house in Beverly Hills, and three appealing children, Katharine, thirteen, a child by his second marriage, Natasha, 6, Natalie's child with her second husband, and Courtney, three, the couple's only child together.

He has a yacht, *Splendour,* which he sails frequently, expensive cars, fine clothes, and probably at least a million dollars in assets.

And yet Robert Wagner is a troubled man. First of all, he is harassed by problems connected with his high-rated series, *Switch,* in which he costars with Eddie Albert; and, seven years after the cancellation he is still smarting at the executive decision at MCA-Universal which prematurely killed off his beloved *It Takes a Thief* series just when it had hit its peak.

I arrived at his house for cocktails late on a typically dry and smoggy Los Angeles afternoon. Black servants ran in and out, shouting boisterously, children yelled from an upstairs playroom, dogs leaped and barked at the doorbell, flowers arrived for the wrong house, and the star conducted an immensely long telephone call to a producer while I waited for almost half an hour in a sunken living room exploding with exotic tropical plants.

The atmosphere was pure Raymond Chandler, all the way to a cocktail bar of the kind seen in 1940s Hollywood films, with the glasses piled up on shelves in the front of the window. The kind of display Kirk Douglas or Burt Lancaster always used to shatter in an outburst of rage following a quarrel with Barbara Stanwyck or Lizabeth Scott.

Wagner turned out to be quite informal, striding into the room in white, short-sleeved shirt and shorts, dark with the sun.

Seemingly casual, he is in fact fiercely committed to improving the quality of his shows. He strode about, emphasizing a point, or, leaning forward in a chair, stabbing the air with a meaningful finger.

"I've never forgotten how Universal killed *It Takes a Thief,*" he said. "One day after shooting was finished a producer came down from his office and told me, 'Congratulations, Bob, your show has the greatest demographics in TV today.'

"The very next day, we were canceled. So that should show you what this crazy TV business is likely to do. The show was a success, the format was perfect, the identification element was strong, and as a result *Thief* was the biggest show in the history of syndication for Universal. And they killed it.

"Let me tell you what happened. I didn't want to do the show initially. Lew Wasserman, the boss of MCA-Universal, who was originally my agent, wanted me to do it. I was against all TV but he talked me into it.

"Then the show was put in as a midseason replacement. I thought, This is the end of my career. Midseason replacements usually die the death. I'm going to be slaughtered in the ratings.

"I was scared. Here I was, a quarterback with the whole team depending on me. If I failed—finish. Well, the series took off with a bang. They kept moving us to new time slots and the audience followed us just the same.

"Then the ax fell. A new executive team came in which wanted to develop its own programs. They canceled *Thief.* I was a joint owner of the show with ABC Networks and MCA-Universal. I couldn't believe they'd pulled the rug from under me. It still makes me sick to think about it.

"I said to them, the new team, 'What the hell's going on?' I just couldn't believe it. I still can't. I said, 'What do you mean by this? Don't you want the show?' And they replied, 'No. We've decided to go in another direction.' Another direction. When they had it made."

Wagner looked out of the window at the well-groomed lawn and the dry trees. "They refused to give a better reason. I finally faced the reality the show had been canceled. I was mad. Then they wanted me—would you believe?—to do guest spots on shows.

"First they wanted me to do a Virginian. Then something else. And something else. I said, 'Look, we're in a very bad situation here. You're in a difficult spot, I recognize that. You have two years to go with me. You can't make a contract for another series. You owe me a great deal of money. I know you're just trying to use me up, to milk me. I'll tell you what I want. If it's in the ball park and you feel good about it, then we can go ahead and make an arrangement.' "

Wagner stood up and paced about restlessly. "I told them, if you want me, I want my own team. And I don't want to play a detective. I want the chance to have my writers prepare three ideas and out of the best of those we'll do a pilot and then I'll be boss.

"I presented one thing, two things, three things, and never got an answer. And then they offered me *Charlie Chan.*" Wagner looked furious. "And *Bureau of Missing Persons.* Oh, God. And *McMillan and Wife.*

"So I'd had it. I said, 'Thanks a lot. That's it, fellers. I've presented my ideas, you've given me these others—which are completely wrong for me. I'm going.'

"They said, 'Oh, no, you don't. You're in breach of contract. You cannot make any TV for anybody else.' I went off to England and did TV anyway for ABC, *Madame Sin,* with Bette Davis, whom I'm crazy about. That's one hell of a lady.

"Universal tried to stop me. They pushed me right to the wall. They wanted part of my residuals on everything I did. They wanted to slice up my salary. Just to let me work at all." Wagner's voice rose in anger again.

"Then they enjoined me from working. I had a bad, bad time. I sued them for the right to be free. I won. I went on my way.

"I'd had it up to here with TV. The interference. Just one other thing in London, *Colditz,* based on *The Colditz Story,* then nothing.

"A guy called Len Larson, I'd helped get started in this business, wrote *Switch.* CBS decided to combine me with Eddie Albert. I decided I'd try again—the chemistry was right.

"And the hatchet was buried at MCA-Universal. I went back and they shook my hand. Lew Wasserman's a personal friend of mine; he comes to my house.

"But there are still problems. Not enough scripts ready— all actors complain about that. You have to rewrite everything, usually on the set. Blue pages, yellow pages, the scripts look like rainbows. It's murder.

"I had a problem with the producer right away. We couldn't get enough scripts. We were behind all the way. There was one very difficult producer I had to fire off the show. Luckily I have two men now who are great.

"For the whole of the first year it was hell. I was trying to get depth into the characters and the writers were trying for situations, angles. They were so busy with connective tissue, the characterizations went out the window.

"There was no time to get good writing. No time even to have good dubbing. The show that went on Sundays had its final dubbing session Thursdays. The print was still wet when it went on the air.

"I found myself on the phone calling up actresses, saying, 'I've got a script that's good for you but it's not finished.' This is not the way to run this business.

"The most important thing in our business is preparation. It's the cry of our whole industry. This year we have a pickup —thirteen developed. So at last we're ahead. We won't be officially renewed until just one month before the first show of the new series, which starts in Las Vegas in June.

"If I hadn't put incredible pressure on for those thirteen scripts in advance, we'd be sunk without a trace in our new season.

"And yet winning that lawsuit made a difference. Lew Wasserman broke backs to set me loose to do *Cat on a Hot Tin Roof* with Natalie for Laurence Olivier in London. They even postponed the starting date of *Switch* to let me do it."

Making *Cat on a Hot Tin Roof* had been the most creative experience of his life. He played Brick, the homosexual husband in Tennessee Williams's play, who is unable to love his wife because of his emotional conflicts.

"I got on a plane to London on July fifth and started shooting on July sixth. I finished on July fourteenth and went back to work on *Switch*. It was rough," he said. "But Lord Olivier—Larry, he's been our friend for years—was incredible. He met us at the airport, at six thirty in the morning, with flowers and champagne. And he was terrific to work with. He was looping *Marathon Man* in Paris, flying to Morocco to do Zeffirelli's *Jesus Christ*, and still playing Big Daddy in *Cat* and producing our show. I never saw anybody with so much energy."

If making *Cat on a Hot Tin Roof* was the most enjoyable

experience of Wagner's life, then making two suspense epics, *The Towering Inferno* and *The Mountain* was the worst.

In *The Towering Inferno*, Wagner had to be in a burning set, in a scene in which he played an executive trapped with his girl friend in a suite of a giant San Francisco skyscraper.

He said, "I didn't actually run through the set with a towel on my head and flames all around me the way you saw the guy do it on the screen. That was done by a stunt man. It was a terrible stunt. If he'd have fallen down and taken one breath —finish. He'd have been dead. The fire would have burned his lungs.

"But I had to be seen in the flames. Just for a moment so the audience would believe it. My jacket caught fire. They put it out with hoses and then cut to the guy. I didn't think he'd make it."

The Mountain also placed his life in jeopardy. Wagner played a mountaineer, with Spencer Tracy as a veteran climber of Mont Blanc.

He said, "That was the worst thing that ever happened to me. The teleferique, or cable railway, went up to the mountain. It's the largest single-span teleferique in the world. There are no pylons. A jet hit it five or six years ago.

"I was afraid to go on it. So Spence said, 'Look, we'll ride up together.' In the middle, with a drop of three thousand feet below us, it went off the rails.

"It slid off the track. The front end went up and banged the cable. It hung there, in space. I thought we were going. I was sure we were going to drop.

"We just hung there. When they realized what happened, they evidently decided to send down a work car, an exposed movable platform, and we were supposed to have gotten out of our car and climbed into the other one with three thousand feet of nothing underneath.

"We couldn't do it. I don't think we would ever have made it. Even if we hadn't slipped during the transfer, we couldn't have clung to it all the several miles to the top. We hung there for forty-five minutes with our car swaying in the wind. A woman and a couple of young kids were there, and the so-called conductor—what a conductor does in a teleferique I can't imagine. Spencer was numb—just stared into the void below.

"They managed to back the car onto the cable again. Inch by inch. I thought the car was going to cut the cable in half. They managed to balance us and up we went. Trouble with a TV series suddenly seems small after that."

Natalie Wood, looking stunning in a swirl of tropical colors, entered the room. "Don't they, Nat?" He hugged her and smiled, and turned to me. "Have another drink?"

Robert Young

This was the first interview I did for *The New York Times*. I was extremely nervous, because I knew that the only thing people would want to hear about was Robert Young's former alcoholism, and I did not want to discuss it with him. However, I felt obliged to do so. I called the press agent who arranged the interview and he told me that I could talk to Robert Young about anything *except* his alcoholism!

I arrived early, and managed to obtain all the information I wanted from Mr. Young before the press agent got there. As it turned out, I needn't have worried. Mr. Young talked of little else but his alcoholism the rest of the afternoon. He was a nice, honest man: one felt that, if he had taken up medicine, he would have been a great deal happier than he was. And surely *he* would always have made house calls.

1971

"Sixty-five million people," says Robert Young, television's Marcus Welby, M.D., "watched the program last week. That's around one-third of the population. It's ridiculous. If I thought about it for two seconds, I'd freeze up on camera and never utter another word."

We are sitting in the leafy patio of Young's Beverly Hills

home. Tucked behind bare elms, the Pennsylvania Dutch farmhouse is as snugly vintage Norman Rockwell as any addict of the top-rated ABC program would expect: Abraham Lincoln bookends, fire flickering around imitation logs, family portrait emitting a faint pastel glow from the living room. At sixty-three, Young is subdued and solid, kindly hazel eyes watering behind contact lenses, face as comfortably creased as a turtle's, hands making schoolteacher's steeples as he emphasizes a point in a phrase. The paternal image is satisfyingly complete, but it's obvious as you talk to him that he is far more complex than his appearance immediately suggests.

Robert Young. The name conjures up three careers. First, as the prototypical M-G-M thirties, smooth-faced juvenile in cable-knit sweaters and Oxford bags, saying "Tennis, anyone?" or changing into white tie and tails, elegantly lighting Joan Crawford's cigarettes all through the Great Depression. Second, as the mature forties actor, playing Boston Brahmin in *H. M. Pulham, Esq.* or scarred war veteran in *The Enchanted Cottage*, David to Dorothy McGuire's classic goody-goody Claudia or urgent liberal detective of the anti-anti-Semitism melodrama, *Crossfire*. Third the all-American Father Figure, photographed at home with wife, four daughters, and five grandchildren, starring for six years on television as Jim Anderson, harassed dad of *Father Knows Best,* finally achieving a humanist apotheosis as king of the Nielsen ratings in *Welby,* tackling seemingly everything from the common cold to sexual promiscuity.

Pleasantly serious and sensitive, Young talks carefully, measuring out his words like prescription doses. "I wanted to do the program because it highlights the role of the general practitioner in a time of increasing specialization. Medicine isn't something I think about in the abstract. It's painfully meaningful to me, and I've based the character of Welby on three practitioners I've known.

"My grandson Robert lived only twenty-four hours. He was killed by hydromembrane, the same thing that took John Kennedy's son. And I've been sick myself. Sick all my life with fear. As far back as I can remember, I was afraid. Of some imagined disaster that never did eventuate. When I was a child, I used to hide in the crooks of trees, just to be alone. When I became an actor I constantly felt I wasn't worthy, that I had no right to be a star. All those years at Metro and even later on *Father Knows Best,* I hid a black terror behind a cheerful face."

Young can't recall a week going by without at least three blinding psychosomatic headaches brought on by his insecurity feelings, smiling at Katharine Hepburn or Margaret Sullavan or Jane Wyatt through a veil of agony. "Naturally, I tried to find a way out. Alcoholism was the inevitable result. It took me more than thirty years to realize I was poisoning myself to death.

"I wasn't cured overnight. I did it myself, over a long period, just by coming back again and again to that moment when you know that if you don't stop a chronic cold it's going to turn into pneumonia. It was an immensely slow, difficult process, but after slipping back again and again, I at last made a kind of giant step and I was across the threshold to sanity and health.

"People talk about Alcoholics Anonymous suddenly ending a bad habit, but it's really a question of the person himself coming to a slow but finally complete understanding of the nature of his own illness."

Alcoholics Anonymous aided him, and he has worked on their behalf, lecturing and arranging meetings.

Young's family life hasn't been all *Father Knows Best,* either. "Last year, one of my daughters got divorced. Another daughter divorced her husband, then remarried him. My youngest, Kathy, hasn't gotten married at all, perhaps because she's seen all the problems her sisters have had to face. It's true, Betty and I have been happily married for thirty-seven years, but I guess to Kathy all that seems rooted in antiquity."

I asked Young if his newly found confidence and enormous television success have encouraged him to think about going into politics in the wake of those other thirties juveniles, Ronald Reagan and George Murphy. "If I'd run against Ronnie in the last California election, as some people seemed to feel I should, I'd probably have won just five votes from my loyal if reluctant family.

"I'd have wanted to increase taxes. We need more money for our colleges, for our roads, and our water, and to clean up our air. If my rich friends complain they should move to Guadalajara. Theoretically, there's no reason why an actor shouldn't go into politics. Ronnie's camera sense gives him a nice unfair advantage. Murphy wasn't so lucky, but he rose up against a weak opponent and second time around he just didn't have the armory to answer Tunney's challenges. And then he'd say things like, 'The war's going great in Vietnam.' Hawk or dove, you just don't say things like that." Unless you're John Wayne? "Well, Wayne marches to—what's the poet's phrase?—a different drum. He still sees the Stars and Stripes unfurling over the regiments."

Young, surprisingly, turns out to be an anticonservative independent, long since a refugee from the Republican party, voting for whichever candidate he likes best at a given moment, furious about what has happened to the American Indian and angered still further by the fact that residents of Rancho Santa Fe, near San Diego, where he has his second home, would not allow blacks to settle there. "It's almost eerily conservative. I was the only one there to disapprove of Proposition Fourteen of an Open Housing Bill calling for discrimination against blacks. I firmly expected guys in white hoods to ride up to my house and set fire to it.

"I actually *like* hippies. I don't approve of their escape into drugs, though I deeply understand it. Drugs, after all, destroy their health and their looks, and by escaping they're simply moving themselves into a special kind of limbo from which often there's no return. I like their indifference to the old American passion for acquiring money—that seems to me a fine progression from previous generations. They aren't as greedy as we were.

"They sometimes fail to understand child hygiene, but just watch them with their children and you see that they're like Indians with a papoose. However they might be drugged, however sick or spaced, they huddle around their families protectively, and I haven't seen any examples of serious desertion or neglect in the visits I've made to their communities."

Young had an uneasy relationship with his father, an Irish immigrant carpenter turned staunch Republican building contractor. "He was very strict, very severe, and I loved him dearly, but the truth is when he was out of town we all breathed a sigh of relief." Young worked from the age of eight, selling newspapers, and the family—living first in Chicago, where he was born on February 22, 1907, then in Los Angeles—often had barely enough to eat. Unsentimentally, he recalls the years working as a Los Angeles debt collector and bank clerk and Keystone Kops extra, and, after his father's final desertion of home when Young was ten, the constant struggle for survival. Marriage to his high-school sweetheart Betty was an immense help, and a kindly schoolmarm helped him to escape his harrowing shyness by coaxing him to act at the Pasadena Playhouse.

In 1931, after months of knocking at studio doors, he at last managed to land a Metro screen test. He was twenty-four, tall and willowy and painfully nervous. "Metro was going through the motions of testing a producer's girlfriend. I read her lines. She was so terrible they kept shooting over her shoulder at me. I was signed and she wasn't." When he went home to announce the news, his mother, brothers, and sister joined hands and danced around the kitchen table.

Oddly enough, his first important screen role was as a doctor in *The Sin of Madelon Claudet,* in which he had to tell his ailing mother, acted by Helen Hayes, that her illness was terminal. For nine years after that, Young walked through a succession of dapper, interchangeable hero roles, the Robert who didn't quite make it into the Taylor or even the Montgomery class. At one time he played in three service movies at once, dashing from stage to stage and invariably getting the uniforms mixed up. One exception was his 1939 role in *Three Comrades* as a German officer, which shocked his fans. "They just couldn't get used to my playing a Hun. There was a similar problem in the forties when I made a picture called *They Won't Believe Me,* in which I was cast as a heel. The picture was correctly named. The public *didn't* believe me. I went right back to playing good guys again after the box-office results came in. Fate, I guess."

Leaving M-G-M in 1946, Young free-lanced successfully, chiefly for RKO. *Father Knows Best* began as a radio show in 1949, moving to network television in 1954. Bored and exhausted by its relentless cheerfulness, and his schmaltzy title role ("It all seemed so pat"), Young abandoned the series in 1960 when it was still highly rated. Seen by audiences from Tokyo to Melbourne, it earned him a fortune from his 50 percent interest.

By the mid-sixties it seemed as though Robert Young was comfortably but definitely washed up. A new series, *Window On Main Street,* in which he played a novelist, flopped. He took off on an ill-fated stage tour as a bewildered father in the comedy *Generation,* collapsing twice of exhaustion in Detroit and Chicago. Returning home, he was forced to treat himself as an invalid, swimming, golfing, resting in the sun.

Gradually, with the help of Betty Young and Alcoholics Anonymous, he emerged during the last three years to the first real happiness of his life. When producer David Victor chose him—Young doesn't kid himself that he was first choice —for Marcus Welby, he was aware that his final chance for regeneration had come. They worked together carefully on the new series, trying to fire a degree of warmth and vigor to the tired, ancient format by *Ben Casey* out of *Kildare*—of old doctor fights young doctor on crucial medical issues, curing one patient per program. Victor's and his wife's encouragement made him go ahead to the big comeback that set the final seal on his career. "At first I resented the help I got. I was the lost child that does not want to find his way home. But I learned. There's a marvelous story I read once that illustrates what happened to me.

"A migrant worker is gathering peas at dusk. He will only be paid if his basket is full when the sun goes down. He's hurrying, desperately, to fill it up before it gets dark.

"A man on the other side of the field is ahead of him. The migrant begins to develop a hatred for the man. The man is filling up a hat. Finally the migrant goes up to him angrily and asks him what he is doing. The man takes the hat and tips the contents into the migrant's basket, filling it to the brim. And as he does so, he says, 'Now *you owe* someone a hat full of peas.'"

David Steinberg

Probably because he's too intelligent, David Steinberg hasn't made it all the way to the top. There was one aspect of the interview I left out because I had no space for it. Steinberg was living at the time in the haunted house which had recently been vacated by Joe Hyams and Elke Sommer. Joe and Elke had seen the figure of a man standing in one corner of the dining room. A fire had swept through the house, emanating from the spot where the ghostly man stood. On one occasion, a Yellow Cab had arrived for an out-of-town guest and had gone up the hill without picking up the guest. When Joe called the cab company angrily, they said, "But the guy did pick up the fare. And the fare disappeared before the driver could get any instructions." Joe asked for a description of the passenger. It was the ghost in the dining room.

At a certain stage in the Steinberg interview, I noticed an odd, stiff, pale figure standing beyond him. Fortunately, the tape recorder was going, and Mr. Steinberg was the kind of comedian who didn't need any questions, for I was far too uneasy to ask one. When it was time to go, I watched the figure move into the dining room. I shivered a little.

Somebody told me it was the tax man.

★

1972

"It's as though I'm living a David Steinberg situation. Here I am, working for CBS in a brand-new summer show. And right next door to my office the CBS guys are preparing to answer to a suit lodged against the network by the Smothers Brothers. I was supposed to be the one responsible for the brothers being taken off the air. And now I'll have to give evidence for the brothers, against my own bosses."

The nimble, surrealist comedian, star of "The David Steinberg Show," is referring to a case due to be tried in the Los Angeles Federal Court involving the cancellation of the Smothers Brothers show in April 1969. Steinberg had taped one of his famous comic sermonettes—ironical comments on Bible texts—for a show to be played on Easter Sunday in the week of Eisenhower's funeral. CBS demanded that certain offensive lines of the sermonette—on Jonah and the Whale—be removed ("The Gentiles grabbed the Jews by the Old Testament"), and the brothers refused. On April 3, Robert Wood, president of CBS, informed them by telegram from New York that not only would the show not go on that Sunday, it would never go on again. Now they are suing for $31 million on a number of counts, including breach of their constitutional rights by the imposing of network censorship restrictions, and wrongful dismissal.

Steinberg is sufficiently fond of the comedy of the absurd to be relishing the situation. And just to give it another twist, he has used his carte blanche status with the network to engage Tommy Smothers as a guest for one of what might be called his anti-talk shows. Steinberg's aim is to expose the character of talk-show hosts—expressing a cheerful sycophancy while tensing up as a commercial looms, flattering a guest while wondering when the hell he is going to shut up, trying to figure out how he can possibly upstage someone very famous while seeming to be modestly overawed.

He is a Magritte among TV clowns. In a preview of one taped show he bounds onto the set with crushing confidence, accompanied by blaring music and giant letters announcing his name, then produces an immense hand, about twenty times the size of a baseball glove, with which he obviously wants to grip the hands of the entire world. It is a ruthless joke many of the audience miss, a comment not only on the desperate eagerness of the idols of the Box, but on Americans as a whole, crying "Love me!" to the universe.

Steinberg has the exact measure of stars: in another show, he has his guests singing in a mood of swooning rapture, "It's you! It's you! It's you!" to giant photographs of themselves. The final visual comment in that same show is the deadliest. On an animated cartoon finale, Steinberg is seen as a middle-aged baby, crawling cheerfully along the floor, only to be crushed into extinction by a giant gorilla foot. Something, he is saying, is waiting out there to squash all you happy people for good. His executive producer and manager, Arlyne Rothberg, even seems to think that image may be prophetic. "I have a feeling the critics and the people will kill us," she says. "We have dared too much, and will they understand us out in Oklahoma?"

Tense, thin, and pale, with shrewd, despairing eyes shyly half-hidden behind smoky-blue spectacles, Steinberg looks as though he has just turned on a shower tap in a Greenwich Village walk-up only to see a cockroach fall out. Instead, he somewhat edgily inhabits a Haunted House Beautiful in a Beverly Hills canyon, all shingled roof and fairy-tale eaves and flowered chintz, green and cool in its interior with a grand piano, the whole thing so relentlessly kitschy you half expect to see one of the Gabors coming around the door to greet you with a wave of a perfumed handkerchief. Steinberg obviously wonders what the heck he is doing there: "If I stay in California much longer," he says, "I'll melt like butter."

Not that it makes all that much difference, because, wherever he lives, Steinberg feels misplaced. From the beginning of his life, he hasn't fitted into any kind of a predictable pattern at all. Sure, he says he likes pretty girls and Jewish food. But in almost every other particular he is on a personal wavelength of his own, and getting "through" to this man is not entirely easy, for all his charm. He was totally misplaced, first of all, in his family; he was the recalcitrant son of a Romanian rabbi, born in Winnipeg, Canada, some thirty years ago.

"I was the only one in my family who wasn't funny," he says. "I was known as 'the quiet one.' They would always be saying, 'Can we get him to open his mouth?' I'd just sit there. I was horrible. I'd listen, and make a note of everything they said. I haven't forgotten a word and now I can play it all back at them. They were a truthful family. I always lied. I felt fine about that after a while because I read that William Blake and Thomas Wolfe were very good liars, too. So I sat quiet, and when I spoke, I lied. Did I say I was horrible? I was very horrible. My mother is always giving interviews nowadays in which she says, 'He was such a sweet boy, so wonderful, we never hit him.' *Who is she talking about?*

"At eighteen I went to Israel to study theology. My father said, 'I kiss the train that takes you away!' In Israel I studied theology and ran after girls. I went to Chicago and studied some more theology and ran after some more girls. By this time I'm sounding like Harpo Marx. I saw Lenny Bruce and something happened to me. I realized I didn't have to pretend when I did comedy in plays at the University of Chicago, where I was studying for an arts degree. I could play roles drawing on my own experience for the interpretations. Then I saw Second City, that brilliant review with Nichols and May, Barbara Harris, and Alan Arkin. Paul Sills, director of Second City, saw me. I was doing *Candide* at the university, playing every single part except the lead. He hired me.

"Did the company accept me? May I say that is not an easy question to answer. These great people could not be funnier onstage but offstage they weren't so funny. They were lions and tigers. Once they added me to their long list of tensions I guess you could say I was absorbed. . . .

"Finally we parted company. I was going to be a Great Broadway Star! I was in *Carry Me Back to Morningside Heights,* directed by Sidney Poitier. It died. I died. I did *Little Murders.* It died. I died. You want to hear more? All right! I made a documentary film in Peru!"

It looked as though Steinberg would sink without a trace when a thin dark girl, Arlyne Rothberg, then entertainment director of the Playboy Circuit, rescued him. She put him into the Bitter End in Greenwich Village. "They wanted to hear jokes about mothers-in-law. The bus tours came, saw, and fled. I stood there, gazing cheerfully into a void."

A New York critic gave him a good review which encouraged Steinberg to struggle on. Finally, Arlyne managed to hustle a film clip of him to the talent coordinators on the Johnny Carson Show, and he zapped his host so completely he took over the show when Carson was on vacation. He also acted as a replacement host for Dick Cavett, evidently noting down some gestures for his lethal parodies of him on his own shows. His move from underground to overground wasn't easy. He tended to unsettle network executives with irreverence and his reversal of the usual TV formulas.

"I did something for ABC called *The Music Scene.* I had to introduce endless canned acts. You couldn't tell where I ended and the commercials began. I was supposed to say glittering things like, 'And now here is that great, great singer, Smoky Robinson, and I think he's wonderful and I just know you will find him wonderful, too, you wonderful people.' And instead I'd say, 'I never saw the singer you're about to see, Smoky Robinson. Maybe he's good, possibly he isn't, but here am I, me and myself, with my big gorilla foot!' ABC would toss in the canned laughter and they'd want to burn me alive."

His appearance on the Smothers Brothers show resulted in the fiasco that took it off the air. "Needless to say, I wasn't really the cause of it at all. The brothers were getting less funny. Tommy was putting politics in his act. And the ratings were going down. I was the excuse CBS needed."

Steinberg's rehiring by CBS is purely for five weekly summer shows, but he may do more later. The network's forgiveness surprised him, although it was evidently due to an urgent need to find something to fill the Carol Burnett time slot, and despite the impending court case, the big brass decided to let bygones be bygones. "I had the condition that they would give me absolute freedom. I've worked with the censor of

CBS, a man called Samuel Taylor, who had been complaining about my material on the Smothers show. This time we got along fine. In other words, he did not do anything about my material. But despite the fact that the big brass bent over backwards, I really got them worried. They didn't like the fact that my humorous sketches and interviews went on and on, that I didn't use quick jokes and blackouts. I doubt if I'd ever do a weekly show again. A monthly show, maybe. Working on a script until two o'clock in the morning after a dinner party is not my idea of living.

"Instead, I want to do a pirate movie. I've written the script and Milos Forman wants to direct it. Ah, yes, yes, yes, I'll be the star! Can't you just see me hanging upside down from a mast with a sword in my teeth?"

Mercedes McCambridge

I am proud to say that this article gave Mercedes McCambridge a new career. At a birthday party for Linda Blair at Chasen's, a representative of Warners flourished the proofs of my article in my face. Asked what was my idea in writing the piece, I said, "What was your idea in smuggling the proofs out of the paper before their removal was authorized?" I received no reply, observed the baleful eye of director William Friedkin, and spent the rest of the party chatting amiably with Linda Blair, who had no idea I had probably cost her an Oscar. The studio's infamous attempt to obtain her the award by denying Mercedes' crucial contribution to her performance was a main reason for my writing the piece.

───────── ★ ─────────

1974

Perhaps the most horrifying feature of *The Exorcist* is its sound track: director William Friedkin and his experts used the cries of pigs being driven to slaughter to produce the scream of the Demon when it is exorcised from the twelve-year old Regan's body. Although Warner Brothers has not made the fact public, Mercedes McCambridge, the Lady Macbeth of Orson Welles's Mercury Theater of the Air and Oscar-winning actress of *All the King's Men,* hair-raisingly spoke the aural role of the Demon itself.

Millions of parents may find it especially chilling that Linda Blair, the horse-loving teenybopper who played Regan, actually spoke all of the brutal obscenities and blasphemies heard in the movie so that Miss McCambridge could dub the words to Linda's lip movements later.

Mercedes sounds demonically furious when I call her in Los Angeles. She feels Warners soft-pedaled her contribution to the film (the fact was leaked in *Variety* and *Time*) because they did not want to affect Linda Blair's Oscar chances: "Maybe," Mercedes snaps angrily, "people will think the sound-effects people simply fixed her voice up—that it was her vocal performance. But her vocal performance was laughable!

"I have nothing against the child. I've never met her. But if people had heard her saying some of those obscenities, they would have fallen over laughing. Of course, she spoke every word. But much too fast. I said to Billy Friedkin, my director, 'Why did you have her babble her words? It's impossible to fit my words to her lip movements.' No, it's not true that some of her words were blended with mine on the final track. All of the devilish vocality is mine—all of it. Every word.

"Just before you called I was thinking, Does God want to punish me for playing the voice of the Devil? I gave the most difficult performance of my life—and then Warners didn't give me a single credit on the picture or in the advertising. The man who supplied the jewels got a credit! I cried. Billy Friedkin promised me a special credit—'And Mercedes McCambridge.' He broke his promise—it's heartbreaking when someone you thought was a friend does that. I put my father's crucifix against my forehead just twenty minutes ago. It was ice-cold, and I thought, God has deserted me. Shall I go off on an ocean cruise? Then your call came—it was an answer to my prayers before I had a breakdown."

Two hours later, when I visit Mercedes in her Westwood high rise, she is still overwrought and on the verge of tears. With much the same magnetic presence she displayed as the gang leader in Orson Welles's *Touch of Evil,* the actress paces against a panoramic view of western Los Angeles.

"Doing that sound track was a terrible experience. I didn't

just do the voice, I did all of the demon's sounds. That wheezing, for instance. My chronic bronchitis helped with that. I did it on one microphone, then on another, elevating it a bit, then a third and fourth, two tones higher each time, and they combined them, as a chorus. The wailing just before the Demon is driven out, that's the keening sound I once heard at a wake in Ireland. I used moaning cries I had used when playing Lady Macbeth for Orson. For the groaning sounds, I pulled a scarf around my neck, tight, and almost strangled.

"I'm a product of sixteen years of convent education, and I am still a devout Catholic, so speaking those vile, blaspheming words was an agony for me. For sixteen years, I sat in front of a pulpit hearing about the horror of Evil Incarnate, and now I had to play Evil Incarnate. How? After hearing Bishop Sheen say that 'Satan is the personification of all Evil,' I can't believe that Satan will sound like Mary Poppins, can I? So I had to think Evil. Every night when I came home, I got down on my knees and gave thanks to God that I had been able to conjure up so much demonic personality. It was in me, of course. It's in you, it's in everyone."

Mercedes McCambridge fixes some tea, sits down opposite me, and looks at me hard in the eye. "I had to imagine Lucifer. I had to imagine the incredible, bottomless agony—the eternal agony of a lost soul. I drew on memory for that. I've been an alcoholic, saved by A.A., and I've seen people in state hospitals, vegetables in straitjackets, the hopeless, abysmal, bottomless groaning and screaming. I used imitations of those hellish cries. I've been through hell, and I thought, Who better than I would know how the Devil feels? I'm out of hell, he's there forever. To be on Death Row for eternity has got to be some kind of sentence.

"So I cried out from my remembered hell. And when I spoke the scene in which the little girl spits out green vomit, when I made the ugly sounds of violent expectoration, I swallowed eighteen raw eggs, with a pulpy apple. To convey the feeling of the Devil being trapped, I had the crew tear up a sheet and bind me hand and foot. Sometimes I was so exhausted and my circulation was so sluggish that I wasn't able to drive home; I stayed in a motel near the Burbank Studios. My voice was ruined. For weeks, I couldn't talk above a whisper.

"So you see after all I went through why I'm mad at Billy Friedkin for not getting me on those credits. Any child could have wiggled on the bed. If there was any horror in the exorcism, it was me!"

Paul Newman

This is the only interview I've conducted at 120 miles an hour. And when I did it, I was still cutting my teeth at *The New York Times*. *And I didn't drive.*

———————————★———————————

1971

"Driving this thing at a hundred twenty miles an hour, and that's what they used to do, it would damn near rip your kidneys out!" Standing on a remote stretch of the huge Ontario Motor Speedway east of Los Angeles, Paul Newman grins appreciatively at a superb museum piece: a 1914 Peugeot, which came second to the post in that year's Cincinnati 500. Ever since he made a routine feature about racing fanatics called *Winning*, Newman has been tripped out on mechanized speed, and now he is commemorating his passion by coproducing, starring in, and narrating a $400,000 ABC special, *Once Upon a Wheel*, which covers the history and dangerous contemporary excitements of the sport.

For days, Newman has been shooting in rain or in bitter desert winds. Now the sky is raw blue, the asphalt curves in dusty planes past the 125,000 empty spectator seats in the red and blue grandstand and along the 2.5-mile oval track, and a helicopter kicks up sandy soil as it rises for its airborne crew to make a shot. Coproducer David Winters, fashionably hippie in embroidered leather, darts about anxiously, while Newman, pink-cheeked and blue-eyed, looks monumentally relaxed. No longer a self-conscious, cut-rate Brando, he has mellowed cheerfully in recent years. Capped and goggled for a period sequence involving the Peugeot, he clowns expertly as he spins the ancient automobile's crank, hops in, earnestly strains for the takeoff—and feigns surprise when the car starts shooting backwards at eighty miles an hour.

It is typical of Newman that he should have improvised the expert visual joke on the spot, laughing uproariously at his own comic invention. Least pretentious of the vintage stars, he believes that a sense of fun and an ability to relax are far too rare in contemporary American society; he insists that driving fast—on motorcycles, in period cars, or in contemporary speedsters—is not so much a burning obsession, more a way of becoming a happy child again. Yet even as he is talking it's obvious that he may be almost as much in love with cars as he is with his wife, Joanne Woodward. His eyes—their blue intensified by imported French eyedrops—glitter fiercely as he insists that it is only an amateur's quiet affection.

He explains his feelings as, in a break between takes, we climb into his apple-red 914/6 1970 Porsche and burn up the straightaway at 120 miles an hour. "I don't go for fancy talk about 'the mystique of speed' or 'escaping the problems of our age,' " he yells above the engine. "I drive for the hell of it. I don't drive competitively, as Steve McQueen does. He's been doing it for fifteen years. He's a great driver, and I would be too if I'd started young enough.

"I get sheer pleasure from just noticing what an automobile like this can do." Effortlessly, we spin around a bend and break out into another straight. "This kind of car makes its turns comfortably at eighty miles an hour, and if you were in a Grand Prix you'd be making turns at a hundred and ten, but this is still no problem.

"Notice how the body doesn't change posture. It stays perfectly level while the wheels adjust to the track. In most cars, if you rounded a bend the way we're doing, you would just roll over and smash. You could even hit a curb in this one and all you'd do is turn around a few times. It's fantastic."

We stop near the grandstand and Newman goes off to confer with the film crew. He walks away with the springy confidence of a star athlete. Three days later we talk again over canned beer and salad at Universal Studios.

"I first learned to drive fast for *Winning.* Up to then I'd done nothing more dangerous than driving the highway from Connecticut, where I live, into New York, in a souped-up Volkswagen with a Porsche engine.

"I didn't plunge into the big speeds all at once. It's like those guys who fall free; they start in at just a few thousand feet and work up. I began driving at eighty, then I'd go up to ninety and a hundred twenty. Finally—the movie company insured me for a million dollars—I went up to a hundred twenty and then up to a hundred eighty-five. The cars I was driving were only supposed to go at a hundred twenty miles an hour, and that was a helluva risk. The insurance guys were shitting in their pants.

"Making a picture is like working up speed. You start slow and before you know it you've gotten into production and the momentum carries you on to the very end. For instance, after years of playing no good sons of bitches in pictures like *Hud* and *The Hustler* and *The Outrage,* I started in as a director with *Rachel, Rachel.*

"Joanne found the original novel, *A Jest of God* by Margaret Laurence, the story of an aging, virgin schoolteacher in a small Eastern town who decides she's going to find a man and lose her virginity. I thought, Who the hell would want to see a subject like that?

"Joanne and I and the writer Stewart Stern went to Palm Springs and sat around and talked the whole thing over. Gradually I started to get involved with the subject. Soon I was warming up.

"I thought, here's this schoolteacher, she's in her thirties, she's gotten this comfortable, quiet loneliness and sadness, and then she decides to risk plunging into the agony and joy of real living. It seemed to me that though there are very few virgins around to identify with the picture, there are lonely people everywhere who would love it. I was right.

"Now I wanted desperately to make the picture. But all the companies turned me down flat. Finally I did get the money and went ahead. And in a little over a month I had the perfect location, the perfect cast, and I was starting. That's the way to make pictures, when it's all in a rush and it's too late to back out.

"I was involved in *WUSA,* too, about a hard-drinking, right-wing radio announcer in the South who doesn't believe a word he says, based on Robert Stone's novel, *A Hall of Mirrors.* I was producer on that one as well as star. It failed at the box office and it got very unsympathetic reviews. Perhaps because it was by inference too frank about the right-wing fast talk of our political leaders. Vincent Canby had the gall to list that picture as one of the ten worst of the year. If he's right, then I don't know my backside from a hole in the ground. I'm mad at him.

"I hope the European reviews are good. Perhaps they'll see it's a portrait of the way America is run. I'd like to take an ad in all the newspapers and magazines here with the European raves and say to the lousy critics in the East, 'Look at this!' New York critics can't direct. They know nothing about pictures! My God, which critic was it? Susan Sontag? She made a movie in Sweden and it was a walking Seconal! It was crap! And those critic friends of hers got up off their fat behinds and said, 'It's so filled with mystery!' Mystery! The only mystery is why it was made at all."

Newman's latest picture, shot in Oregon for Universal, is *Sometimes a Great Notion,* from the novel by Ken Kesey, a story of labor disputes in backwoods lumber camps, which Newman directs and costars in with Henry Fonda and Michael Sarrazin.

"I wanted to do the picture because, like so many of my best pictures—I'm thinking of *Hud* and *Hombre* especially—it shows the life of simple Americans. There are wonderful things in it. Hank Fonda has a death scene that, goddamnit, is one of the finest things I ever saw. I fired the director after three weeks because he didn't understand the subject in the way I thought he should and I took over the directing because how could you hire a new guy in Hollywood and train him to understand the logging business in three weeks?

"I love *Sometimes a Great Notion* the way I love the world of *Winning* and this TV special, because they show ways in which we can return to simple actions. After *WUSA* I wouldn't exactly be asked to the White House. It was a good deal too frank about right-wing demagoguery, but *Notion* will probably be seen with murmurs of approval from the onlookers in the Oval Room, it's so much a picture of grass-roots Americans. Not that I give a damn either way. I don't care for Washington's opinion and I don't care for New York's.

"The theater's no good at all there anymore, though my next picture will be *The Effect of Gamma Rays on Man-in-the-Moon Marigolds,* from Paul Zindel's Off-Broadway play. I'll direct with Joanne in the Sada Thompson role. I hate Los Angeles because of the deadly smog. I want to go to Australia and live by my wits with just a little food and water and see if I can really be a pioneer. Wouldn't that be a good life for a son of a bitch?"

Mary Pickford

This is an introduction without an interview.

In 1969, I was asked by an Australian women's magazine to interview Mary Pickford. Surprisingly, she agreed to it.

I arrived at Pickfair on a dry, sunny winter afternoon. A housekeeper ushered me into the writing room. I sat there for a time, admiring the slightly faded elegance of the room.

The telephone rang. It continued to ring. It never stopped ringing.

Naturally, I didn't pick it up. Nobody knew I was there, and one doesn't normally answer the phone in somebody else's house. Especially if one hasn't been there before and most especially if the house happens to be Pickfair, the Buckingham Palace of Hollywood.

The ringing went on. The housekeeper put her head around the door and said, "Aren't you going to answer the telephone?" I replied that I wasn't expecting a call. "Miss Pickford is calling," the housekeeper said.

I answered the phone. A female voice (presumably Miss Pickford's) said, "Welcome to Pickfair."

I began to think it was a gag. Then she said, "Look to your left." I obeyed. She went on: "You see that table with the lamp on it?" I couldn't deny that I did. "There's an ivory-colored book on the table. Why don't you pick it up and bring it back to the telephone?"

I did so. I picked up the phone. "And now," the voice said, "please turn to page one twenty-two."

I made my way through the pages. On the page suggested, I found the autographs of Lord and Lady Mountbatten.

"You see, Lord and Lady Mountbatten stayed with us. They were so charming. Being British, I thought you'd appreciate it. It's been so nice talking to you. Good-bye!" And with that, she was gone.

Tiny Tim

Like Mrs. Miller, Tiny Tim is one of those strange phenomena flung up by popular culture. I was surprised to discover that I had seen him before: when he was the Human Canary in Hubert's Museum on Times Square. In that dungeon, reached by a winding flight of stairs, a bedraggled figure in yellow feathers with a plastic beak and claws stood flapping its imitation wings on a summer night, trying to pipe a medley of birdsong. The real eyes looked through the glass ones, and seemed to be staring out of a private purgatory.

I hope Tiny Tim saved his money.

1970

The *O* in wonderful, printed over his name on the enormous purple book advertising Tiny Tim, is shaped like a heart. Yet the image presented to us by the articles, the publicity handouts, is more horrendous than sentimental: he has been described as Boris Karloff in drag, Dracula's mother, Cyrano de Bergerac crowned by a dishrag, and Joan Baez as Mary Poppins.

Delayed half an hour Tiny Tim finally received me in his hotel suite. I expected John Barrymore as Hamlet crossed with Judith Anderson as Mrs. Danvers and equipped with the voice of Yma Sumac at the age of eight. Astonishingly, Tiny

Tim—the biggest thing to hit the pop scene since the Beatles
—turned out to be a quiet, masculine, intellectual Jewish New
Yorker, with the intonations of a Norman Mailer and a manner no more effeminate than Glenn Ford's.

Recovering slowly from the shock, I asked him about his
passion for ancient 78 rpm records, which he flawlessly imi-
tates in a reedy soprano an octave above his own light-brown
tenor voice.

"I've always written down songs from old discs," he said.
"Songs from as far back as 1908. They're so old not even the
American Society of Composers can get a lead on them today.
The sheet music has vanished. When I was very small"—he
is forty-six—"I always had a windup phonograph. I would
hear Henry Burr's voice, recorded in 1918, singing 'Beautiful
Ohio,' and I loved that. It was on a Columbia Blue Label. I'll
never forget it.

"I played it over and over again. I'm still fascinated by
old-time phonographs. The arm that goes down. The little
silver needle that makes the record play. The sound box—
looking into those interior workings and listening to the tiny
echoes. I have a 1909 Victor horn phonograph in my apartment in California and I sit many times in a day, especially
after a romance has broken up with a girl, and I put my head
inside the horn. I cut off the light and the phone, and just
picture the girl in my mind as I peer into the darkness and the
dust. Or I might put my head or my nose tip right on the label
as it spins, and feel the record going round and round, as the
singer gives a sweet, sad song of 1906."

Tiny Tim looked reflective for a moment. His manager
came in, a pretty, slender blonde, and said the authorities
were after his honey as well as his seeds. He looked slightly
flustered, as well he might, and sat down, hard. "There's just
this honeycomb," he said sadly, looking at it. "Oh, dear. Now
where were we? Oh, yes, my early days. I kept getting hold of
new old records. . . . I was like a vampire, I wanted to suck
in everything, every last drop of vintage blood.

"Maybe I'm a medium the old-time singers can sing
through, who knows? I did messenger jobs, sang around ama-

teur competitions, parties. The teachers would chase me out because I'd sing to the kids in their lunch hour and the kids wouldn't eat. I sang 'Rain or Shine.' " And Tiny Tim sang it for me, Rudy Vallee style.

He learned to imitate Arthur Fields, Gene Austin, Ruth Etting, Russ Columbo and other vintage, half-forgotten stars. "I didn't graduate from high school because I was too crazy about beautiful girls in class. It was like a baseball team—the Dodgers, say—winning the pennant every time I sat next to one. I didn't concentrate, so they threw me out."

After leaving school, he wandered around for years, failing his IQ tests at army call-ups (he was confused by the task of comparing drawn cubes), until finally he volunteered for service in the Korean War. "This time I passed everything— except the psychiatrist. When he asked me why I wanted to join up I told him I wanted to go to the moon. I was before my time. I wanted to go there for real. But he sent me home with a free subway token and classified me 4G, one below 4F. He said: 'We'll never call you unless we're desperate.'

"In 1951, I found an old Rudy Vallee record in a store in New York. I identified with him, as he portrayed himself in his book, *Vagabond Dreams Come True.* I knew how he felt, playing the saxophone at Yale and seeing all the beautiful girls come in on the rich boys' arms and he had to sit there and play.

"I became him, I sang him—in a higher-pitched voice: 'Every time I see a pair of love birds up in the trees.' Thank God for His blessing; it was my turning point: I had a start.

"I also sang Patti Page hits, to give a contemporary note. I didn't use my 'male' voice after that. My father was upset. I said, 'Something just came over me. The good Lord knows I'm not that way, and so long as He knows I'm not, that's all that counts. I'm no sissy.'

"Dad made sweaters in the garment jungle and had no real understanding of my music. He was like a cold wall, though I love him dearly. But I went on. In 1954—all my dates are accurate—I grew my hair to go with the voice. Long before the Beatles. I wore white makeup, too, to go with the hair that went with the voice. I kept myself cleansed, I creamed my face all the time, for the image, you see. If girls looked at me and giggled, 'Who is that idiot?' at least they'd look, and that was what mattered. . . . It didn't only help me in show business, it helped me in my love life.

"The relatives looked at me like I was a fixed statue when they came to visit. When I went to the library, the clerks said, 'Here IT comes again.' I'd go into Macy's perfume department and they'd say, 'May I help you, madam?' and I'd shrill, 'Oh, my goodness, yes, you can!' It was all a put-on.

"Finally, I got a job. On Forty-second Street near Times Square, New York, there's a gigantic penny arcade called Hubert's Museum. In there, they had freak exhibits. There was a guy who could turn his head all the way around to the back, and his face would look at you directly when his back was turned to you.

"And there was a woman with feet exactly like an elephant's. And a flea circus. I stood in a cage from one in the afternoon until ten o'clock each night—nine hours straight— and for fifty dollars a week I was on after the fleas and was Larry Love, The Singing Canary, a kind of human bird."

Tiny Tim smiled bravely at the memory. After more struggles in various seedy dives in Greenwich Village, he finally got a break at a place called The Scene, and he developed his act, blowing kisses, plucking at his guitar, sporting a sheriff's badge and a shopping bag, smothering his face with powder from a compact, and shrilling Mother's favorites in the voice of the Shirley Temple of 1934. From being down and out, really poverty-stricken, he hit the big time. His record "God Bless Tiny Tim" sold 150,000 copies right off. And he got religion: Billy Graham and Norman Vincent Peale became his idols.

"I never asked the good Lord to make me a success, to make me famous. I only asked Him to make me do what He wanted me to do. But He saved me; if my parents had passed away before I made it, I would have been in the streets, that was how little I had.

"As long as Christ was with me, and I obeyed his commands, I couldn't go wrong. I worked in The Big Fat Black

Pussycat, and the Page Three. I loved the girls. *Cosmopolitan* magazine wrote me up: 'There seems to be a weird spirit at large,' they wrote, 'with a shopping bag and a ukulele.'

"I moved on; Christ was with me." Just as well: at Expo 67, eight thousand Canadians pelted him with bottle caps, but he survived that to become the most bizarre smash hit in the recording world, and a sensation at the Albert Hall in London. "I have such ambitions for the future! I want to be in a horror movie! And I want to play Scrooge, with someone else as Tiny Tim." Phyllis Diller, one presumed. "Everything's exciting now, oh, goodness me . . ."

And Herbert Khaury, Vernon Castle, Emmett Swink, Rollie Dell, Darry Dove, Larry Love, The Singing Canary, and Tiny Tim picked up his ukulele and giggled.

Edward G. Robinson

Edward G. Robinson had only a short time to live when I interviewed him. I didn't realize it then. He had courage. He was probably in unimaginable pain, but he talked to me fluidly and eloquently for hours. It was the last interview he gave. Our mutual friends, Sam and Bettye Jaffe, told me that the article lightened and made happy the last weeks of his life. Because of that I am prouder of this piece than of anything else I have done.

———————— ★ ————————

1972

The voice is still Little Caesar's: harsh, stabbing, authoritative. The eyes still have a fierce intensity, the wide frog mouth as tight with determination as ever behind the grizzled Hemingway beard. The body may be shrunken now, even smaller than one remembered it on the screen, but the hands, graceful and darting, are constantly expressive. In the snug, richly upholstered den of his Beverly Hills mansion, flanked by part of his great collection of French Impressionists, Edward G. Robinson is still, at seventy-eight, very much Edward G. Robinson. And after years of character roles and "guest appearances," he is starting work on a genuine starring assignment as the aged sidekick of Charlton Heston in Richard Fleischer's sci-fi film about the New York of the future, *Soylent Green*.

Robinson gives an impression of iron stoicism, the kind of True Grit that had him in there slugging it out with men twice his size in *Bullets or Ballots, Five Star Final,* and *Kid Galahad* in the golden years of Warners, or discovering the treatment for syphilis in *Dr. Ehrlich's Magic Bullet,* or sending a *Dispatch From Reuters,* or wringing from a craven Francis Lederer the *Confessions of a Nazi Spy.*

Seeing his old movies today, it's easy to understand the thrill Depression audiences felt as the squat, runtish figure got in there fighting, haranguing crooks or journalists or silver miners just two inches from his nose as though they were at the other end of the Yankee Stadium, slamming a fist the size of a child's on tables with all the authoritative emphasis of a heavyweight boxer's.

In his own life, Robinson has needed as much determination as any of the onscreen characters he has played. He has had enough Joblike tests of endurance to quell all but the fiercest spirit; being short and uncompromisingly ugly would have stopped most aspiring actors dead in their tracks at the outset. He has not only been blacklisted, but suffered from a heart attack, lost $3 million worth of paintings in a divorce suit, and had a son, Edward G. Robinson, Jr., who has followed the classic show-biz younger generation route of suicide attempt, drink-and-drugs, and mental disorders.

As if that were not enough, Robinson has suffered in recent years from increasingly severe deafness, that deadly hazard for an actor which has driven more than one famous player to suicide. Yet Robinson seems largely unfazed: clearly, he is determined to go on, loud-voiced and heckling, fists held high against a cruel world, until the day he drops.

I ask him whether his increasing deafness hasn't hindered him in making *Soylent Green.* "Is it a handicap? I won't say it is. I tell the directors in advance what to expect. They hire me anyway. When I'm on a set and the instructions are spoken from a distance, I just say to the actor next to me, 'What's the director saying?' and I get along somehow. Picture-making is as much a club effort as it ever was back when I started out. You have to help each other."

Robinson sits absolutely still for most of our interview. A little frail, he was at first supposed to see me for only a half hour at a time on several different days. To my surprise, he continues talking for nearly three hours on my first visit, recalling his heyday in the thirties and forties—and the troubles that came later to threaten his career.

In the fifties, Robinson played a real-life cliff-hanger: a battle with the House Committee on Un-American Activities on the matter of his secret blacklisting. "Suddenly, around 1950–51, I found I couldn't get work. I was handed lousy B-picture assignments. Those goons, those vigilantes, and so-called 'good Americans' confused some of us with really sinister, genuine Communists in our midst. It was true that I had supported various pro-Russian organizations during World War Two. But who hadn't? We were supposed to be Russia's ally, weren't we?

"I was never subpoenaed by the House Committee. But that awful paper *Red Channels* began insinuating that I was a Communist. I decided to do something about it and go before the committee voluntarily to clear my name. They said, 'We have nothing on you.' But I was sure they thought they had. I demanded to be put under oath. They refused. I insisted. Finally they agreed. I told them I was clean. They accepted that. But the press still kept bandying my name around. I went back and once again they commended my action. But the implications went on and on.

"I went before a third hearing still, when Congressman Sam Yorty, who is now mayor of Los Angeles, asked me to. Congressman Jackson, who was my congressman from California, was on the committee. I asked him point-blank, 'Do you believe that I am or have been a Communist?' He said, 'No, I don't. But I do believe you have been keeping bad company.'

"I was furious. I said, 'What do you mean, keeping bad company? I merely subscribed to certain causes, and I would again today.' He said, 'You are clean, you are a good American, but you have given comfort to the enemy.' I said, 'That's ridiculous.' My name was never really cleared. I made more B pictures, terrible pictures.

"The shadow hung over me for six years. Finally Cecil B. De Mille decided he wanted me for a part in *The Ten Commandments*. He said, 'I've had you investigated, and you're as clean as a hound's tooth.' He reinstated me, but it was only a character role.

"That whole period was a bad dream. I may have been an unsuccessful father and husband, and have taken money under false pretenses as an actor, but the one thing they can't take away from me is that I am a true American, a good citizen."

No sooner had De Mille broken the blacklisting of Robinson, than the beleaguered star was faced with a new test of endurance in 1956: in order to comply with the California community property laws in his divorce from the former actress Gladys Lloyd, whom he had married in 1927, he had to sell more than half his superb collection, started in 1933, of masterpieces of art.

"It was so brutal—the worst ordeal I ever went through. I went to everyone I could think of—rich men who had an affinity for art—Winthrop Rockefeller, Bobby Lehman, Kirkeby out here—to try to arrange for a loan to pay off the estimated worth of half the paintings, but these men played games with me; they only agreed to help provided I would sell them four or five of the paintings for little or no money. And so I said; 'No deal.'

"My wife had been very ill, and it proved impossible to reach any kind of sane agreement with her. I had no real estate, very few stocks, nothing else I could sell. I had put my money, my whole life's blood, into paintings. Finally, some dealers took the paintings for over three million on behalf of Niarchos, the Greek shipping millionaire. He acted very miserably in the whole matter. He wouldn't let me buy back what I wanted when I finally got the money. Just a few things he condescended to part with, crumbs from the master's table. It was horrible.

"The worst blow of all was losing Rouault's 'The Old Clown.' It was the king of my collection, I used to call him 'Everyman.' The symbol of man's inhumanity to man. After that divorce suit, I realized just what the phrase 'inhumanity to man' really meant."

Robinson's eyes cloud over with tears. "As for the remainder of the pictures, I don't know what I'll do with them. For years selected groups, classes, have come to see them. I have never closed them off from the public. You don't own any painting, you pay for the privilege of being a custodian. But I don't like the idea of them ending up in a museum. It's like putting a beautiful dead man or woman in a morgue. Last December, I was in the Prado and I was horrified: the paintings there are badly hung, badly lit, you can't see the details. And it's supposed to be a foremost tourist attraction of Spain. No, I don't want to leave these lovely things to a museum, although I suppose inevitably they will end up there. What will I do with them otherwise? I don't know. I don't know."

In the 1960s came the long professional struggle back to the top, despite the consolation of millions, and a marriage to the couturiere, Jane Adler, in 1958. Most stars would rather be buried under the sod than billed under the title of a movie, and Robinson often had to accept that humiliation. One of his few decent roles was in Alexander Mackendrick's *Sammy Going South*, shot in Africa in 1963. But shooting was interrupted when, high up on Mount Kilimanjaro, he suffered a heart attack. Characteristically, he won't accept the fact that it was a heart attack at all. ("Doctors are a Mafia. They all support each other.") He went on and finished the picture, saying that he had been slightly affected by the altitude. In the 1960s, his son was in the news on drunken driving charges, finally suing the dead Gladys Lloyd Robinson's estate when she left him penniless. Robinson refuses to discuss his son.

At last, via successful appearances in *The Cincinnati Kid, The Biggest Bundle of Them All,* and the noisome *Song of Norway,* Robinson fought his way back, despite deafness, to stardom in *Soylent Green.*

"Increasing deafness isn't much of a prospect, but then

what is today? Looking at commercials on television, I feel genuinely afraid of the future for the first time in my life. Of what's happening to us.

"*Soylent Green* is, I believe, an important picture, a harrowing projection of our existence fifty years from now. It shows very clearly what may well become of us if we don't look out. It is set in Manhattan, a city of forty million people living miserably and horribly in a depersonalized Orwellian state.

"The character I play is symbolic of the weakest of liberal intellectuals who aren't doing enough to stop the rot in our society. He is a brilliant man, a close friend of a policeman played by Charlton Heston, who has foreseen the worst, but, in common with many others like him, has done nothing. Finally he submits to euthanasia. Will what the film predicts come to pass?" Edward G. Robinson takes a deep puff at his Little Caesar cigar. "I guess I'll stick around just a little longer and try to find out."

The
Ringmasters

Francis Ford Coppola
I and II

Francis Ford Coppola is a nice man. But my experiences with him
have not been comfortable.

I ran into trouble on both these articles. In reply to the profile, he
wrote to *Action: The Director's Guild Magazine,* in which it
appeared, complaining that he had not fired the cameraman Haskell
Wexler from *The Godfather* as I had claimed, but that Wexler had
left the picture of his own accord. Since Haskell's brother Yale was
a friend of mine, I knew differently. But *Action* was an organ of the
Guild, and Coppola was allowed the last word on the subject. I was
not permitted to correct his misstatement.

Several years elapsed. I saw Coppola once, at a party in San
Francisco, and he was understandably distant. In 1976, I decided to
do a piece on *Apocalypse Now.* Almost nothing had been in print
about the film, and since Coppola had gambled at least $8 million
of his own money on it, I felt it might make a fascinating subject for
a piece.

I called the press agent for the film who coolly informed me that
I must interview nobody, that I would not be given any information
or photographs, and that Coppola would not be available for
comment. My back was up. The red rag, as they say, had been
shown to the bull.

I had no idea what the picture was actually about, beyond a
rumor that it was based on Joseph Conrad's novel, *Heart of
Darkness,* which had fascinated, among others, Orson Welles and
the Polish director Andrzej Wajda.

I knew that Coppola, like Hitchcock, couldn't work without illustrative sketches covering virtually all the master shots of his pictures. A visual continuity had to be worked out for him. I knew that only six men in the business were capable of doing this, and that the best of them was Hitchcock's man, Tom Wright. Knowing that Hitchcock was between movies, I guessed that Wright would have worked for Coppola. I called him at Universal. Sure enough, he had done a complete visual breakdown for *Apocalypse Now.* Would I, he asked, like to see what the picture looked like?

I drove to the studio immediately. Tom Wright showed me his inventive and detailed sketches which told me all I needed to know about the look of the film, its story, and most of its characters. Then I heard that John Milius, who had written the script, was dissatisfied with Coppola and would grant me an interview. I saw him, and he fleshed out further details for me.

Through the Army, I found Vietnam veterans who told me more still. I reached the art director, Angelo Graham, in the Middle West, figuring that in a motel on a long, dreary night after a day's work he would want to do nothing except talk to someone in Hollywood. I was right. We talked for two hours.

The Times rightly felt that we needed an actor in the picture to comment on its making. Marlon Brando turned out to be as elusive as ever. He no longer had an agent. His lawyer was uncommunicative, and Brando seemed permanently en route to Tahiti. Dennis Hopper had been asked to say nothing. He had been effectively silenced by Coppola. Martin Sheen, also, would say nothing, and Harvey Keitel flatly refused to give an interview. That left only Robert Duvall among the principal players. The play in which he was appearing on Broadway, *American Buffalo,* was in difficulties, and needed publicity. The press agent for the show agreed to let me talk to Duvall in his dressing room on the telephone for half an hour before he went onstage for an evening performance, provided I mentioned that he was the star of the play. This seemed only the mildest of bribes, and I couldn't seriously object to it.

It took several days for the press agent actually to reach Duvall. The actor seemed not to be answering his telephone. Just as I was leaving to do the interview with Milius, set for 3:00 P.M. one afternoon, the press agent called from New York to say that Mr. Duvall would speak to me at 4:00 P.M. our time, 7:00 P.M. his, at the theater.

It was an impossible situation. I needed at least two hours for the Milius interview. I also needed the Duvall interview. How could I possibly squeeze in both? And then, the press agent said, Mr. Duvall would only grant the interview if I tape-recorded it through a rubber plug attached to the telephone.

I did not own a plug of that kind. Somehow, I had to conduct the interview with Milius, buy a plug, find a telephone, and make the call. I rushed over to Milius's office only to find myself confronted with a twenty-minute delay, while he was in conference with his associates on his first film as a director, *Big Wednesday*.

Figuring that I had about twenty minutes to buy a plug and reach a telephone, I realized I would only have ten minutes for the Milius interview. There was no time for preliminaries. I zeroed in on every main point, obtained some sharp quotes, and fled, no doubt to Milius's amazement, from his office.

Disliking freeways, I was forced to take one. When I reached a well-known recording equipment shop, I found they were out of plugs. I made my way down La Brea Avenue in dense traffic and found another store. They had one plug left: the cheapest kind available. I looked at my watch. There was no time to get home. I couldn't record the interview standing in a booth because there would have been nowhere to balance the recorder. I had to get to a hotel. Fast.

The nearest hotel was the Hollywood Roosevelt, once the haunt of Tennessee Williams. As I drove into the parking lot there was a scene only Hitchcock could have shot. Hundreds of pigeons completely covered the parking lot from one end to the other. The asphalt, the cars, even the shoulders of the people.

I had no alternative. Despite screams of fury from the bird-fancying parking attendant, I let off a blast from the horn that sounded rather like the last trump, and the birds flew up into the sky. I parked the car, and found I only had a $20 bill in my pocket. I thrust it into the attendant's hand and broke the Olympic mile into the hotel. Only to find (it was exactly one minute to four) that all of the telephone booths were filled.

At exactly 4:00 P.M., a woman rose from the seat in one of the booths. As she did so, her pearl necklace broke and she was on all fours looking for the pearls.

I scooped them up and, my English gentlemanliness deserting me completely, took her by the fanny and pushed her out of the booth. She screamed, and I slammed the door shut. I called the theater. The line was busy.

It was busy for the next ten minutes. I could have spared the pigeons, the woman's fanny, and my nerves, while Mr. Duvall conducted a leisurely conversation at the other end. At last the line was clear. He gave me a very entertaining interview, with little or nothing good to say for Coppola.

The article was published. In the meantime, Coppola and his lawyers were on the phone to my bosses at the paper, doing their utmost to quash the story. They failed, but Mr. Duvall suddenly decided to withdraw the interview, presumably under the influence of Coppola.

For a week, the piece was delayed, and I suspect even trembled in the balance. But at last it was run with a much-cleaned-up version of Duvall's remarks run minus his name.

I still couldn't understand what Coppola was beefing about. He had no reason to believe I would write damagingly about his film. Yet he had even had his press agent threaten the paper with legal action if they printed any stills from the film.

A few nights after the story appeared, my editor, Guy Flatley, was at a party when he met Anita Loos. She said, casually, "Did you know that my friend Maureen Orth of *Newsweek* has just been in the Philippines writing a story on Francis Ford Coppola's new picture?"

Guy called me to tell me this. Now I understood everything. Coppola wasn't annoyed because I had broken through the smoke screen on the picture. He was annoyed because I had scooped *Newsweek*, with which he and his company had clearly made a deal: no interviews and no information to the other media, in return for a *Newsweek* cover story.

But the joke, finally, was on them. First of all, my story beat Maureen Orth's so that hers had to be held over a week. It would have seemed too much like a rip-off of mine. By delaying the story two weeks, it ran slap into the Jubilee of Queen Elizabeth of England which supplanted it as a front-page story. It was pushed into the back and was barely noticed. Poetic justice.

I

1974

Francis Ford Coppola's house on Pacific Heights in San Francisco is a monumental Queen Anne pile, with stained-glass windows, turrets, and an imposing doorway. Built in the late nineteenth century, former home of a spice king, it should probably be crowded with ornate, gilt-edged antiques suggesting the habitat of the hottest young director in the country. Instead, it is almost bare of decoration: a Joan Miró, a pop art sofa representing a pair of scarlet lips, liver-brown chairs like slices of rotting beef, a huge brown painting of windows almost hidden in smog, a beer-hall mirror—we might well be in an expensively chic New York art gallery.

Plenty of time to contemplate the various shocks to the eye: the director, is almost two hours late. Panting apologetically, reached by a frantic secretary in a telephoneless eighth-floor office of a building he just bought in downtown San Francisco, he pads into the room in a pair of ancient shoes. Black-bearded, unabashedly fat, he looks in his early thirties like a student's imitation of Topol in *Fiddler on the Roof,* or a shorter Castro. Mild dark eyes behind smoky spectacles hint at a surprising gentleness. At thirty-three he is mellow, considerate, quietly intelligent, deeply committed to the idea of conveying, through the medium of popular mass entertainment, a punishingly severe critique of this country today.

His very topical new film, about bugging, *The Conversation,* is totally obsessing him at the moment. "I began thinking about the project some five or six years ago. I had been terrified by the whole question of bugging, of the invasion of personal privacy, and an article in *Life* by a bugging expert sparked off a further interest. I realized that a bugging expert was a special breed of man, not just a detective, and I thought how great it would be to get into the mind and experience of such a man.

"I was fascinated to learn that bugging was a profession, not just an example of some private cop going out and eavesdropping with some fairly primitive equipment. I spent years, on and off, working out a script. Now, of course, the whole thing has become tremendously talked about. But I don't want the film to be a lecture on the subject. I'm not interested in 'messages.' As in *The Godfather* I want to get inside a very specialized individual, discover what motivated him. And I feel that the only way to show his character in the action is to show something horrifying, a nightmare, the nightmare we live in, in which any personal privacy can be invaded with too much ease.

"Gene Hackman plays the expert. He's ideal for the part, because he's so ordinary, so unexceptional in appearance. The man he plays is in his forties, and he's been doing this strange job for years. It's significant, I think, that the character is an extraordinarily private man. It's as though by being very private himself, by guarding his privacy, he has known what barriers may be set up against invasion, and how those barriers may be removed. And it's important to show that he absolves himself of all responsibility, that he's the instrument of other people."

Coppola pauses for a moment, listening to the cries of his young son bicycling around the hall. "He's just a businessman. He feels he's morally absolved by the nature of his work.

"We begin the picture with an apparently harmless conversation between a young couple in a San Francisco park. They are played by Cindy Williams and Frederick Forrest. The Hackman character records them, and he doesn't know why. Gradually he begins to realize that the couple will be murdered. Their imminent death is due to him—and yet he's taken orders from an impersonal head of a corporation, a man with enormous power. During the picture, we see the conversation over and over again. Just as you see a sequence in a cutting room, in different contexts assuming different meanings, so in his memory Hackman recalls what he saw, and the scene changes and changes. At first it seems sunny and bland, and then you begin to see that even though the couple are talking about nothing, buying this, buying that, underneath it all they are very frightened."

The film, Coppola says, most thoroughly explores the bugging "industry" (still continuing even though it is now illegal), and its complicated products. He engaged two specialists in the field to work with him; one had testified at the Watergate hearings.

I asked him if he had any particular problems with the production. "Yes, I came on the picture not quite fully prepared. I have gotten myself involved in too many different things. I started the picture right on top of doing the opera *The Visit* here and it was too quick. The unit didn't function properly at the outset and I had to make some changes. A major example was Haskell Wexler. I began with him as a cameraman. He's good, of course, but when the rushes came in I just didn't feel he was getting what I wanted on the screen. I was a little embarrassed to 'push' this important man, so I felt the best thing to do was make a clean break. I went back to Bill Butler, who did *The Rain People* for me, and I began to get the effects I wanted.

"The film came in at a million six or seven . . . very reasonable considering the cost and so on."

The Conversation represents a continuing line of subdued American naturalism which began with *You're a Big Boy Now*, several years ago. A graduate of UCLA, Coppola was one of the few alumni who actually made it into movies. He was given his first break by Roger Corman, who hired him as general factotum on several horror films, and tossed him the chance to direct a story of a doomed family, shot in Ireland, called *Dementia 13*.

You're a Big Boy Now was made under a Warner contract when that studio was conducting a nervous flirtation with young directors in the belief that whiz-kid picture-makers would automatically drag in a college audience. They were proven disastrously wrong, along with M-G-M and Universal, when the whiz kids turned out to have no commercial pull. But of the films that emerged from that period, *You're a Big Boy Now* was clearly one of the best, the story of a very eager, young Jewish librarian in New York, trying his damnedest to lose his virginity. Typically, Coppola opted for the entire movie being made in New York.

You're a Big Boy Now establishes his style: fluent, immediate, physical, energetic. He shot it, with Mayor John Lindsay's blessing, in the markets, streets, and even in the sacred precincts of the public library. He concealed his cameras in boxes of goods, showed his young hero roller skating through the library stacks. It was a fresh, very attractive work. *Finian's Rainbow*, a gigantic flop, he took on because he very much liked the score. When he saw the book, he was horrified, and he was still more dismayed when Warners told him he couldn't go to the Kentucky location that would have been perfect for the story but would have to shoot the film entirely on the back lot. He liked working with Petula Clark, but felt that the picture was damaged by the miscasting of Tommy Steele, who was too brash as the shy, tender-spirited leprechaun of the original.

His *The Rain People* was more personal: the story of a footballer who suffered from brain damage, played by James Caan, and the disaffected married woman (Shirley Knight) who picks him up when he hitchhikes. "The guy was based on a man I knew at college, who used to sweep up leaves. I wanted to show the sympathy and attractiveness in simple, backward people. This time the studio let me shoot the picture the way I wanted, over several states. Bill Butler, my cameraman, did a wonderful job of capturing the landscape. But the picture was another flop. And my Zoetrope outfit here, designed to help young filmmakers, collapsed after a terrible struggle when Warners withdrew their finance."

Coppola was completely penniless when he was offered *The Godfather*. He turned the subject down, picking it up again only when his financial situation was so desperate he had no alternative.

Chosen because of his ethnic background, he made the best possible job of material to which he wasn't attracted in the first place, though he denies rumors that he directed the picture "with his left hand." One advantage of his newfound success is that he has been able to form, with two other "hot" directors, Peter Bogdanovich and William Friedkin, a company which allows the members of the triumvirate freedom and gives them the right to produce one picture each. Bogdanovich's production is to be Orson Welles's *The Other Side of the Wind,* which was in fact begun two years ago, and which Bogdanovich hopes with his money and influence to help to its long-delayed completion.*

Coppola has a complex attitude toward *The Godfather,* at once enthusiastic and defensive.

"When I made *The Godfather* I underwent a new experience. At Warners, I'd had quite a lot of freedom. But at Paramount people began telling me no. My argument over that picture is that I would make a decision, use up endless periods of time discussing the decision, arguing over it, and then at the end finding out that they were prepared to accept it, when they could so easily not have wasted three months and accepted it in the first place. My director's cut was much shorter than the one released: I was told in no uncertain terms that if I came in with a picture longer than two and a half hours they would pull the whole thing right from under me. So I made a picture two hours and twenty minutes long; it would be safely below the length limit to give nobody an excuse to fire me before I did a finished cut. And Bob Evans and the others at Paramount said, 'It's too short.' They realized it just had to be longer. The final cut was pretty close to everything I had shot. But there was some beautiful Sicilian footage removed, a scene between Brando and Pacino early on in which they go

*All these plans subsequently disintegrated.

and visit a dying associate, and a scene in which James Caan tells his mother that his father is dead, which didn't work on the screen.''

How much of himself had Coppola put in it, and how much of it was simply a commercial venture? "I feel that a great deal of my background as an Italian-American, with very strong memories about family rituals, the weddings, the funerals, went into the picture. I was deeply anxious to show that world as it is, not as it's often portrayed. But of course there's no doubt there's more of Mario Puzo in the picture than anybody else. The film, after all, is extremely faithful to the book.''

What about the suggestion of some critics that the film was too sympathetic to the Mafia? "I don't agree with that at all. After all, at the end of the picture we see Michael telling a mortal lie to his wife. We see that after everything has happened he's no longer a man, he's a monster. The film doesn't soften that, or sentimentalize that. It shuts the door right in your face. Villains are people, aren't they? They believe that they're doing something which by their moral code is good. For me, the Mafia was just a metaphor for America. It is transplanted from Europe; it is a capitalistic, profit-seeking body; it believes that anything it does to protect and sustain itself and its family is morally good. We Americans go to Chile and unhesitatingly subvert and cause a revolution. . . .''

Wouldn't he agree, though, that the picture was unreal? "O.K., yes, it's unreal. But it's a fairy story, an allegory. It's the story of a 'royal family.' The story had a classic quality.

"Could I show these people as monsters in their own homes? No one would go to see it.''

But wasn't Brando too genial? Could one see this man as a former murderer?

"You may have a point there. The real problem is we don't see him throughout. He's on the screen infrequently, but vocally and physically he is perfect: I based him on an actual figure of the Mafia, high-pitched or soft-voiced, according to his mood and when he is doing nice things. I hope in *Godfather II*, which I'm currently scripting, to show the character in much more detail, at different times of his life. The problem

I have is whether I can get Brando again. He's in ego problems, angry with Paramount because they publicly criticized his refusal of the Oscar. He may not want to go back to work for them.

"Brando liked the idea of having the beginning of the story and its aftermath told this time, and setting the story in all kinds of different periods, with a very free narrative structure, but it's by no means certain he'll do it. That's rough on me, because I'm writing something with no very clear idea of who'll be the star. All of the other players from the first *Godfather* will be in it. Eventually it'll make a six-hour movie. I hope Brando will do it."

Coppola strolls into the kitchen of his mansion to play with his lustily screaming children, looking like a benign young Godfather himself. "All I can do is to go on working at it. Right?"

————————★————————

II

1977

"Coppola went wild," recalled one participant in the arduous shooting in the Philippines of *Apocalypse Now*, Francis Ford Coppola's epic about the Vietnam War. "He had temper tantrums. There was a scene in which I am screaming that the napalm has ruined the surf. I was supposed to yell something and then walk away. By this time, I was so sick and frustrated with the picture that when I did the scene, I did something which wasn't in the script. I threw a prop twenty feet in the air. Coppola screamed, 'Cut! That was terrific!' He came over to me and said, 'How did you have such an inspiration?' I said, 'I did it because I couldn't take your goddamn tantrums any longer!' "

"Yes, indeed, Francis did throw tantrums from time to time," conceded an official spokesman for Coppola, since the director himself was unavailable for comment. "Being so far from home and in such adverse weather conditions did make several people throw temper tantrums. But in general Francis was one of the least temperamental directors one could hope to work with."

This tantrum-inducing *Apocalypse* has been in production for over a year and has cost well over $22 million before a single print of the 70-millimeter film could run as high as $10,000. The script has been changed day by day, scene by scene, and one well-known actor has made an angry exit. Harvey Keitel was either fired or voluntarily withdrew from the cast after just four days on the job; Martin Sheen has reportedly been hospitalized with dysentery and exhaustion. There have been a typhoon and an earthquake, quarrels and more quarrels, accusations and counteraccusations. And over the whole massive enterprise there hangs the most crucial question of all: Will the public spend a total of $70 million—the sum necessary to permit the film to show a profit?

From the beginning, a smoke screen of secrecy has descended on *Apocalypse Now.* The production company even sent a memorandum to some of the actors, asking them to cooperate by not giving interviews and advising them that Gerald Rafshoon and Patrick Caddell, the Atlanta-based advertising team that handled President Carter's campaign, would be handling the picture and that all statements must first be checked by them and United Artists. The actor Dennis

Hopper's press agent, Robert Raison, would not allow Hopper to be interviewed without the permission of United Artists, which in its turn has declined to supply any information on the film whatsoever, or even to release a single photograph to the press.

There has been considerable conjecture about the reasons behind the soaring budget, the delays in shooting, and the clashes of personality which have plagued *Apocalypse Now.* In addition to complaints about the weather and the grueling working conditions, it has been said by one close observer that there were costly last-minute script changes and extravagant expenditures for such marginal items as birthday parties and shipments of pasta for the Italian members of the crew.

The primary problem, however, seems to have been a surprising indecision about what kind of movie *Apocalypse Now* was meant to be in the first place. The history of the project has been a complex one, and its progress has been impeded by emotional antagonisms as well as ideological conflicts.

Apocalypse Now was a brainchild of the feisty, individualistic screenwriter John Milius, who as long ago as 1969 wanted to make a 16-millimeter feature based on Joseph Conrad's *Heart of Darkness,* to be directed by George Lucas. Conrad's novella dealt with the corrosive effects of power on the personality of an ivory trader who sets himself up as a god in the African jungle, and Milius's plan was to place this story in Vietnam and to give it a heavily hawkish point of view. Later, when Milius's friend Coppola developed a passionate interest in the project, the latter expressed a desire to direct the film and to turn it into a strong liberal statement.

After a period of bitter disagreement, Milius and Coppola decided that their film should make no political statement at all, that it should focus instead on the monstrous adventure of a man who is so consumed by his thirst for power that he is willing to cut himself off from the civilized world. This is a theme which has long fascinated both men and one which runs throughout both of Coppola's *Godfather* films, as evidenced by that final, haunting image of Al Pacino, the new head of the mob, gazing out across the water, realizing that he is totally isolated from the rest of humanity.

It took a long time for Hollywood studios to see this offbeat variation on *Heart of Darkness* in a favorable light. Indeed, after seven years, Milius and Coppola seemed to have reached a dead end. Warner Brothers and Columbia both turned the project down, believing that few moviegoers would be interested in seeing a picture about the Vietnam War. But Coppola was determined, and in 1975, he finally made a deal with United Artists. "Francis told me one day, 'I've got to do this picture,'" Milius said. "'I consider it the most important picture I will ever make. If I die making it, you'll take it over; if you die, George Lucas will take over.'"

Milius's script tells the story of the ferocious Colonel Kurtz, who becomes a Great White God to his South Vietnamese followers. Arriving by helicopter, he sets up headquarters in an Angkor Wat–like ruined temple. Another officer, Colonel Willard, is sent upriver by the military authorities to compel Kurtz to resign. In the latest of several script versions, the picture will end in a *Walpurgisnacht* of exploding napalm during which Willard murders Kurtz. In Milius's original version, the wounded Kurtz died on his journey home by boat to court-martial.

Joseph Conrad's story was not the only inspiration for the character of Kurtz. "I based the character on Colonel Robert B. Rheault, the Green Beret officer in charge of all Special Forces operations in Southeast Asia in the late 1960s," said Milius. "Rheault was imprisoned with his command and forced to resign from the Army for having executed a double agent. The Army wanted to discredit him because it believed he was working for the CIA. I firmly believe that Rheault was framed. Francis Coppola wanted to cut out all the parallels with Rheault, saying that the public wouldn't identify with a character like that. But, in going over the numerous drafts of the script, Marlon Brando said he could use the character of Rheault as a satisfactory basis for his portrayal of Kurtz.

"Rheault is a great man," said Milius. "I believe in his kind of warfare. In having specialized units. Men like Rheault could've helped us win the war. We almost did win it. We lost the war, not in Vietnam, but on the campuses. It's a shame. We're soft in this country. We have a soft underbelly. We have a President now who is giving way to the Russians. We're handing over Africa. I believe such a character as Rheault would be valuable in times like these."

Although Milius believes the Vietnam War was justified, he insists that the film is apolitical and that he decided from the outset not to make Kurtz/Rheault represent either good or evil. And, of course, he opposed Coppola's impulse to turn *Apocalypse Now* into a pacifist film. "Francis thought he was a liberal, but now he's got more sense. How can he be left-wing when he's so concerned with money and power? He's a capitalist now, isn't he? A millionaire several times over? And now he's met the guys who fought in that war. He knows they are not ashamed. They're proud, good men. Francis no longer wants to liberalize *Apocalypse Now*. The liberal press in this country has deliberately discredited the Army. I think today Francis sees the folly of that."

Hero or villain, Marlon Brando seemed the ideal actor to play Kurtz from the start. The other roles were not so quickly, or permanently, filled. Steve McQueen was sought for the part of Willard, and Gene Hackman was to be the outrageous Kilgore, the surfer-turned-air-commander who lands Willard at the mouth of a river for his journey upstream to kill Kurtz. Coppola offered McQueen $1.5 million to play Willard, but the actor's price turned out to be $3 million. This Coppola flatly refused to pay, and since he had obtained distribution guarantees on the basis of McQueen's name, he was forced to return part of the money put up for the picture, and to invest some of his own money. It is currently estimated that he has put up several million dollars.

Harvey Keitel replaced McQueen, but after four days of work in the Philippines, he left the picture. According to Coppola, Keitel was unsuited to the part; according to Keitel, there were differences of opinion over the terms of the contract. Jack Nicholson was then offered the part but he turned it down. Coppola ran into Martin Sheen at the Los Angeles Airport between planes and offered him the chance to take over Keitel's role. Sheen, an excellent young actor who has yet to become a major star, accepted instantly, though it is possible that he has come to regret his hasty decision. Not only has he been ill, but it has also been reported that he has quarreled with Coppola over the interpretation of his role. In the meantime, Dennis Hopper, cast as a photojournalist, remains silent.

Tom Wright, the well-known artist who has also worked with Hitchcock, did many of the sketches for the picture. "We did something on *Apocalypse Now* we never did on any other movie," he said. "We made a film of all the sketches cut together and Francis put a score on it. When the helicopters soar over the jungle you hear 'The Ride of the Valkyries,' and when the temple is burned at the end, you hear the rock number, 'Light My Fire,' which the GIs were so crazy about.

"Here's the opening shot," he said. "We begin with a spiderweb, very delicate, in subdued greens. The camera moves over it, into the jungle. Suddenly various heads rise up: the maverick force run by Kurtz. Look." Wright held up sketches of Indian headdresses with feathers, fantastically decorated flak jackets, strings of jewels, loincloths, all rendered in brilliant greens. "Then the mood changes, and the color with it. The climax is strictly red and white."

The climactic sequence, in which Willard reaches Kurtz in his jungle hideout, shows flares and exploding bombs and the giant brooding faces of ancient gods on the temples. And, dominating everything else, Kurtz—in profile—bemoaning the destruction of his world. Image after image was of a striking power and immediacy, vivid as a nightmare. "Francis wanted a psychedelic look, a look of hectic exaggeration, as you would get under LSD," said Wright. Since this whole design was worked out over a period of seven months, Coppola has considerably modified it, opting for a more realistic approach.

Once the casting and preliminary sketchwork had been completed, *Apocalypse Now* was ready for the next giant step. In February 1976, a 450-man unit was airlifted to Baler, on the northeastern coast of Luzon, in the Philippines, in old C-47 Gooney Birds and Mitsubishi jets to build a fishing village of bamboo and tile according to the dictates of the script, and a replica of the Saigon red-light street, Tu-Do. Then, in May, Typhoon Olga caused much of the partly constructed temple set to sink in mud. One complete set on an island in the river was submerged, and many members of the cast and crew were left stranded.

Finally, work began in the jungle itself, and the conditions there were horrendous. The huge stone faces on the temple of Angkor Wat had to be constructed on the spot. "We were seven months on the job," art director Angelo Graham recalls, "in terrible heat and humidity, up to our knees in mud. Fungus crawled over our skin and our clothes. The pressure to finish the job from Francis, from the associate producers, and from United Artists, was even worse than the weather conditions. At night you'd simply drink and smoke and collapse into bed. Constructing the entire fishing village was a tremendous task. We had to have a seven-hundred-foot bridge and twenty-five or thirty buildings, plus huts. Three hundred Filipino workmen toiled on this. Each structure had to be fully furnished so you could see everything down to the pots and pans when the roofs caught fire and fell in."

The bombing of the village by fifty helicopters, supervised by stunt coordinator Terry Leonard, is one of the two biggest set pieces of the picture. The other is the grand climax in which Kurtz's empire in the temple ruins is blown up. These sequences added considerably to the film's budget. But apart from the cost of the sets and the delays caused by illness and weather, there was also Coppola's refusal to be rushed in his painstaking perfectionism. "It took forever," said one weary veteran of Coppola's war. "One shot in one day. I was over there for three weeks in March and April 1976, and back for three more weeks last November. I never was able to develop the character fully. Scenes were shuffled around. Some of the lines were rewritten. There were shots I wanted, touches to put icing on the cake of my performance. But these pickup shots were never done. It was difficult. Now it's too late. I can't go back there a third time.

"When I wanted to see scenes that I had shot the previous year for matching purposes, to make sure my performance had continuity, Francis got extremely vague. I hardly saw anything. The picture is way over budget. There were birthday parties, and more birthday parties, and one of the associate producers accidentally paid the people who flew the pasta in for the Italian crew eight thousand dollars instead of the correct amount, five hundred. Then the producers had to pay sixty thousand dollars to some of the local military guys to get the right number of helicopters for the bombing scene. And they cut corners with the actors to compensate."

Gray Frederickson, coproducer of *Apocalypse Now*, confirms reports of heavy expenditures. "Two hundred thousand dollars was spent in buying spare parts for Philippine Air Force helicopters," he said, "plus sixty thousand dollars to buy, at cost, the flying time at two hundred and fifty dollars an hour, which would pay for the pilot, the fuel, and the maintenance.

"The Italian crew expressed the wish to have pasta, spaghetti, and other Italian foods brought in from Italy," admitted Frederickson. "It was decided to bring it in with the lighting equipment which had been ordered from Rome, and the Filipino customs accidentally overcharged about five thousand. Nobody connected with the company noticed the error."

When they weren't filling up on pasta, what did the *Apocalypse* crew members do for recreation? "We'd play pelota in the massage parlor," recalled one actor, "and eat ice cream with chocolate cake in a local café. I never put on an ounce, it was much too hot. When I started to play tennis, it was impossible. I was soaked through with sweat."

Meanwhile, Francis Ford Coppola sweats on and on, waging his seemingly endless battle to achieve a great film in

Apocalypse Now. "I just wish I could finish the goddamn thing!" he said to Tom Wright on a visit to Los Angeles last July, just before jetting back to another stage of his remarkable adventure.

William Peter Blatty

I did this interview for *Los Angeles* magazine. The publication was then in its early stages and totally disorganized. I wrote the interview on a very tight deadline and delivered it by hand. Two days later, I received a frantic phone call: where was the article? I described rushing up several flights of stairs—their elevator had broken down—to press the article into some woman editor's hands, and I added what happened: After I had told her it was a piece that had been promised for that day, she turned to me and said, "We'll be very glad to consider it." I had resisted the temptation to kick over the chair she was sitting on.

It turned out that the article was lost. I had made no copy. There hadn't been time. I had exactly four hours to reconstruct the entire piece. I've never been asked to write for *Los Angeles* magazine again.

No doubt William Peter Blatty would find a psychic explanation for the mysterious vanishing of the article. I found a more rational one. It came back to me in manuscript a week after it was published—with a rejection slip.

---------- ★ ----------

1976

"Not long ago, I went to lay flowers on my first girlfriend's grave. She died twenty years ago. When I got home I began to feel ill. Within a few days I was down with hepatitis. And you know what my first girlfriend died of? Hepatitis."

William Peter Blatty, author of *The Exorcist,* is talking in an office at Warner Brothers. Searching, slightly clouded dark eyes and a faint touch of yellow in the skin suggest not only his illness, from which he is painfully recovering, but the psyche of a man who has spent most of his life on the brink of the supernatural. Despite the powerful physique, the confident bristle of the beard, the hands firm as a surgeon's, he exudes a fragile, sensitive temperament deeply attuned to intangibles. He looks like a man who has recently returned from Purgatory, if not actually Hell.

Is it true he has the power of precognition? He nods, deadly serious.

"My very first experience was preschool. My mother played the numbers game. She asked me to pick a number for her. That night I had a dream. I was standing by a man playing a pinball machine. The man had a mustache. He told me to play 059. The following day our janitor, who was the local numbers taker, came to collect the money. Mother had no money so she gave him some milk bottles instead. I told her to play 059. She won.

"Two weeks later I had another dream—789. She won again. I did not have any more dreams until I was a sophomore at a Jesuit high school. Brooklyn Prep. For a period of exactly seven weeks I dreamed the scores of my high-school football team.

"When I was an adult, and was losing my shirt in the convertible bonds market, I dreamed in Encino that I was in a hotel lobby in New York. That I was arm in arm with a man named Hal Lehrman who had been a book reviewer for the old *New York Herald Tribune.* Lehrman and I advanced to the desk and I said to the clerk, 'Check box one thirty.' When I awoke I picked up my copy of the *L.A. Times* and looked for anything on the stock market page at a price of a dollar thirty. There was one. Allegheny Ludlam. I prepared a cryptograph with HAL LEHRMAN printed out under ALLEGHENY LUDLAM. I found if I eliminated the *H* in Hal I had the first four letters.

Alle. I called my broker and told him to buy Allegheny Ludlam. That same morning someone had dumped a large parcel of fifty thousand Allegheny Ludlam shares. I sold everything I had and bought them. They went up—and up."

Blatty's eyes grow even more remote.

"When I was married and working on the book of *The Exorcist,* I was awakened by pain in a dream. In the dream I was eating a shrimp cocktail. I reached for a shrimp with my left hand—odd, because I'm right-handed—and a shrimp bit me. As I woke I was thinking, 'Crabs bite, not shrimps.' My finger was still throbbing. I found a note from my wife saying she had taken the boys to the beach. When they returned, my son David had a bandage wrapped around his left index finger —the same finger that I had felt hurting. She told me, 'A sand crab bit him.'

"Later, I was in Las Vegas with my wife. I played black-jack, she played roulette, I had exhausted my quota for the day at the blackjack table, she did fairly well at roulette, and that night, just before I fell asleep, I saw the number twenty-two as if it had been burned into my forehead. White on black. I thought, what does it mean? It's a 'bust' in blackjack. Next day I was standing next to my wife at the roulette wheel and I remembered the number. I leaned over to tell her to play it. There was a woman placing five-hundred-dollar bets all over the table who gave me an ir-ritated look. My wife said she would not play twenty-two. I insisted. Right in the middle of the argument the croupier called, 'Twenty-two.' "

In addition to precognition, Blatty has had numerous ex-periences of psychic phenomena. "I was staying in the home of a former classmate of mine at Georgetown University. We were sitting in his dining room talking about the projected motion-picture deal on *The Exorcist.* The telephone rang and stopped ringing. My former wife, Beth, cried out from the other room, 'My God, the telephone jumped off the hook!' She actually saw the receiver lift off the hook and fall to the floor. Two days later the phone rang again. I looked at the phone and it lifted off the receiver and fell to the ground. My host, Dick, and Beth both saw it. I'm convinced now that it was my dead mother, trying to contact me.

"No doubt many people, hearing these comments baldly, would think I was certifiably insane. But I believe that when we die we retain an electromagnetic field which can in fact move physical objects *also* within an electromagnetic field. That explains poltergeist phenomena, and my mother's ability to move a telephone."

Blatty's powers of precognition helped him in writing *The Exorcist*. He found he had imagined the entire work subconsciously, so that the actual writing of it, not consciously preplanned, was simply the discovery of preexisting territory. He seemed to know instinctively that it would be filmed, and would be an overwhelming success.

His problem as producer in making the film was to convey the kind of supernatural experience he had so frequently experienced in visual and—still more important—aural terms. "We wanted to create in an audience a feeling of absolute terror. So we used sounds that cannot be identified consciously but which part of you recognizes. For instance, when the little girl arches backwards and an apparition of the Devil appears. There was a fantastic sound there, the sound of a demon in pain as it is being driven from its earthly habitation. It was the sound of bees trapped in a jar, trying to get out, multiplied hundreds of times, combined with the screams of swine being led to slaughter. The sound of terror. Your unconscious knows what that sound is. It works on an audience fantastically."

Such cinematic contrivances, executed under the guidance of director William Friedkin, have indeed had a profound effect on audiences. Hollywood publicity-mongers once staged phony fits and faintings to dramatize the "impact" of movie thrillers, but such shenanigans have hardly been needed for *The Exorcist*. Ushers, as has been widely reported, regularly apply smelling salts to fallen customers at every performance, while other patrons are overcome by nausea or simply flee to the lobby to wait it out.

"We have a sound of a woman's voice," Blatty continues,

"heard on the tape which the exorcists make of the girl. This bears out the Demon's assertion that the young priest's mother is inside the girl as well. But you don't actually hear the mother's voice; it goes through too subliminally. You absorb it unconsciously."

The film, therefore, actually uses the supposed methods employed by supernatural presences to contact the human mind. Blatty believes that a "demon" is not so much a creature with horns and a tail as a malign, disembodied intelligence capable of seizing on the human body and possessing it. "It wants the kick of being married to a nervous system. Like Henry the Eighth wanting to eat a thirty-course meal again!"

Although Blatty wants to avoid being quoted directly in the matter, he doesn't seem particularly defeated by film critic Pauline Kael's savage personal attack on him in *The New Yorker*. He claims that he doesn't know what she's beefing about. First of all, says Blatty, she attacked him for having exploited the Church and then attacked him for following a strict Church line in the treatment of the subject. What is really wrong with her, Blatty feels, is that she's against the Church itself, and has gone on record as saying she despises films about the supernatural, religion, and children. Since Blatty's film boldly contains all three, she was naturally against it from the start. As to Kael's charge of exploitation, Blatty claims many learned Jesuits, all of them specialists in exorcism, have praised him for the sensitivity and accuracy of the concept and execution of the novel and the film.

Further, Blatty rejects the charges of several critics that in some way the child in the film, Linda Blair, was affected adversely by the requirements of her role. Despite the fact that her voice, intermingled with that of Mercedes McCambridge, was heard uttering obscenities on the sound track and that she went through a physical ordeal, Blatty says she remains a normal, healthy child, saw the picture without a qualm, and cried at the end, saying, "This is so beautiful." Blatty adds that the only thing Linda objected to was having to spit out mouthfuls of pea soup in key scenes, representing vomit.

That, according to Blatty, was because she hates pea soup more than anything else.

Blatty's fascination with the supernatural is currently leading him into an even more extraordinary area: he now believes—and this will be the theme of a future book—that man was not a mere development of nature, but was planted here by creatures from another galaxy. "Grimly enough, Crick, the Nobel Prize-winning scientist, has come to that exact conclusion. He cites molybdenum, an essential to the building blocks of life. He points out that nature would not select one of the rarest elements on earth.

"Furthermore, if life was generated spontaneously, why was there only one genetic code? There should be a multitude, a proliferation of different genetic codes. Crick believes this smacks very strongly of artificial creation. Of course, this means that unidentified flying objects must be 'checking the livestock,' surveying us on behalf of our Creator.

"I have no doubt of the existence of UFOs. Pursuing this idea one step further, we come to the concept of devils and angels, to the idea that angels were the benevolent creators of the race from another galaxy. That God created them, that they were the intermediaries. And that the demons were from that same or another galaxy and have interfered. This is one explanation of the existence of evil. I believe *creatures* created us. It should be quite a theme for a novel, don't you think?"

Robert Aldrich

I have always had a weakness for Robert Aldrich's films, starting with *Kiss Me Deadly* (1955) which starred a memorably smoldering young Cloris Leachman. The sexuality of the film, its brooding dark images, represented *film noir* at its peak. Aldrich's decline has been noted by many. Nevertheless, I continue to find an electricity and vitality in his work not equaled in his more approved-of successor in the field of violence: Sam Peckinpah. The Burt Reynolds–Catherine Deneuve feature, *Hustle,* mentioned here under another name, was a disaster, but *The Longest Yard* I thought a virile and vividly edited work, still the best picture Burt Reynolds has made, and the movie which best displays his aggressively *macho* gifts as a star.

I like Aldrich personally. He is a blunt, down-to-earth, humorous man. He makes a splendid interview. And it's virtually all his own work, since he scarcely waits for the questions. . . .

---------- ★ ----------

1974

Robert Aldrich gives an impression of massive strength. His forearms could be those of a heavyweight boxer. His chest is enormous, his stomach heroic, his face heavy, alive with a shrewd intelligence. Dark eyes twinkle sharply in nests of wrinkles. He grabs a telephone as though picking up a gun.

He wouldn't be a man for the unathletic to trifle with. One blow of his fist would flatten most men.

He talks with a formidable directness in keeping with his build. In his appropriately huge office in Hollywood, overlooking the stone desert of Larchmont Avenue, he suggests the humor, the rapid-fire energy, the thudding toughness of his pictures. He is the master of stories of men in action—his first picture, *The Big Leaguer,* and his latest, *The Longest Yard,* both deal with men on the sporting field, and he has shown men at war, in *Attack!, The Angry Hills, The Dirty Dozen,* and *Too Late the Hero,* in criminal gangs *(Kiss Me Deadly, The Grissom Gang),* and in the West *(Vera Cruz, 4 for Texas, Ulzana's Raid, Emperor of the North).* All of these pictures are marked by a boisterous humor, a love of the physical life of muscle and sweat, and a dynamic command of camerawork and editing which makes him one of the greatest Hollywood craftsmen. Fainthearted critics object to his gusto, his sheer, exuberant lustiness which is in the direct tradition of John Ford, Tay Garnett, and Jack Conway. But Aldrich goes on making his ruggedly slam-bang pictures just the same.

He sums up his recurrent, obsessive theme at the outset of our conversation: "Since it's impossible to 'win' everything in life, whether you're a football player, a soldier, or a politician, your interior self-esteem comes out of how hard you try to win—the degree of your struggle. That's the yardstick whereby effort, whether it's heroic or imaginative, is really measured. I'm concerned with man's efforts to prevail against impossible odds." Thus, in almost all of his pictures, he has portrayed the struggle of beaten, nondescript characters in search of their manhood in extreme situations: the seedy detective played by Ralph Meeker in *Kiss Me Deadly,* the grab-bag assortment of dropouts turned professional soldiers in *The Dirty Dozen,* the railroad men in *Emperor of the North,* Burt Reynolds's woman-beating ex-jock turned prisoners' team captain-coach-player in *The Longest Yard.*

It isn't surprising that the theme of man's struggle fascinates Aldrich. His own life has been a powerful battle against seemingly impossible odds. In his early pictures he was faced with problems of casting, censorship, and tight budgets; he had several flops followed by the huge success of *What Ever Happened to Baby Jane?*, the less tremendous but still very real success of *Hush, Hush, Sweet Charlotte,* and then his commercial blockbuster, *The Dirty Dozen.* Recently he has been through a harrowing period of box-office failure, with four flops in a row; at time of writing, *The Longest Yard* seems to have taken off very promisingly. It would take a man as physically and mentally rugged and resilient as Aldrich to cope with this roller-coaster career; fortunately, he is a very popular man within the industry, crews love to work with him because he's funny and vigorous and very much a member of a team, and his shrewd showman's instincts make it easy for him to talk to the top men of the studios.

Aldrich remembers: "I got into pictures in 1941, just as I was about to leave the University of Virginia. My uncle had some interests in the movie business in California—he got me a six-month job as production clerk at RKO. I became a third assistant, then a second—and finally I got a real break. I was thrown out of the Air Corps after a day and a half because of an old football injury. There was such a manpower shortage I became a first assistant in my mid-twenties, and then a production manager.

"During that period I assisted many of the best, and learned from all of them. They could honestly be called great: Milestone (three pictures), Losey (two pictures), Wellman, Renoir, Chaplin, Rossen, and Dassin. I firmly believe you could learn more about comedy assisting Les Goodwins on a two-reel Leon Errol than you could spending two years at a film school. And during this same period, I had extraordinary exposure to important writers like Steinbeck, Faulkner, Irwin Shaw, Odets, and Remarque. If you'll remember, that was the golden age of screenwriters, and I had the good fortune to work on films by Trumbo, Polonsky, Butler, and Lardner. People often ask if an aspiring director can learn anything from producers and my stock answer is, 'Naturally, from the good ones.' During those same years—again being lucky—I worked with some super-producers: Sam Spiegel (two pictures), David Loew (three pictures), Val Lewton (three pictures), and Hal Wallis. The important thing to remember, however, is that you learn as much from the dogs—about what not to do—as you can from the giants about what to do.

"Between forty-one and forty-five I was fired twice: once by Adolph Zukor for telling his nephew that he didn't know his ass from a hot rock, and once by Louis B. Mayer because one of his 'important' directors had told him I was a Communist. Zukor was right and Mayer was wrong.

"Later, I left RKO for Enterprise, an independent outfit releasing through United Artists and M-G-M. Unfortunately, that group only produced one hit, *Body and Soul*—and several disasters. It was a sensational organization, very creative, but it was dead after three and a half years. Afterward I got an opportunity to direct soap operas in New York. Finally Dore Schary gave me a chance to do my first feature as a director, *The Big Leaguer* for Metro. It was a baseball story and I enjoyed doing it, but it was hardly memorable.

"I did a great deal of television, including the China Smith series with the late Dan Duryea; the cameraman on the series was Joe Biroc, who's still with me—he photographed *The Longest Yard*. Doing an independent thriller, *The World for Ransom*, I even had to shoot beer and Eversharp commercials to pay for the last day of the picture. It took nine and a half days to make and I loved it. I am reluctant to admit that I went a day and a half over."

Aldrich smiles his veteran campaigner's smile. "Hecht-Lancaster let me do a Western, *Apache*, because I was young, ambitious, eager, and inexpensive. It was a moderately expensive epic that I should have done better. Burt Lancaster was the star. The script had an ending in which Lancaster as the Apache hero was shot in the back by Federal troops. United Artists insisted on a happy ending, even though Lancaster and I disagreed. Jean Peters played Lancaster's Indian wife and was wonderful in the part.

"I did *Vera Cruz*, also with Hecht-Lancaster, and then Victor Saville, who owned the rights to Mickey Spillane's works, offered me *Kiss Me Deadly* to produce and direct. I took the title and threw the book away. Al Bezzerides did a sensational script. The picture represented a breakthrough—I really got away with a lot of original effects in the picture. But I ran into censorship trouble. In one scene, a black girl was singing a song and caressing the microphone. The Legion of Decency screamed. The picture was cut as a result, and I was furious about that. By the way, that picture had the young Cloris Leachman in the cast, and she was wonderful."

After *Kiss Me Deadly,* which acquired an underground reputation as a powerful, disturbing, anti-Establishment gangster story, Aldrich formed his company, The Associates and Aldrich, and made his fine version of Clifford Odets' stage play about a falling Hollywood star, *The Big Knife.*

"The trouble with that one was audiences couldn't identify with a situation in which a man is worried whether or not to accept five thousand dollars a week. Many people in the audience weren't earning that much *a year.* I based the character of the producer so wonderfully played by Rod Steiger on Harry Cohn. Steiger cried and pleaded like Mayer, but basically, with all of his rages, he was Cohn.

"I guess it was self-survival that made me do *Autumn Leaves,* with Joan Crawford. People were critical of the cruelty and violence in my pictures and I decided it was time to do a classy soap opera. I didn't realize it would turn out to be just that; quite so full of soap. Ms. Crawford announced that unless I used her writer she wouldn't show up for work. Actually, I didn't use her writer and she did show up. But she didn't talk to me for five days. She took direction perfectly and professionally, but she wouldn't say anything except the dialogue. Then, one day, she played a very sad scene brilliantly, at the conclusion of which she saw me wipe away a tear. She came over to me, embraced me, and from that moment on we were very good friends.

"The picture did well, but then I made a few pictures in Europe which didn't make money. I spent my last dime in Yugoslavia trying to put a picture together entitled *Taras Bulba* that never got off the ground; Hecht-Hill-Lancaster made a different version of my script two years later in Argentina. *The Last Sunset* was really a disappointing picture. Even though Dalton Trumbo was responsible for my getting the assignment, I had certain difficulties with his screenplay, plus the fact that I didn't get along with Kirk Douglas, whose company was producing the picture. But I liked working with Rock Hudson; he was enormously helpful and cooperative."

Nineteen sixty-one and sixty-two were bad years for Aldrich. After *The Last Sunset* sank slowly in the west, he got embroiled in something called *Sodom and Gomorrah*, shot in Morocco and Italy. Luckily, a new success was just around the corner: the camp Gothic thriller, *What Ever Happened to Baby Jane?* Lukas Heller worked on the script and the result was a nice black comedy, with Joan Crawford and Bette Davis at their best as two aging ex-movie queens living in a run-down house in Hollywood. Aldrich remembers: "Right from the beginning, Crawford and Davis were my only choices for the parts." What about their legendary differences on the picture? "They didn't fight at all. I think it's reasonable to say they detested each other, but they behaved perfectly. There was never an abrasive word in public, and not once did they try to upstage each other. They were perfect pros. Davis—more than I—decided to wear an ugly, chalky makeup. When she saw the picture with me at the Cannes Film Festival, I heard a quiet but desperate sobbing and I looked around. It was Bette. 'I look awful,' she cried. Bette had never seen any of the rushes.

"I thought *Hush . . . Hush, Sweet Charlotte,* was a much better picture. And I thought Bette was much better in *Charlotte* than in the all-out Gothic of *Baby Jane*. I cast Joan again but she fell ill—genuinely ill—and I replaced her with Olivia de Havilland. I had to fly to Switzerland in midproduction to discuss it with Olivia. She didn't want to act a villainess. But I persuaded her that the part was much more complex and multidimensional than a simple villainess. And she was wonderful— she and Bette were old friends and she entered into the spirit of the thing magnificently—despite her fears, she made a great villainess.

"*The Dirty Dozen* has been just about my most successful picture—M-G-M had bought the novel after I had tried to buy it myself. Several scripts were written, the last by Nunnally Johnson, but I wasn't satisfied with any of them. Then John Wayne was cast without my knowledge or consent. I was very distressed, but fortunately Wayne withdrew. I called in Lukas Heller to write a new script. The result was something I could be proud of; I think most people were fascinated by the picture's first two-thirds and tolerated or were excited and/or stimulated by the last third. Ken Hyman was the producer of *The Dirty Dozen,* and I've always been grateful to him for giving me that assignment.

"I'm sorry to say that *The Legend of Lylah Clare,* about a film director played by Peter Finch who tries to recreate a star that he had once loved in the image of Kim Novak, was a disaster, and none of it was Kim's fault. Audiences didn't understand the picture. I tried to make everything explicit, but it wasn't clear enough. I was much more disappointed with the box-office results of *The Killing of Sister George,* from a play concerning the lives of three London lesbians. I was very proud of that picture. I thought Beryl Reid gave a great performance, and I was astonished that she wasn't nominated for an Oscar.

"*Too Late the Hero,* a World War Two film set in Singapore but shot in the Philippines, came out at exactly the wrong moment, after the student revolution had begun, the country was polarized, and Vietnam was the most unpopular war in history. *Emperor of the North* not only had a title that didn't appeal—obviously partly my fault, because I thought the title was sensational. But nobody knew what it meant. Also Ernest Borgnine and Lee Marvin as two men fighting on a railroad were apparently too old for the youth audiences to identify with. There was a wonderful young character played brilliantly by Keith Carradine that made up the trio, but in the end his youth didn't help. *The Grissom Gang* should have been a hit but wasn't; I don't know why." Could it have been, I ask Aldrich, because the central character of a gangster played by Scott Wilson was sexually impotent? Didn't this frighten men in the audience who would want to identify with him? Aldrich

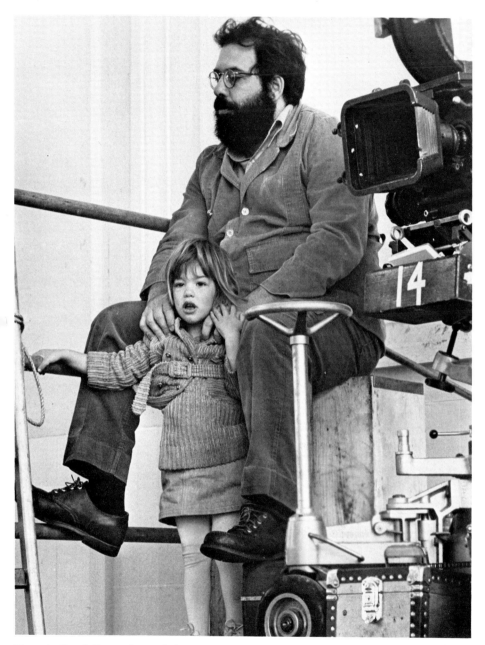

Francis Ford Coppola and daughter Sofia Carmina

William Peter Blatty (PHOTOGRAPH © 1978 JILL KREMENTZ)

Robert Aldrich
(COPYRIGHT © 1977
ALLIED ARTISTS
PICTURES CORP.)

Don Siegel (SAM FALK)

Martin Ritt

Brian De Palma

(TONY ESPARZA)

Christopher Isherwood (PHOTOGRAPH © 1978 JILL KREMENTZ)

King Vidor (TONY ESPARZA)

Roger Vadim (PHOTO BY BRUCE MCBROOM © 1978)

Alfred Hitchcock in Covent Garden for *Frenzy*
(COPYRIGHT © UNIVERSAL PICTURES)

George Sidney
(COBURN, COPYRIGHT © 1960 COLUMBIA PICTURES CORPORATION)

Paul Schrader (TONY ESPARZA)

William Wyler and Samantha Eggar during filming of *The Collector*

Roman Polanski

Robert Wise

Maria Rasputin, 1977 (ASSOCIATED PRESS)

Ralph Bakshi (TONY ESPARZA)

Raoul Walsh (TONY ESPARZA)

Jacqueline Bisset with François Truffaut in *Day for Night*

Orson Welles (TONY ESPARZA)

looks very thoughtful. He suddenly darts back, "What about Warren Beatty in *Bonnie and Clyde?*" "But he was cured of impotence." Aldrich shrugs. "Well, maybe that was the reason *The Grissom Gang* went down the drain. . . . Who knows?"

Certainly, that isn't a problem with the present picture, *The Longest Yard,* in which Burt Reynolds is every man's macho fantasies rolled into one. I ask Aldrich about the making of this picture. "It began as a story written by Al Ruddy five years ago that nobody was interested in. My guess is that nobody was interested because sports pictures have notoriously not been successful. After *The Godfather* Paramount figured that Ruddy could do no wrong—so they finally allowed him to develop a screenplay, and Tracy Keenan Wynn did the first eighty-seven fabulous pages. I'm not kidding myself I was the first guy to be asked to do this picture. I read the eighty-seven Wynn pages and I saw the nucleus of an exceptional movie. I'm a football nut—a real freak. At high school I played tackle and at college a guard. I guess I would have done the picture for nothing—fortunately they didn't know that at Paramount. It took someone who has played football—is freaked out about it—to do that kind of movie. If you fancy yourself an ex-jock and you've suffered with the Rams as long as I have, there's not much you don't know about the game.

"So I had to do it. All the players in the picture were experienced. Burt Reynolds had played very good football at Florida State before getting injured in his senior year.

"I enjoyed coaching as well as directing the team in the picture. Coaching is the last retreat of a would-be dictator anyway, so I had a good time. If Hitler could have gotten his kicks as a film director–football coach, we wouldn't have had World War Two."

Did the story have any parallels in fact? "Yes—Oklahoma State Prison had a football team made up of guards; it was semipro and had its own stadium, and the administration had a passion for it to succeed. Originally, we were going to shoot the picture there, but the inmates made short work of our plan —they rioted and burned the whole institution to the ground. Nothing to do with our planned picture. Suddenly there was no prison in America with a built-in team or a stadium on the grounds.

"Luckily, we had support from Georgia, the most progressive state in the 'New South.' Governor Jimmy Carter has a genuine interest in filmmaking, offering all kinds of enticements to Hollywood. Burt was born in Georgia, which helped us when we went to see Governor Carter and told him our problem. He offered us Reidsville, which is the maximum security prison, and we arranged to build a stadium and solicit the help of the prisoners in making the movie. I didn't realize until after we'd completed the film that we had had no real protection from any prisoners who might have acted against us. By giving us total flexibility of movement the authorities also gave us total vulnerability. Had I known that, I might have approached the problem differently.

"The Georgian penal authorities elected to take a chance the prisoners would welcome the picture being made and wouldn't seize us as hostages. I was never aware of any threats. One night some prisoners escaped and my wife was evacuated from the house we occupied on the prison grounds. Otherwise, no trouble." Weren't the authorities shocked at the portrayal of the mean, weak, chiseling prison warden as played by Eddie Albert? "Well, we set our story in Florida. Georgia was never the setting of the picture." Obviously, this helped to placate the official reaction.

What will Aldrich be doing next? "A picture called *Home Free*,* with Burt Reynolds as a policeman who falls in love with a five-hundred-dollar prostitute played by Catherine Deneuve. One of the things I like best about the picture is that it will be shot entirely in Los Angeles. It's so strange, in these days of location pictures, that we seldom see our city the way it is now. I'm excited by the idea. But then, win or lose, picture-making always is the next most exciting thing in the world. It's almost as rewarding as coaching a football team. . . . Don't you agree?"

---

* Later entitled *Hustle*

Don Siegel

Writing this was an interesting experience. I spent several nights on the set of *Dirty Harry*, starring Clint Eastwood, and noticed Don Siegel's forceful, vigorous handling of the actors. He has always been one of the best of the action directors in Hollywood, and Eastwood has learned virtually all of his own directorial techniques from him.

The interview had the most spectacular setting of any I have conducted. The whole of San Francisco lay below us, all the way to the Golden Gate Bridge.

———————— ★ ————————

1977

"Godard called me an artist. Well, that's all right. John Cassavetes introduced us at a party in Hollywood. Here was this dark little Frenchman telling me what a great director I was, and all I could do was stand there stupidly, saying, 'Thank you very much.' I hadn't seen anything he'd done."

At a hotel window high above the rain-swept plunging hills and beige and white buildings of San Francisco, director Donald Siegel modestly broods on his huge European reputation, sipping an afternoon glass of herbal tea commended as an energy builder by Clint Eastwood. He needs the energy; pushing sixty, this hard-bitten, likably laconic man has been working close to dawn for nights at a stretch on his and Eastwood's fourth Malpaso Production, Warners' *Dirty Harry,* a movie about a racist cop (Eastwood) who tracks down a sniper. The filming has been done almost entirely in the business offices, police stations, and streets of the city. Oddly enough, Siegel's first picture, *The Verdict* (1946), was another story about a psychotic cop. It, too, was made for Warners, but it was typical of the studio during that period that it should have been set in London.

Cahiers du Cinéma's Eric Rohmer, Truffaut, Godard, and other critics took up Siegel before they became directors, and his sardonic, casually improvisatory style undoubtedly influenced them.

Talking about this, Siegel, with his tousled steel-wool hair, sleepy Walter Matthau eyes, scrubby mustache, and rumpled jump suit, looks like some veteran mystery writer dragged out of bed to learn that he has just won the Nobel Prize. He seems genuinely astonished that after twenty-five years of making what are, for the most part, essentially fast-moving B pictures, he has become a French idol, a high campus figure like Howard Hawks or Budd Boetticher, and the subject of a National Film Theatre retrospective in London.

In Hollywood, Siegel has the reputation not so much of a major artist as of a skilled action director who works very economically (his last film with Eastwood, *The Beguiled,* was not a box-office success, but he puts that down to poor selling and distribution). Auteur theorists like to link his films together as reflecting a common theme of the antihero (the heartless cop who turns out to be right all along, the apparently insane GI who is in fact the only man capable of leading an army unit). Although Siegel dismisses the idea that his pictures have a consistent point of view, it is certainly true that he has always tried to eliminate the hard blacks and whites of the old-fashioned Hollywood *roman policier,* to show that the police can be crooks and the criminal can have unexpected streaks of decency.

"We're all victims of a pattern of accidents," he says. "I learned that when I was making a picture called, *Riot in Cell*

Block 11 back in the fifties. I met this young guy who had had a relationship with a very young girl, and her mother handed him over. He went up for a stretch and when he came out, two girls approached him and he serviced them. It was his luck that he should have been caught once more. He's probably become a hardened criminal by now; most of his youth has been spent in jail. That boy's face has haunted me ever since. Some policemen think criminals are a special breed. I don't agree at all. I think they're made, not born.''

Siegel's tough but sympathetic attitude toward young criminals (exemplified particularly in his excellent picture about delinquents, *Crime in the Streets,* starring his friend John Cassavetes) has endeared Siegel to college students; so, too, his very harsh and frank portrait of the police (which hasn't prevented the same police from giving him aid both in New York for *Madigan* and in San Francisco for *Dirty Harry*). He is proud that students admire him, and prouder that his son, Kristoffer Tabori, who starred in *Making It* and has a cameo role in *Dirty Harry,* also has a strong campus following. Tabori, the child of Siegel's first marriage with Viveca Lindfors, is the stepson of novelist-playwright George Tabori; Siegel is now married to another actress, Doe Avedon.

Born in Chicago in 1913, son of a mandolin virtuoso, Siegel started work in the San Quentin–like atmosphere of Warners, getting his first job there in 1934 after his father's failing fortunes canceled all plans for a lavish education. Down on his luck in Los Angeles, he had drifted into the Warner film library, graduating to shooting inserts (Bette Davis lighting a cigarette, Bogart holding a gun), then progressing to directing full-scale scenes when the actual directors proved too lazy to shoot them. He became famous for his surrealist montages for such sequences as a marathon dance contest *(City for Conquest)* and a jazz band's cross-country tour *(Blues in the Night),* learning well the Warner rule of shoot 'em hard and fast, a lesson which has remained with him to this day. After *The Verdict* and *Night Unto Night* at Warners, Siegel (even then dissatisfied with Hollywood scripts) fled to other studios, making low-budget features marked by his sardonic cool.

His first famous picture was *Riot in Cell Block 11* (1954), about an outbreak at Folsom Prison. "We had a hell of a job persuading the warden at Folsom to let us stage the riot in his own sacred four walls. Finally, he noticed that one of my assistants looked familiar. 'Isn't your name Sam Peckinpah?' he asked. Sam nodded. 'Well, I know your dad. Anything you need?' 'Just one thing,' Sam replied. The warden looked at me and growled: 'O.K., you get the prison.' "

During the shooting of the picture, Siegel developed his technique, deeply admired by the French, of using amateur actors to play themselves. "Why use Hollywood guys who looked like convicts when they actually had convicts? They had a ball, and thoroughly enjoyed wrecking their own cells. When they went back, they were as mild as you please. Of course, we had guards with guns at double strength just in case anyone had any ideas of trying a real escape."

Through such good films as *The Line-up, Coogan's Bluff,* and *Madigan,* Siegel has continued to use his improvisational methods. On *Dirty Harry,* I watched him hastily convert a portion of an office into a hospital ward, dress up a black second director as intern, and shoot the scene in defiance of studio orders. "The scene shows the cop, played by Clint, learning to tame his hatred of blacks, then his wounded leg is checked by the intern," says Siegel. "The studio thought it was unnecessary, and had it taken out of the script. I've put it back. I don't give a damn if the studio disapproves. The scene cost only five hundred dollars and it says a hell of a lot about Harry—that he isn't just a bundle of prejudices, that he has a certain amount of humanity as well. We just rigged the whole thing up with a couple of sheets and some borrowed instruments. You were wearing white pants last night. If necessary, I could have used you as an orderly. That's the way I work."

Siegel's improvisations often infuriate writers. Albert Maltz, author of *Two Mules for Sister Sara,* and coauthor (with Irene Kamp) of *The Beguiled,* told me he thought Siegel had ruined his work, chopping and changing the scripts for the two films until they were travesties of the originals. He and

Irene Kamp were so angry with Siegel's reworking of their writing on *The Beguiled* that they insisted pseudonyms be used on the picture's credits—John B. Sherry and Grimes Grice. Siegel says: "Martin Rackin, the producer of *Two Mules for Sister Sara,* a man I despise, and Maltz put the script together and sold it to Clint. They saw it in terms of a crude and stupid burlesque and I had to humanize it. It was the story of a nun and a Texas guy played by Clint—the nun turns out to be a whore. I rewrote most of it, and had several run-ins with Rackin over that.

"*The Beguiled* was an even worse headache. Here is a story about a Civil War soldier who is wounded and lies around in a girls' school, and the effect he has on the younger and older women there. Maltz saw it as a romantic love story, and he showed a young girl running away with Eastwood. I was horrified by the softness and sentimentality of his treatment and I showed him a print of *Rosemary's Baby.* I said, 'If you'd written this script, Mia Farrow wouldn't have given birth to the Devil. She'd have given birth to healthy blond twin sons.'

"Maltz didn't like it, but he took it anyway and rewrote the whole thing. It was worse the second time around. I threw his new script away and went off in disgust. The studio—Universal—hired a woman, Irene Kamp, to rewrite the script. They said she, as a female, would know how to treat a story with several women and one man.

"I nearly threw up when I saw what she had done. It was far, far worse than Albert Maltz's worst work. I don't even remember how she handled it. Mercifully, my memory blocks out when I think about it. So I just took over the whole thing and handed it to my associate producer, Claude Traverse, and we did something else. We showed how these girls and women could be evil, how they were capable of murder when their passions were aroused. I came out with a tougher picture. It had a stronger visual style than anything I've done, because how do you keep an audience looking when your hero spends most of the action flat on his back?

"*Dirty Harry* began as a Malpaso Production of Clint Eastwood's company for Universal, but they didn't want to do it, and after being sold to another company it finally was resold again to Warner Brothers at a vast profit. I'm in the wrong business. Originally, Frank Sinatra was to have starred in it, with Irvin Kershner directing, but Frank had trouble with his hand and withdrew and Kershner got left out. When they finally offered the part to Clint, I naturally came along. The script was terrible—it has gone through several drafts already. It was begun by a married couple, a scriptwriting team called —believe it or not—The Finks. It's very different now. You have to keep changing things around if you're a director.

"I think it will be fascinating now. I'm trying to show the character of the policeman again, as I did in *Madigan*, with Richard Widmark. Dirty Harry is a tough cop, a racist sonofa-bitch, who's faced with a crazy sniper and naturally blames everything on blacks and other minorities. We show that within the force there are 'pigs' like this, but we also show that not all are pigs—the way the students see them—that a great many are ordinary men dealing in extraordinary, horrible situations and people.

"I think I've improved the Finks' writing. Albert Maltz and Irene Kamp can complain as much as they like, but I notice that by using pseudonyms on the credits of *The Beguiled*, they can still collect their residuals. They think I did a great deal to improve their writing, too, and I think I've done a great deal to improve many scripts I've worked with. After all, I'm a director-*auteur*. Aren't I?"

Martin Ritt

This interview is one of the few I've ever suggested myself. Since the interview, Ritt has continued to do fine work which hasn't been sufficiently acknowledged: *Sounder* (1973) and *Conrack* (1974) express the continuing humanism of his vision, his interest in simple people, his strong sense of the American bucolic scene, and his warmth and tenderness in dealing with human relationships.

———————★———————

1969

Massive in a coverall, the Hollywood director Martin Ritt suggests great energy and his best films—the Oscar-winning *Hud,* with Paul Newman, *The Spy Who Came in from the Cold,* with Richard Burton, and *The Molly Maguires* with Sean Connery and Richard Harris—have considerable force.

It's understandable, then, that Ritt has been chosen to direct what promises to be the most exciting entertainment of 1970: *The Great White Hope,* from the Tony-winning Broadway smash hit about the career of the black boxer Jack Johnson, who was ruined by the white world because he cohabited with white women.

In his cramped office at Paramount, Ritt took a break from cutting *The Molly Maguires* to talk about this story of the Pennsylvania coal mines in 1876. "It's about these bitter, tough

Irishmen, who committed arson and murder and were hanged, and about a man who goes in among them as an informer. He is played by Richard Harris, and the workmate he drinks with, chases after women with, plays football with, is Sean Connery, head of the Maguire clan. He betrays Connery, destroys him. . . .

"We had hoped to shoot in the actual coal mines, but it proved impossible; you couldn't move the walls to make room for your lights, and there just wasn't enough space for camera movements. So we reconstructed the whole mine in the studio, importing tons of anthracite, and you couldn't tell the difference.

"It was a very tough job to light. I wanted complete realism and some scenes were lit only with the gleam of the miners' headlamps. We had to use special lenses so that the black faces of the miners became fully separated from the black backgrounds.

"The whole picture has been designed to suggest a grim, overcast, black world. Today, that part of Pennsylvania has red houses and green leaves. It looks too fancy. So we painted the houses a very dull green, and we sprayed the leaves with black paint. We shot only on bad days. We even put coal dust all over the new roads to make them look like tracks as black as cinder paths. Every shot in the picture was designed for darkness.

"In the opening there's one complete reel of silent film in which you meet the men and discover their working habits, the way the Maguires plan to destroy the mine because of their bitterness at the working conditions.

"We have a football sequence on a Sunday afternoon when for a moment these grim Irishmen break out and are living, happy men. The wake sequence is a high spot, an Irish wake wilder than anything you heard of. And when the Maguires loot the general store, it's very strong. But our top moment dramatically is at the end: Harris has turned in the Molly Maguires and they're waiting to hang; he goes to see Sean Connery, the friend he betrayed, in jail; and it's very tense.

"These are all based on real people. The informer character went on after the Maguires died and got a very good job; twenty years later, when the government was out to get the Wobblies, the labor agitators of that time, he coached the chief police informer as to how to entrap them. Darrow defended the Wobblies and got them off; but the Maguires had the whole Establishment against them: the railroad, the church, the mines.

"Even today, the people of Pennsylvania fear and hate the memory of the Molly Maguires.

"And you can see the parallels today; I was looking at the rushes when I saw the line of black-faced miners at the pay office, and I said to my writer, Walter Schumann, 'My God, they're like Negroes!' The scenes of looting and arson by these black miners were written before Watts, but the dramatic link is too obvious to need spelling out."

Raised in the toughest areas of New York, where he spoke with his fists before he uttered a word, Ritt battered his way inch by inch from squalor to the antiseptic luxury of Beverly Hills. He survived the jungle of television to make mass-appeal films ("It costs too much to make pictures here for us to handle art pictures"), but these blockbusting stories were always informed by his knowledge of suffering and the struggle of urban men. Blacklisted in the early fifties because of apparent left-wing sympathies, Ritt got a job finally on the strength of his direction on Broadway of Arthur Miller's *A View from the Bridge*.

He shot the first feature he was given, *A Man Is Ten Feet Tall*, on location in New York in twenty-eight days, a white and black story of conflict, with the young Sidney Poitier and John Cassavetes. It flopped, because its theme was ahead of the times, but it made Ritt's name as a realist.

He was hired by 20th Century-Fox for several years on contract. "I hated it. I was just off a blacklist, I was in hock up to my ears, and I had to take orders. I served my time like a jail sentence. I made *No Down Payment*, a film about suburbia, with Jeffrey Hunter; I wanted to tell the truth about the boredom and hopelessness of suburban life, but the then head of the studio wouldn't let me have a realistic ending.

"I made *The Black Orchid,* with Sophia Loren, and *The Long, Hot Summer* and *The Sound and the Fury.*

"Orson Welles was in *The Long, Hot Summer* and he was difficult. I said to him: 'I grew up in the toughest part of New York City. I can kill anybody with knives. I can stone them to death. If they don't cooperate, the hell with them.' He cooperated!"

Ritt's version of the early life of Hemingway, *Hemingway's Adventures of a Young Man,* he felt had been damaged by the casting of Richard Beymer in the central role, and the fact that the public cannot identify itself with films about authors. Breaking with Fox after that, his career took a tremendous leap forward with *Hud,* about a cowboy (played by Paul Newman) in Texas, which exposed the whole myth of sexy, jeansy, teenage heroes and showed its essential hollowness: the cowboy "hero" turns out to be a cheap crook.

"We shot it around Amarillo in the flat, panhandle country. The people there have a joke: 'There ain't nothing between us and the North Pole but a barbed-wire fence.' It's a windy infinity of dust and emptiness. The tornadoes whistle down from the north, and sometimes it's as cold as Alaska.

"I'll never forget the dry humor of that region. I wanted a scene in which Paul Newman's brother, played by Brandon de Wilde, chases a steer. He wouldn't do it. I insisted. Finally he turned on me and said, 'If you're so tough, you do it yourself.' So I went wild. I jumped over the fence and ran after the bull through the corral. I jumped on the animal and I got dung all over me. The stench was terrible, and I fell over, feeling like hell. A cowpoke was sitting on the fence chewing a straw. He looked me up and down in my misery and said out of the corner of his mouth, 'Stuff ain't nothing more than grass and water, boy.' There I was, the big Hollywood director, covered in filth . . . and I laughed and laughed. I'll never forget it as long as I live."

Ritt went on to make *The Outrage,* a story of rape and murder based on the Japanese classic, *Rashomon,* and *Hombre,* also with Paul Newman.

And then *The Molly Maguires.* He believes that today, following the collapse of American censorship, there is a period of freedom in which an American director can do almost anything he wants on the screen.

"The Europeans taught us that any subject can be tackled. That we could deal with adult matters and get out of the candy-floss period we were in. *The Great White Hope* is going to be a really tough, harsh picture. But a problem we still have here is handling stars. They've got so big they don't want to be directed. Burton, for instance, in *The Spy Who Came in from the Cold.* We argued constantly. Sometimes he'd come on a set unprepared. I let him have it. He wasn't used to that. Finally he came through. And gave the best performance of his life.

"Of course, in *The Great White Hope* I've got the greatest star of all. James Earl Jones, who played on Broadway, was stunning. He won a Tony and the New York Drama Critics' Award hands down as Jack Johnson, Negro heavyweight champion of the world. We'll shoot it in San Francisco, New York, Paris, London, and Berlin.

"Johnson was an extraordinary man. The white world hated him because he went to bed with white women. *The New York Times* cleared its whole front page to call for a Great White Hope to defeat the Negro. When he beat the White Hope, the whole country was outraged. They finally closed in on him to the extent he was in fear of his life. He was forced to throw a fight. He was broken; he even wound up playing in *Uncle Tom's Cabin* in Vienna. He came back to Mexico, his white girl suicided, and he died. It's a tremendous theme for today, of course, and an explosive theme." Dangerous, too? "Maybe. I'll have to be careful. It's the biggest challenge of my career. I only hope I can rise to it. . . ." By the way he slammed his fist on the desk as he said that, Martin Ritt almost certainly will.

Brian De Palma

Brian De Palma has gone on to make *Carrie* and *The Fury*. He has moved from strictly physical horror to supernatural mishaps and adventures. At the time of the interview he seemed already to have one foot in another world. He looked like a nineteenth-century medium. If anyone ever made the life of Daniel Dunglas Home, the great spiritist of that time, he would be perfect for the role. He is spooky. Spookier, I feel, than his films, which are too crude for my taste. He may well scare us more subtly in the future.

———————— ★ ————————

1973

"I'm almost completely oblivious to my surroundings. I have no desire to own anything, I've never married and don't want to marry. The outside world means little or nothing to me. I'm completely obsessed with film. Everything meaningful is right here in my head, behind my eyes."

And the eyes, a pale and pebbly gray-blue, look inward at what seems to be a desolate, joyless world. Brian De Palma, whose films *Get to Know Your Rabbit* and *Sisters* are earning substantial critical acclaim, is, at thirty-four, the coldest hot young director in town. His films, bleak and jaundiced, make the spectator a voyeur of hopeless lives.

Get to Know Your Rabbit, starring Tommy Smothers as a male dropout from the business world who becomes a traveling magician, and *Sisters,* about the murderous surviving half of a pair of French-Canadian Siamese twins, are visually ugly films filled with pessimistic humor about human behavior. They are the work of an obsessive artist who may one day produce a major work.

De Palma is staying in the Hollywood high-rise apartment of Martin Scorsese, celebrated young director of *Mean Streets,* while Scorsese is in New York. Tiny, and so dark that lights have to be lit even in the blaze of early afternoon, the apartment is as drab and impersonal as the one occupied by the insane twin in *Sisters.* No paintings on the walls, only crude movie posters. And the convertible sofa I am sitting on bears an alarming resemblance to the one in which the twin hides her stabbed black lover in *Sisters.* One almost expects a demented girl with a French-Canadian accent to come rushing out of the kitchen, brandishing a carving knife. If that were to happen, De Palma would no doubt take it very calmly. He seems prepared for anything in a demented world. From the beginning, he has been aware of the physical horror of so much of human existence.

"My emphasis on horror isn't arbitrary or exploitative," he says. "When I was a child in Philadelphia, I was thrust up against the reality of physical pain, disease, the terror of the operating theater. My father was an orthopedic surgeon and I used to watch him operate. I was facinated by his complex and, at times, gruesome operations."

De Palma rummages in the refrigerator and pours me a grape juice in a long narrow goblet. "When I went to Columbia University, I began to be obsessed by movies. Particularly the films of Roman Polanski. I was fascinated with his *Repulsion,* about a psychotic girl's nightmares. And Hitchcock's *Rear Window* and *Psycho. Sisters,* of course, was influenced by all three films. They seemed terrifying and wonderful to me, and suddenly I knew that I could convey my dreams on the screen. No other art form would do."

De Palma began making experimental films, and when his *Murder a La Mod* was shown at Tambellini's Gate, in New

York's East Village, in the spring of 1968, his bizarre imagination began to attract wide attention. It was followed by *Greetings,* a harsh political satire which won the Silver Bear Award in Berlin in 1969, a screen version of Off-Off-Broadway's *Dionysus' 69, The Wedding Party,* and *Hi, Mom!* One of the starkest episodes in *Hi, Mom!* dealt with a stage production called *Be Black, Baby,* whose all-black cast, in whiteface, mingles with, steals from, and finally beats and rapes the white liberal audience.

Whether comedy, farce, outrageous satire, or horror flick, all of De Palma's movies are grim commentaries on a psychotic society. His *Get to Know Your Rabbit,* flawed though he claims it was through interference by Warner Brothers, is among his most savage *films noirs.* "It's a movie in many ways close to Woody Allen in that it creates a feeling of an absurd, mad, and rather threatening universe. It came from a story by the novelist Jordan Crittenden. I added some low humor, belly laughs; I like that kind of thing. But the humor isn't warm, it has a cruel twist that's part of me.

"And I changed one very basic concept in the story. There's a character, played by Allen Garfield, who is Tommy Smothers' boss. Crittenden had him dropping out of the business world, only to make a comeback in a new line of business. I changed it so that he became rich through starting a school for dropouts. I tried to show that there's no escape. That the 'hip' world is big business, too. Revolution, black or otherwise, is commercial. The whole rock music world, supposedly representing the voice of revolution, is utterly commercial, with its own fashions, its own set rules. Look at the *Village Voice.* It started out being revolutionary. Now it's as square as anything else."

What about the end of *Get to Know Your Rabbit* in which the hero, after being trapped in various forms of commercial compromise, does finally shake loose and become a traveling magician once again? Doesn't this suggest that at least there is a possibility of escape to a simpler life?

"I had a much more complex ending. Originally I showed Donald, the dropout, ending up on the Johnny Carson show doing his routine, and talking about how 'fresh' and 'spontaneous' he had become. Gradually, it dawns on him he's being exploited all over again. So he does his magic trick, sawing his rabbit in half, but seems to be really sawing it in half by mistake. The audience screams, Johnny Carson loses his cool, and Donald flees. But it *was* only a trick, the rabbit is O.K., and at last Donald is free of everything. Nobody wants him after he saws a rabbit in half on television. This is much better than the studio ending, which simply shows Donald disappearing from his brand-new office in the dropout business for no reason at all.

"Tommy Smothers didn't like the picture. Although he agreed to play the part of Donald, he felt that the character wasn't forceful enough. He didn't believe that Donald would smilingly accept everything in the way that he did. Smothers has always made a point about being strongly individualist and opinionated, and his left-wing opinions have kept him off television for a long time. He took the part because it seemed to symbolize his struggle.

"But when he got into it, not only did he feel the man weak, he identified Warner Brothers with the commercial monolith Donald was dropping out of—and he even disappeared from the picture for two days. He refused to come back for retakes, which I desperately needed to shoot, and as a result some scenes in the film are very bad and unfunny. He also refused to back me up when I fought with Warners over the new cut they made. But I'm sorry for him. From being a great television star, where is he today?

"Warners took the picture from the producers and gave it to a project coordinator named Peter Nelson who cut it, rearranged some scenes, directed a new sequence, and put in other scenes that I had decided to eliminate."

De Palma gets up, coldly answers a persistent telephone caller, and then sinks back in his chair, looking tired and puffy. "I'm much happier with *Sisters*. That is mine from beginning to end. American International took on the distribution—but they didn't tamper with it at all. It was shot in location on Staten Island. I liked the idea of a very suburban setting for a horror story about a small-town girl reporter who sees a murder from her apartment window."

Not all of *Sisters* was shot on Staten Island, however. "We built the set of the apartment where the murder takes place on East Fourth Street, right next to the Cafe La Mama. I loved the voyeuristic mood of the story— Here is the girl, this amateur sleuth who gazes through windows and sees a man murdered and all kind of horrifying things going on. Things half-seen. Like most directors, I'm a voyeur at heart. I loved dragging the audience through the whole psychodrama of an insane situation. The audience *becomes* this girl; the people out there can be her, too."

De Palma's next film will be *Phantom of the Paradise,* a Gothic horror story, based on *The Phantom of the Opera,* but set in a replica of the shrine of rock in New York. "There will be a hideously scarred musician who wears a beautiful mask and plays the organ," De Palma says with a grisly grin. "Then I'm going to do *Obsession* with the writer Paul Schrader, a story similar to *Vertigo,* about a man in love with a dead woman."

These films, like their predecessors, will emphasize the horror, the madness, the violence, the meaninglessness of life in our time. And, above all, they will stress De Palma's belief that everyone is busy exploiting everyone else in our society. "Take that girl reporter in *Sisters,*" De Palma says as he rises to leave for a doctor's appointment. "No sooner does she spot the killing than she becomes eager to push her own career by writing about it. I used to do talk-show appearances, talking about my left-wing, anticapitalist views, and all I was doing was filling in spaces between soap commercials.

"So now I have no political views. How can you be a non-capitalist film director? It's ridiculous, a contradiction in terms. If you're buying or selling. Everything is a product. I'm a product, you're a product. Take this interview for instance. I'm supplying. You're demanding. My films are *products.* But they have one advantage over most I see around. They come out of my dreams, my nightmares. If I can get at least a percentage of those dreams across without interference, I'll feel okay. Maybe."

Brian De Palma turns out the light and suddenly the room is pitch-dark.

Christopher Isherwood

This is the earliest of the interviews in this book. I had a most curious experience after I met Isherwood again, years later.

We had gone to Mae West's, a group of us, for a Christmas party. During the evening, Isherwood arrived. He seemed mysteriously hostile toward me. Since I scarcely knew him, I couldn't imagine why.

I woke at about three o'clock the following morning, drenched in perspiration. Something was in the room. I saw Isherwood's figure standing by the bed, looking down at me with intense dislike. I was wide awake. Against the curtains, I could see the reflection of a fire which was consuming a building across the street.

I felt my life drain away. It was as though Isherwood's doppelgänger were willing me to death. I was drowning. I could hardly breathe. The temperature of the room dropped seemingly below zero and I began to shiver unbearably.

I forced the figure to go away. I did not sleep the rest of the night. It was hours after the figure dissolved in the darkness that the room resumed its ordinary temperature.

Whenever we have met since, Isherwood has been charming.

Call this paranoia, if you will.

———————★———————

1967

Christopher Isherwood's house stands high above the romantic, plunging slopes of Santa Monica Canyon, looking down
across a wilderness of cactus and yucca and tangled scrub,
past scattered red-roofed houses to the broad, beating waves
of the Pacific. At the gate, two young people, pale, pimply,
black-clad, and patently English, are consulting a road map in
their Mini-Minor at the head of the drive. Clearly, they have
been visiting Herr Issyvoo in his aerie.

The house is modest: Spanish in flavor, with low-lying
couches, an enormous coffee table, theatrical posters on the
white-painted walls. Isherwood is informally dressed in open-
necked white shirt, black slacks, and slippers. Against the
deep California tan the eyes glitter with a nervous brilliance,
blue and sharp, nervously darting like a bird's. He is at once
inviting and cold. He looks extraordinarily compact and
young, only a thin film of age laid over the Issyvoo of the
Berlin drawings, and the voice, eager, high-pitched is the
voice of a boy.

Isherwood has lived in Santa Monica or nearby for almost
thirty years. Since he came to Hollywood just before the outbreak of World War II, he has written five novels: *Prater Violet,*
based on his experiences writing scripts at Gaumont-British
in England before the war; *The World in the Evening* and *Down
There on a Visit,* set respectively wholly and partly in Hollywood; *A Single Man,* a story about a homosexual professor in
an American college; and *A Meeting by the River,* about the
monastic vocation, told in an epistolary form.

What were his methods of work? "I write in spurts. Some
days I work all day long—for hours and hours—and other
times I realize, like an unlucky angler, I'm not going to 'catch
anything that day,' so I switch to some other job. I used to
make endless notes when I was young; now what I do is write
in a purely probing way; I do a rough draft without knowing
where I'm going, and then rewrite it again and again, redoing
every word. To be specific, my latest novel, *A Meeting by the
River,* was originally written straight, not in the form of letters

and diaries as it is now. I was about twenty pages in when I suddenly understood it wasn't going to work. So I changed the whole structure. I wrote three complete drafts." In longhand? "No, straight onto the machine. Luckily, I formed that habit very early in life. Now I couldn't possibly write in longhand. I have arthritis in both thumbs."

How long, I asked him, does it take him to write a book? "Anything up to three years. And sometimes I can see another book emerging from the one I've written. *A Single Man*, for instance. I was fascinated by the character of the Englishwoman in that, the woman who couldn't settle in California. I'd like to write another novel about her.

"Of course, settlement hasn't been my problem. I like the feeling of being abroad. Now England seems just as fascinating as America does. And they both seem foreign." If they both seem foreign, what doesn't? "I don't know; heaven, I suppose."

He talked about his attitudes to literature. "It really doesn't matter what you write. What really matters is what you say. You can set up some kind of plot, but it's all really in aid of something you want to give voice to. Often you don't know what it is; it's something instinctive, something in the unconscious. Whether it's a novel or a history of Charles the Second it might be the medium by which you get certain things said which you deeply want to say."

Who are his idols? "Of course, there's Forster, the great master, whom I come back to constantly. In an odd way, Willa Cather, although she is a totally different kind of writer. And Henry Green, he's a wonderful writer. Edward Upward, of course; he's just finished the second volume of his trilogy, and it's fascinating. Oddly enough, I feel very drawn to Kerouac. There's something in his whole approach, the way he wanders into the experience or chain of experiences, and in his theme of wanderlust itself. For the same reason I love George Borrow and *Lavengro*." What about the new experimental French writers? The "concrete" novels? "I find them absolutely unreadable. I always feel they're writing films, not novels. I'll look at the damned thing so long as you want if they photograph it, but I don't want to hear it named."

I asked him how he came to settle in California in the late thirties.

"Auden and I had written *Journey to a War,* based on our experiences in the Orient, and we came back to Europe by way of Canada and the States. We made up our minds then that we would live in the States. We were delayed by the Munich crisis and we didn't leave finally until January 1939.

"I chose California because I wanted to meet Aldous Huxley, who had moved out several years previously, and Gerald Heard, whom I already knew. I had been very curious, too, to see the West." Had it fulfilled his expectations? "I was simply stunned by the classic West: Yosemite and the Sequoia forests were incredibly wonderful. Our first night in Los Angeles was squalid—a seedy hotel after a long bus journey—but I soon came to love the city. Olive groves everywhere, and the hills untouched by bulldozers."

How had he gotten into movies? "Through Salka and Berthold Viertel, the film director whose character formed the basis of *Prater Violet.* I had worked on a script for him at Gaumont-British in the early thirties: *Little Friend.*"

Salka Viertel's salon in Los Angeles was famous: to it came the great European expatriates who had settled in California for the climate and the possibility of film work: Thomas Mann, Franz Werfel, Leonard Frank, Brecht; and in addition to them Lotte Lehmann, Fritzi Massary, the great comic opera star, and Stravinsky. Huxley, Isherwood said, had settled with unusual ease into California. He had loved the terrain, the desert, the wild flowers, and wrote fascinating essays about them in *Tomorrow and Tomorrow.* "Huxley had an enormous interest in everything that went on around him. He was supremely intelligent, and perhaps interest and intelligence are really synonymous. There was nothing he could not relate to the whole structure of his knowledge and add a brick to the wall."

Isherwood said he had worked on *Rage in Heaven,* with Ingrid Bergman, *A Woman's Face,* with Joan Crawford, and *The*

Hour Before the Dawn, a story he had intended to be a pacifist film but had wound up after rewrites as a glorification of war. What did he think about the theory that so many writers were ruined by Hollywood? "It's ridiculous. If you're going to be ruined, you're going to be ruined. Something will come along and ruin you if it can. I think it's very good for a writer to be forced to visualize. You have to stop relying on the word and start thinking in terms of images and of possible silent sequences. And film writing is of artistic value to me, no doubt of it."

He had written a good deal of the script of *The Great Sinner,* a version of Dostoevsky's "The Gambler," with Ava Gardner; and Gregory Peck, of all people, as Dostoevsky. "I remember one thing that happened during the production. The voice of Christ had to speak from the crucifix in the church when Gregory Peck robs the poor box. They asked me to do it. They said: 'To make the words reverberate, Chris, you should speak the lines in a little concrete entrance hall.' There I was in the hall clutching the mike, and I had to produce this terrible booming voice. Suddenly a door opened, just as a red light went on indicating I should deliver the speech, and a *carpenter* came in. There was nothing to be done, I had to go on, they had the whole thing wired for sound. So I looked him right in the eye, and I said as loudly as my lungs could manage, with every word echoing round the room, 'And they parted my garments among them, and they cast dice for my robe!' I've never seen anyone as frightened in my life!"

Isherwood's next project, never filmed, had been a life of Buddha. "The whole thing was predicated on a very simple dramatic base: would or would not the prophecy that Buddha would become a monk, that he would renounce the throne, be fulfilled? We didn't have anything about the enlightened Buddha, because that isn't allowed to be shown in Buddhist countries. We showed the young prince growing up, in a barbaric Gordon Craig type of castle with a sort of Alice in Wonderland little door in the back, guarded by two tremendous men, one with a sword in his teeth and another with a sword in each hand.

"When you went through this door you came to a marvelous pleasure park, where everything was very Chinese with little hills and peacocks and ivory pagodas. And here the young prince lived with his companions and girlfriends."

On the film version, directed by Tony Richardson, of *The Loved One*, Isherwood said he had written the scene in the chapel when the wedding becomes the funeral, and the board-meeting sequence; most of the rest of his work on the film had been recast by Terry Southern. He had never met Waugh in California, or elsewhere, and winced at mention of his name. "I didn't like the book. The ending isn't at all resolved, and, in fact, you couldn't have shot it as it stood, it didn't amount to anything. The hero is such a boring kind of heel that it's all rather distasteful. And snobbish. And to laugh at Forest Lawn seemed so trivial, so obvious, and so thin a reason for condemning the whole of California life."

How did he feel about Swinging Britain now that he had just revisited it? "I love the mod thing. I was given a kind of press conference when I was last there recently. They started asking the usual questions about England—how did I feel about it, and so on. And I said, 'I think it's just ideal. In other words, everything that I hoped would happen to England when I was young has happened.' And somebody said, 'Oh, you mean the total destruction of England!' And I said, 'No! Not at all, you're quite wrong, you don't understand!' England today is a marvelous place."

King Vidor

King Vidor is one of nature's aristocrats, an immigrant from Texas to California who ennobled the American film. We have been friends for years, which is why it was especially difficult to do this interview. When you know someone very well indeed, it's almost impossible to ask him those conventional questions to which you already know the answers.

There was one story which I cut out of the final draft of the piece, and which I'd now like to restore. Katharine Hepburn told me it was the loveliest thing she ever heard.

In 1921, King Vidor directed Colleen Moore in *The Sky Pilot*. They had a brisk jazz-age romance. At parties, they indulged in a performance which Scott Fitzgerald attended more than once. And must have appreciated.

King would stand on the stage in a ballroom or living room wearing a black tuxedo, blindfolded with a white cloth. Colleen would pass through the crowd picking up various objects. King had to identify them without being able to see them. Colleen would say, "What is this that I hold in my hand?" And King would instantly say, "A lady's handbag." Colleen would call out, "Quick! Now! What is this?" And he would say, "A wedding ring." The explanation was simple. Each phrase had been prerehearsed and memorized to match a particular object. Audiences never discovered the code. Occasionally, when some possession which had not been coded was held up, King would say, holding his head,

"The image is not clear. Dark vibrations are swirling through my brain." And he would admit defeat.

Fifty years went by. King had barely seen Colleen after their affair ended. She had moved to Chicago. He had settled on a ranch in Paso Robles, California.

One afternoon about seven years ago, King was wandering down the Champs Elysées. A woman's voice behind him said, "What is this that I am holding in my hand?" Without turning around, he said, "A handbag!"

"Right the first time!" the woman's voice said.

There is no need to say who the woman was.

1973

It is just like the journey to Spanish Bit, Lionel Barrymore's grandiose ranch house in King Vidor's celebrated baroque Western, *Duel in the Sun.* The driveway sweeps through yellow rolling fields and clumps of eucalyptus and conifer, up a steep incline through a roughhewn gate to a low-lying house at the crest. Youthful and handsome at seventy-eight, Vidor comes to the front door himself, wearing a Western ranch tie clipped by a sterling silver medallion with the initals KV in turquoises, a white Western shirt, cotton pants, and handmade brown leather boots. He walks from the hall to the window of his living room, gazing in a manner befitting his kingly name over his 1248 acres of choice central California territory. In the remote distance, Hereford cattle graze peacefully, horses frisk in a paddock, clumps of oak trees toss in a breeze. It is a classically appropriate setting for this master of the American rural film.

Though he retired from feature filmmaking in 1959, King Vidor is still active as a moviemaker: like a young student of the medium that fascinates him as much as it did sixty years ago, he has created a beautiful short film on 16 millimeter, *Truth and Illusion,* an abstract work consisting of images of nature, pure distillations of his vision of life. The Museum of Modern Art in New York showed a major three-month retrospective season of his movies, ranging over fifty years, from *The Jack-Knife Man* (1920) to *Truth and Illusion.* He will be in New York with Colleen Moore, the deliciously amusing comedienne of such twenties classics as *Flaming Youth* and *Ella Cinders,* to introduce his 1928 Marion Davies vehicle, *Show People,* at the museum, and to join in the festivities.

King Vidor's romance with Colleen Moore (b. 1900) is already a Hollywood legend. They first met in 1921, when he was married to his boyhood sweetheart, Florence Vidor; he directed Colleen in *The Sky Pilot.* They fell in love, and their affair continued until 1924. They met again exactly forty years later; Vidor heard from Hedda Hopper that Colleen now lived in Chicago, and when he was there he made a point of seeing Colleen again. They resumed their romance with much of its original intensity. Now she lives some fifteen minutes drive away across the Paso Robles hills, in her own splendid homestead, El Rancho. "We have the same sense of humor, and we both love to travel," Vidor says. They have just returned from a two-month cruise of the South Seas and the Orient, where they bought paintings and carvings and screens for Colleen's collection of Oriental art.

Above all, they share a passion for the land. Vidor has always been a poet of the American landscape, creating vivid images of rural life in such films as *The Texas Ranger, Billy the Kid, Hallelujah, Northwest Passage,* and *Duel in the Sun.* He has been from the outset a rebel in the Hollywood system, striking out for his own ideas. At the beginning, he championed the common man, most notably in his masterpiece, *The Crowd,* and in *Our Daily Bread,* more recently the rugged individualist, in such less admired films as *The Fountainhead* and *Beyond the Forest.* But his humanism, his passionate love of life, have never deserted him.

"When I was a young kid in Texas at the beginning of the century, I used to hate movies. I hated their phoniness, their fakiness, the makeup which used to mask the actors' expressions, their dreadful unreal acting with overdone pantomime gestures.

"People found them laughable *then*. I felt drama would be more vital if you could believe events were really happening while you were looking at them. I wanted to focus on small, important things. I decided in my teens to make pictures which would make people feel they were reliving their day-to-day lives through the characters."

He began by shooting small films in Texas, with borrowed money—mostly documentaries about small-town life or the life of the soil. Later, a team of businessmen supported him in making a work exemplifying his own Christian Science principles—*The Turn of the Road*. He and his young wife, Florence Vidor, started out for Hollywood in a Model-T Ford and arrived with fifty cents between them; they landed jobs as extras, and he also worked as a general handyman. His first important break came with a contract from First National, which allowed him to make a simple film about an old man and a boy on a Mississippi shantyboat, *The Jack-Knife Man*.

Vidor went on to make a number of famous silent films, including *Happiness* with Laurette Taylor (which opened the museum's season) and *Wine of Youth*. None of these really exemplified his principles of subdued realism, but in 1925 at last he got his chance with *The Big Parade*. "I wanted to make an honest war picture. Until then, they'd been all phony, glorifying officers and warfare. There hadn't been a single picture showing the war from the viewpoint of ordinary soldiers and privates, not one that was really antiwar.

"Before the picture was released, I anticipated an attack from militarist factions. But there was none. In fact, one of the Du Ponts, who was one of the big war matériel manufacturers, visited the set and said that if exhibitors refused to handle the picture, he would supply a tent to show it in. He liked it very much. Actually, the picture was a huge success, nobody criticized it, and it made a fortune. It really put me on the map as a big director.

"Irving Thalberg asked me what I could do to cap it. I came

up with the idea of *The Crowd,* which I made in 1928. *The Big Parade* was one man's view of war. A simple man. I thought, Why not do a movie reviewing life in peacetime? Thalberg said, when I gave him the whole outline, 'Well, I guess we can afford one experimental film.' So he let me do it. I showed a young couple, poor and struggling, getting married, going to Niagara Falls for their honeymoon, having a baby, the baby gets killed, we see the man in an office with desks as far as the eye can see, and at the end they are simply swallowed up in a mass of humanity.

"The male star was an extra I discovered, James Murray. Later on he fell or jumped into the East River during a drinking bout and drowned. The girl was my then wife, Eleanor Boardman." [Married in 1926, Vidor and Miss Boardman were divorced in 1933.] "Louis B. Mayer didn't like *The Crowd* at all. In those days the Academy Awards were decided by a handful of people, including Douglas Fairbanks, Joe Schenck, Louis B. Mayer, and Sid Grauman. The others wanted the picture to have an award, but Mayer wouldn't go for it. It was his own picture, but it was unglamorous, against the studio's image."

From then on, Vidor tried to sustain his vision by bargaining, making one realistic film for every three or four "studio pictures." In 1929, he succeeded in inducing Thalberg to let him make the all-black *Hallelujah,* about a revivalist minister in the Deep South who falls in love with a good-time girl. "M-G-M let me do it, but the New York office wouldn't distribute it. Loew's Inc. turned it down flat. They feared that too many black people would come into the theaters. It barely got released at all."

In 1934, when Vidor wanted to make *Our Daily Bread,* a film about out-of-work people in the Depression who join together on a cooperative farm in order to survive, Thalberg of M-G-M said it was out of the question. Vidor mortgaged his house and sold everything he owned to do the picture. "It could have ruined me. Luckily, it made its money back out of individual theaters which booked it. Of course, I was accused of being a Communist. And then, when it went to the Moscow

Film Festival, the Russian critics said it showed 'evidence of Capitalist thinking.' "

The Big Parade and *Our Daily Bread,* which is currently being rediscovered through its showings on public television, were the first and second parts of a trilogy Vidor thought of as "War, Wheat, and Steel." It was not until 1944, after a string of conventional successes, including *Stella Dallas, The Citadel,* and *H. M. Pulham, Esq.,* that Vidor got the chance to make the "Steel" portion. He called it *An American Romance.*

"It was the story of a simple immigrant who rises through his own efforts in a world of machines, but doesn't lose his common humanity. I wanted to show how a man can become a major figure in an industry and still put on a pair of overalls and sweat and fix something when it goes wrong. The studio cut so much out of the picture, so many of the realistic scenes of factory life, that it was ruined." Disappointed in the film, many critics noted that Vidor was now celebrating the individualist against the masses in his central figure of a Ford-like tycoon.

Vidor's earlier movies had tended to emphasize the virtues of the common man. But gradually he came to believe that the individualist was the most important of beings, that a man must ignore received opinion and hold ruthlessly to what he believes. Just recently, he has even gone a step further, developing a Berkeleyan theory of solipsism; today he believes that nothing in the world exists except in the individual consciousness.

"In 1948 I got a chance to show how I felt about individualism in *The Fountainhead,* from the novel by Ayn Rand. Miss Rand's central character, Howard Roark, an architect who follows his own principles of avant-garde design regardless of the consequences, who has a contempt for mass culture, appealed to me tremendously. Miss Rand certainly lived up to her own principles. She said, 'I have a bomb in my pocket and I'm going to blow up the studio if they change a line of my script.' She wrote the script for nothing rather than let the studio, Warners, use an inferior screenplay.

"When I made the picture, with Gary Cooper as Roark, I

thought the hero's action was too extreme in blowing up an apartment building because it had been a travesty of his original concept. Now I'm not so sure."

Beyond the Forest, which followed *The Fountainhead* in 1949, was the story of a woman, Rosa Moline, played by Bette Davis, trapped in a marriage to a small-town doctor. Like Howard Roark, Rosa strikes out for individual freedom. "I had some trouble with Bette on that picture. I suppose I exerted my will over hers. I told her to throw a bottle a certain way in a quarrel scene and she wouldn't. She stormed off the set and said to Jack Warner, 'Either he goes or I do.' Her career had been on a downgrade. He told her who would go. A couple of days later they cleared out her bungalow. She came to me and said, 'After sixteen years, they can do this to me?' I'll never forget, years later, going to see *Who's Afraid of Virginia Woolf?* When Elizabeth Taylor said, just like Bette in *Beyond the Forest,* 'What a dumppp,' with all those p's, I was stunned. It brought on an overpowering sense of total recall."

The Fountainhead and *Beyond the Forest,* with *Ruby Gentry,* in which Jennifer Jones played a ferocious "free woman," became a trilogy. "People said these pictures were unrealistic, exaggerated. But they weren't. They emphasized, in a heightened realistic form, the frustrations and ambitions of real Americans. Let me give you an example. In *Ruby* I had a scene in which the lovers drive their cars into the moonlit sea off a beach. Unreal? Exaggerated? No. I added it to the script myself because I had recalled something from my own experience I wanted to use. In my part of Texas, lovers would drive out to the shore, gaze at the moon, neck, and by the time they wanted to move, the tide had come in and they were stuck. At other times they would just, in the heat of the moment and for a joke, drive right into the sea deliberately. Crazy? Yes, but it really happened."

After the much-criticized *War and Peace* in 1956 and *Solomon and Sheba* in 1959 (ruined because Tyrone Power died during the shooting and the film had to be hurriedly reshot with Yul Brynner), Vidor retired. He had bought his great ranch at Paso Robles in 1946, when he was shooting *Duel in the Sun* (he shot some of *Ruby Gentry* there). He was glad to spend more time there, and he began writing philosophical essays and a screenplay based on the life of Mary Baker Eddy, the founder of Christian Science. After *Truth and Illusion* he plans to make a film called *Solipsism,* about which, he feels, it is too early to talk. Despite his years, he gives an impression of immense vitality, talking vividly about the Paso Robles country, about his travels, about his undying love of motion pictures.

"My first pictures back in Texas were documentaries. I guess you can say the wheel has swung full circle. And one thing I've kept all along. My feeling for the soil."

The great director strides back to the view of his 1248 acres. In the amphitheater of hills, during the hours we have talked, the light has changed. The shadows are lengthening across the valley, the horses are as still as statues in the paddock, the cattle have moved out of sight. King Vidor stretches out his arms like a patriarch. "I love this country," he says.

Alfred Hitchcock

Alfred Hitchcock and I have an interest in common: the case of Haigh, the acid-bath murderer. It's a favorite of his and a personal story of mine. In 1947 when I was still at school, I used to visit my grandmother at the Royal Court Hotel in Sloane Square in London. She should have been a musical comedy actress, and spent much of her time singing old songs in an agreeably high-pitched voice at the piano in the hotel's Palm Court Lounge.

A little man kept paying court to her. He was mousy, with brown eyes and a small brown mustache, and pale English skin. He wore tweed suits and smelled of second-rate tobacco. I disliked him at once. I interfered with his wooing, telling Grandmother that I found him creepy. Finally, she dropped him. A few days later, I opened the paper and handed it to her without a word. Her suitor, Mr. Haigh, was in the headlines for having murdered a rich widow, Mrs. Durand Deacon, at the Onslow Court Hotel, only a stone's throw from the Royal Court. If I hadn't been so bothersome to Grandmother and her wooer, she, too, might have been dissolved in an acid bath.

Hitchcock loved the story. I could talk to him about murders anytime.

★

1969

The eyes, now wickedly darting, now still and dark and sad, look out from a face that has the slightly threatening babyishness of a fledgling rhinoceros. The body seems more enormous than ever, the vast protruding stomach comfortably clasped in flawlessly manicured hands. A charcoal-gray suit, cut to perfection, and the shoes shining like black ice, indicate a surgeon's precision; one can almost imagine him, on stepping into his office each morning, running a tentative forefinger over every table to detect the faintest hint of dust.

Upon waking on his first morning in a West Indies hotel some years ago—a hotel so palatial it might even stretch the Windsors' resources a trifle—Hitchcock is said to have remarked: "I can notice the smell of fresh cement from the tennis court." When Ray Milland fluffed a line in the middle of a take in *Dial M for Murder,* the master's only observation was, "I wind it up and put it on the floor. And it doesn't work!" He is, clearly, impatient with people and things which don't perform like a well-made clockwork toy.

Sitting in his tiny "English" cottage at Universal Studios, dogs barking at a visitor's arrival, this creator of disturbing and haunting images is like a Buddha in the midst of a crumbling empire. Hollywood as an entity is in the process of being destroyed—extravagance and an inability to understand the young in a golf-playing community of nostalgic oldies clinging to the past have brought it to its knees for the second time in a decade. But Hitch, perennially youthful, will, one feels, go on forever, spinning his spider's web of lethal fantasies.

I asked him about his new picture, *Topaz,* a spy story with a cast almost entirely composed of unknowns. "It's narrowed down and made more compact than the rather rambling novel Leon Uris wrote," Hitchcock told me.

"It deals with the personalities behind the Cuban missile crisis. For some reason the author doesn't want to discuss his sources, but I believe the central figure is based on a French intelligence man called de Beaujolais.

"He worked for the Americans—there were some articles

about him in the Sunday London *Times*—and he disclosed that the French bureaucracy contained certain Soviet agents. Perhaps for this reason the book has never been published in France, and appears in a French-Canadian edition only. It hasn't to date been passed by the French censor.

"Of course it's never the government that objects to subjects like this, it's Intelligence itself. Remember Philby? That caused severe differences between different intelligences: some felt that the story should be told, others that it should not.

"So I've not referred to the Sûreté, the Deuxième Bureau, and so on. I just treat them as shadowy bureaucratic bodies. Of course, we had to submit an outline of the story to the Paris police, because Paris is one of the very few places in the world where you can't shoot without a police permit.

"Just before I left Paris they gave me this honor." He turned his lapel to show me the small insignia—Officer of the Order of Arts and Letters. His face changed from a look of pride to a typically ironical smile. "I hope that, after they see the picture, they don't take it back."

In the film, the plot is set off by the action of a Russian defector who leads the American authorities to the truth of the Russian-Cuban collaboration. The French informer and his mistress later become involved, and she in fact obtains the secrets of the missiles in Cuba with the aid of a hidden tape recorder. She is murdered and the Frenchman recalled to Paris; the tension of the last third springs from a question whether he will release the facts to the Americans or the Russians.

As always, Hitchcock planned the whole production in advance, despite its widespread locales. He likes to prepare a full visual narrative, like a novel without dialogue, accompanied by sketches of every single sequence so that every actor and actress is placed like an article of furniture in a setting.

Then he works line by line on the dialogue with his writers. He was forced into the picture by the fact that several previous projects he had planned had failed to come off. "The problem was the authors' egos," he said. "They all get nervous when they work on one of my projects, because they think: Oh, it's going to be known as another Hitchcock picture. They want their names above the credits, too. And the result is they fall out with me, and we can't get anything done."

Wasn't it true that he would rather have been a painter or a novelist, that the actual physical job of direction bored him after he had fully preplanned it? "Oh, yes. I'd much rather not direct at all. Once I've planned it in my own mind, seen it in full, it's over for me. Physically putting it on the screen becomes rather a bore."

Another problem is that in making his pictures Hitchcock sometimes has to shoot scenes in normally inaccessible locations. On *Topaz*, for instance, he needed to get into Cuba. He sent a cameraman to sneak out some background shots, but the man hung around for two months in Mexico City and finally got cold feet and wouldn't go to Havana at all. Later, a British photographer in New York plucked up courage, went in, and produced a batch of color stills, which were carefully reproduced in Hollywood, and on northern California locations.

Being a semidocumentary, the film is a departure from Hitch's usual methods. Many of his works have been like self-enclosed dreams; this one, in keeping with current fashion, is a reflection of the world we live in. "Of course," Hitchcock said, "I have tried to use real locations in other pictures. In *North by Northwest*, with Cary Grant, I wanted to have him involved in a chase scene over the great stone heads of the presidents of Mount Rushmore, but they wouldn't let me. I had to reconstruct them in the studio, because to have Cary Grant get a sneezing fit in Lincoln's nose was considered an insult to the shrine of democracy."

His pictures are often about a chase, after what he is often quoted as calling the "McGuffin," a pointless objective that the audience cares less about than it cares about the chase itself. "In Kipling's time, it was the plan of the fort, or of the Khyber Pass. Later on, it was the secret of an aeroplane engine. The characters in the story worry about it, but we don't. In *Topaz*, the missile plans are a real McGuffin. That's unusual for me."

The idea of the McGuffin came from a story Hitchcock has remembered from years past: two men are on a train, and one says: "What's that above your head?" And the other replies, "A McGuffin." "What's a McGuffin?" the first man asks. "It's an apparatus for trapping lions in the Scottish Highlands," the other man replies. "But there are no lions in the Scottish Highlands." "Well, that's a McGuffin!"

Controlling these stories as tightly as Hitchcock does presents him with problems that might crush a lesser man. He might want to shoot a snow scene in Central Park and wind up, as he reminded me David O. Selznick did years ago in a picture with Jennifer Jones, *Portrait of Jennie*, with slush and mud on the second day. And then actors' quirks might get in the way of the exact interpretation he needed: he preferred a James Stewart or a Cary Grant, who could do exactly what was expected of him, and who never varied. "Let's face it, you hire a star like that and you can't change them or characterize them. They're there, that's all. And there's an enormous advantage in that kind of immutability."

Hitchcock's greatest fascination is with the bland and genial man who gradually begins to display, like cracks threading through marble, greater and greater strains of psychosis. "People who are really evil are always charming. The heads of the great criminal organizations are perfect gentlemen. They don't kill anymore. They arrange for it all to be done very peacefully and without fuss.

"Just think of Haigh, the acid-bath murderer. He lived in the Onslow Court Hotel in London and picked up various well-to-do women. He had great personal magnetism. He disposed of the bodies very smoothly indeed"—there was a touch of appreciation in Hitchcock's voice—"and he was only caught because he went out with one woman and came back without her, and a girl at the front desk became suspicious.

"I'll tell you something very strange about that case. When Haigh was caught, he was tried before Mr. Justice Humphries, the hanging judge. Long after Haigh died, Humphries's wife, a member of the Ealing Borough Council, passed away, and Humphries left the large house they lived in. He sold it, and his belongings, his bags, his trunks, his crates, the possessions of a lifetime, were piled onto a truck. He drove off to his place of retirement. And do you know where it was? The Onslow Court Hotel! As he entered the hall, one of his aides remarked on the extraordinary coincidence. And it is recorded that the learned judge merely laughed, sardonically."

Warming to the subject of murder cases, Hitchcock revealed that he had had a lifelong desire to make a film of the Crippen case. "The real fascination of English law is the calmness of the procedure that sets the path to the gallows in motion. The moment you start the process, everyone is so charming . . . but it grinds on all the way to the condemned cell and the gallows, and no one is unpleasant anywhere in the whole progress. Genial, nice, considerate, even when they have the killer trapped; they'll say, 'I don't think we'll have the handcuffs, do you?' And, 'Would you like some magazines?'

"Of course, Crippen was the first man to be captured by radio. He and his mistress, Ethel le Neve—who is, I believe, still living and was looked after for years by the novelist Ursula Bloom—were crossing the Atlantic on the S.S. *Montrose* when they were caught.

"As in all such cases, the whole thing broke partly because Ethel le Neve wore the wife's jewelry. Of course, Inspector Dew made a hash of the case. He kept going to search the house for signs of Crippen's missing wife—a blowsy, Sophie Tucker–like singer of her day—without finding anything. He went back for a last look, to close the case up; he was going to have to accept Crippen's story that his wife had gone abroad.

"But as he searched the cellar for the last time he accidentally dislodged a stone that disclosed the body.

"Then the Montrose's captain noticed that 'Mr. Robinson' (Crippen) and his son, 'Master Robinson' (Ethel le Neve, disguised as a boy), seemed very affectionate as they walked down the deck.

"So he became suspicious. He asked Crippen to dine at his table, and kept telling him jokes to make him open his mouth to verify that he had upper and lower dentures, which Crippen was known to have. He also noticed that the 'son' had paper in his cap and that his trousers were held together with elastic; that nothing fitted. So he radioed the information to London. And Inspector Dew came by a faster ship, and waited for the *Montrose*—and Crippen—at a pilot's landing stage in the St. Lawrence River.

"He went on board with a pilot and said, very nicely, 'Good morning, Mr. Crippen.' After that, everyone was very pleasant until finally the noose went around Crippen's neck. And that's the way with English murder cases, a feeling I've tried to convey in my films."

Hitchcock drew deeply at his expensive cigar and sipped quietly and with relish at his favorite tipple, Byrrh. "Pleasant people, pleasant murders. Pleasant, polite arrests. A quiet, orderly trial. And then, at the final moment, the hangman saying, 'Good morning, old chap.' And on the gallows, just before he pulls the lever, nothing violent, nothing nasty at all. Just a light, friendly tap on the arm."

Roger Vadim

I liked Roger Vadim. He made only one film I admire without
reservations: his glacially clever version of *Les Liaisons Dangereuses*.
Nevertheless, I was impressed by his genuine intelligence and
sophistication, and by a personality more genial and relaxed than
the movies suggested. I could understand why Jane Fonda had fallen
for him.

———————★———————

1971

A fist, wrapped around a wineglass, punches the air. Eyes
glitter skeptically under a forehead bronzed by the Malibu
sun. He crouches in the chair like a tomcat about to spring.
Late Sunday wraps his tension in a cocoon of heat. Ice clinks
in red Burgundy, children trot in and out, French voices echo
from the beach patio, vines trail untidily from the ceiling of
the long, sandy room over a scatter of mattresses and cushions. Outside, the Françoise Sagan afternoon will probably
never end. On the table there are photocopied pages from
Byron's poem, "Don Juan," and I notice two lines: "Oh,
Pleasure! you are indeed a pleasant thing / Although one
must be damned for you, no doubt."

Roger Vadim is uptight. Phones have been ringing all day
about his first Hollywood movie, *Pretty Maids All in a Row*. God

knows where Jane Fonda is (picketing the Pentagon, most likely). The offspring of various marriages keep up a charming but insistent demand for attention, and there is always the irritating, persistent hum of the interviewer's tapes, preserving even the most casual words, together with the waves, the seabirds, and the sexual murmurs of a couple outside.

Even though he is dressed for comfort—bare to the waist and shoeless, in casual pants—there is nothing relaxed about Vadim's air. The frown under the bristling hair thatch is intense, then he'll grin, and brood blackly again. He'll look at you quizzically always, as though you are about to ask a question about his investments or even his potency. His tall, wary brownness pounds pumalike around a room no decorator would call home. But it's a comfortable cage to pace in.

It seems only appropriate that Vadim's first words should be, as he pores over some script pages: "How do you spell energetically?" Energy, and a flair for erotic detail, have enlivened his work. He has been married to three of the world's most desirable women (Bardot, Annette Stroyberg, Jane Fonda), and in between he has had an intense, unconsecrated affair with Catherine Deneuve (just as he mentions her, their fair-haired son walks gravely in). At any party, it's obvious that half the women in the room would all but kill for him. Not quite handsome, his animal vitality irresistibly attracts, as well as his astonishing list of conquests.

Vadim's celebrated shock-tactics have tended to obscure Vadim, the artist—a pictorialist with a consistent attitude to eroticism, an aesthetic of the flesh. Born forty-two years ago of a Russian Catholic father, he has fought the Church all his life through the medium of his work, and it has fought him back; he has had constant and rather overreported clashes with official bodies. Several of his pictures have been condemned by the Legion of Decency—thus earning each one a flood of free publicity. He has been condemned by the Society of Authors in France for updating the eighteenth-century author Laclos; and his modernizing of De Sade, Zola, and others has upset many an overly sensitive soul.

Vadim has shown Woman as an emancipated amorist *(And*

God Created Woman), husband's aide in procuring other women *(Dangerous Relations),* vampire predator *(Blood and Roses),* protector of the weak *(Warrior's Rest),* collaborator with Fascism *(Vice and Virtue),* victim of her own desires *(The Game Is Over),* and silly, charming animal *(Barbarella).* He is obviously fascinated by women as desirable strangers, and has said that "marriage is science fiction. No contact between the world of a man and the world of a woman is possible. Everybody knows that they are alone and alone until death."

His knowledge of this does not prevent him from being protective of as well as wary toward women. He was furious when his now estranged wife, Jane Fonda, was spread all over *Playboy.* He was deeply anguished when she developed a curious virus after being attacked by twenty thousand hummingbirds in *Barbarella.* Yet he could often be startlingly masterful and sharp with her in public.

Vadim's father was a Russian aristocrat who became a Parisian and joined the diplomatic service in France; his gift of composing jazz numbers has influenced Vadim's lifelong passion for jazz in his pictures, most notably in the Thelonius Monk theme for *Liaisons Dangereuses.* Vadim's mother was a writer, and a frustrated actress who encouraged him powerfully in his career. He still has a marvelous actor's voice—and played briefly on the stage under the celebrated actor-director Charles Dullin.

He spent his early childhood traveling through exotic locations, including Africa and Turkey, where his father was a member of various consular staffs. He wrote his first novel in Turkey at the age of six. It was about an engine—a train engine—propelled by a strange gas that made it move so fast it was quicker than the speed of sound. "At six I had invented the sound barrier! And jet propulsion!"

Vadim has been traveling at jet-propelled speed ever since. His early loss of his father also seriously affected him; it produced that streak of fatalism in his work, that recurrent image in which everything is bright and sunny and happy before disaster strikes from a clear blue sky.

"It was just before my father was to take up a post in Israel.

One morning, in a lovely little town in the Haute Savoie, we were all at breakfast. The walls were gay with little flowers. The sun was shining so brightly! It was the perfect, the ideal, painting of a family group. Suddenly—he was just in front of me —my father slumped over. His face went into a cup of coffee. My sister started to scream. I knew he was dying, and yet something said to me, 'That's no reason to lose your control.' "

After Vadim's father's death, the family was desperately short of money. Vadim *père* left no legacy or insurance, so sometimes the family even had to sleep in a tent. Roger was at eighteen different schools, and during World War II he lived a wandering existence, sometimes isolated in snow-storms without electricity or gas, filling the nights by mediu-mistic table-rapping sessions, all the time learning a deep skepticism, shared by his generation of young intellectuals, about the effectiveness of religion, setting off his lifelong reciprocated hatred of Catholicism.

"I shook off tradition, religious conservatism, in one mo-ment during the war. A school friend of mine in the Alps was a devout Catholic, always going to church on Sunday. One Sunday, when we were foraging for food as we always did, he asked me to go to church. I refused. Because I didn't go I escaped a horrible fate. All those who went to church were seized, forced into a house, and burned to death."

After the war, Vadim became deeply involved in the existen-tialist movement. "We rejected Christianity—and I have re-jected it ever since." Skepticism, anti-Catholicism, and a ruth-lessly frank approach to life have since marked his work. He longs to make a film about that postwar period of disillusion-ment, so much a seedbed of today's anti-Christian revolution.

Vadim moved from art school to work as a small-part film player, and assistant to the director Marc Allegret on such pictures as *Blanche Fury* and *The Naked Heart*. It was while working with Allegret that he met the fifteen-year-old Brigitte Bardot, who had appeared on a cover of *Elle* magazine. "She was elegant, enchanting, from a grand bourgeois family.

"I fell in love with her the second time we met. But her Catholic family blocked our marriage for years. Even on our wedding night I could not be with her, because only the civil and not the ecclesiastical marriage had been performed. I slept on her parents' living room couch." He got a temporary job as a journalist on *Paris-Match* to convince her parents that he would make a good husband.

This rather conventional marriage scarcely suggested the extraordinary collaboration of their first film together, *And God Created Woman,* a Molotov cocktail which made his name and Brigitte's famous overnight. It was the most notorious director-star triumph since Dietrich and von Sternberg's *Blue Angel.* He was given his break by the producer Raoul Levy, who had admired his work—with Marc Allegret. "The story was of a young girl, Juliette, who in Saint-Tropez lived a life of pure, sensual freedom. My camera made love to her like a poet." Almost at once Vadim developed a fleshy eroticism of style as intense as in Renoir's paintings.

Ironically, just when Vadim made his passion for his wife visible in the camera, making the whole world voyeurs, she left him for her costar, a handsome whippet named Jean-Louis Trintignant. "We were already at the high point of our relationship when the picture began, and the picture was our baby," Vadim says, adding with perfect French logic: "It was only correct that at that moment we should drift apart, that the marriage should come to an end."

After that experience, Vadim cooled off toward women for a while, devoting himself to his work. After his divorce he married an unknown girl called Annette Stroyberg, whose body his camera explored with erotic intensity in *Les Liaisons Dangereuses.* "I adored the novel, which was published in the eighteenth century, and through it I understood deeply the 'libertine philosophy' of its author, Choderlos de Laclos." It was the story, updated to the late fifties, of a French diplomat, Valmont (played by Gerard Philippe, who died just after it was finished), and his wife (played by Jeanne Moreau) who helped each other to find lovers (Annette Stroyberg among them) and reject systematically every rule of conventional society.

Here the visual tone of the film, cool and laconic as the literary style of Laclos himself, showed Vadim in full strength as an artist, making his own ruthlessly sophisticated commentary, as it withdraws coolly to note the absurdities of a fashionable cocktail party, watching with complete detachment while the couple plot the conquest like a complicated chess move, staring blankly when the diplomat's wife scars herself symbolically as she sets fire to some incriminating love letters. Vadim in this picture proved that the camera could not only be a lover—but a philosopher as well. And in this work, his masterpiece, he developed once and for all his *auteur*'s aesthetic.

"I've always approached eroticism with a sense of humor. I am deeply affected by the fabulous eighteenth century in France, when society did at last escape Christian philosophy and morality. It was a period, among the wealthy and cultivated, of great spiritual freedom. I am, like the people of that time, in my life-style a *libertin*. It's a word hard to translate into English. It doesn't mean libertine, exactly—it's a person with an exact philosophical position who absolutely and calmly rejects Christian morality together and makes his own clear set of rules.

"Our society is based on the sense of sin. That infuriates me. Maybe that was a necessary concept long ago in the Middle Ages when the barbarians invaded civilized society and strong rules were needed. Ever since then, it's been an anachronism.

"All our lives we are ashamed. It's anticivilized. I adore, as well as the eighteenth century, the golden age of Greece, when people were really adult and free in their mind. That was before the Christian conscience.

"I'm not only against Christianity. I'm against Hinduism, Muhammadanism, and the others all of which are repressive in different ways. Today, the idea is to go to Yoga classes and to go to India—all this mystical philosophy—which is all very well insofar as it helps people survive in this grimly materialistic world.

"But I don't think it's very healthy. I hope it's just a phase. When I see someone like Jane, my wife, come back from India and say, 'I understand, I've changed,' then all I can say is, 'It's not true.' She is the same person—she has just sacrificed herself to what, if I were not nice, I would call a fashion."

In his next couple of pictures, after *Liaisons,* Vadim's career ran into shallows—with *Blood and Roses,* a clumsy version of Joseph Sheridan Le Fanu's vampire story "Carmilla," which he claims was butchered by Paramount, and with *Warrior's Rest,* a not entirely successful attempt to present Bardot as a serious actress in a story of a typical Vadim woman who makes her own libertine's decision by rejecting a conventional fiancé for an affair with a drunk.

By this time Vadim had shed Annette Stroyberg, who had met and fallen in love with a troubadour named Sacha Distel; and after an earlier meeting that notably failed to strike sparks, fell heavily for Jane Fonda who was in Paris for a show. He starred her in a cool remake of Max Ophuls' more romantic *La Ronde,* switching the locale from Vienna to France in a story of sexual ring-a-ring-of-roses in 1914.

"I did *La Ronde* because if I hadn't I'd have gone to jail on tax evasion charges. I wanted to show the absurd formalities of a doomed society on the verge of World War One. Here was a story of men making love to women who discover other men—a chain of love that comes full circle, like a snake that has swallowed its tail. It shows a world all rather silly and fixed in its patterns, not free as it should be."

In *The Game Is Over,* in which Jane Fonda plays a wife who discovers the freedom of a happy relationship with a younger man, he pursued his theme of erotic freedom more poetically, more lyrically than in any other work. "In this film I not only caressed Jane's body, as I had caressed Brigitte's and Annette's, with my camera, but I also followed my feeling for abstract patterns of light, of flesh and shadow in observing her making love.

"I think and feel like a painter and I have an abstract artist's approach, more and more in my work, to sensual things. I believe, too, this is an essentially masculine thing, a kind of detachment, an ability to see the abstract beauty of a sexual experience even when it's happening, which I don't think most women have. Colette, and perhaps my friend Françoise Sagan, are two who have had this quality, but they are rare."

In his last picture, the science-fiction comedy *Barbarella,*

Vadim showed another planet in which sex ruled everything. "I wouldn't like to live there. I wanted to show a world ruled by morality in reverse, and how this reverse morality, as seen by a free living girl, Barbarella, played by Jane Fonda, would be as threatening as the real moral world was to the heroines of my other pictures."

The wheel of Vadim's career has swung full circle, because his next picture, *Peryl,* will be a companion piece and a successor to *And God Created Woman.* "It's about a supposedly perfect, glossy-advertisement married couple. He is forty, respected, a successful lawyer; she is twenty-five, young, beautiful, they have a little child. Then the man's eighteen-year-old daughter by a previous marriage comes into his life. By her example—she lives utterly freely—she shows up the tensions of her parents' apparently ideal relationship which is in fact extremely precarious.

"In my new picture, *Pretty Maids All in a Row,* which I have made for M-G-M, I for once show a man, played by Rock Hudson, who makes his own rules.

"If you asked me to sum up the destiny of an artist like myself, who cannot help but destroy convention despite the consequences to himself and others, I think of a story told by Orson Welles.

"It is the story of the frog and the scorpion. The scorpion wanted to cross the river, by riding on the frog's back. 'No,' said the frog. 'No thank you. If I let you on my back you will sting me, and everyone knows it is fatal to be stung by a scorpion.'

" 'Don't be silly,' said the scorpion. 'If I sting you, I'll drown.' The frog was forced to admit the logic of this and let the scorpion ride on his back.

"But just in the middle of the river, the frog felt a terrible pain. The scorpion had stung him. As it sank, taking the scorpion with it to death, the frog cried, 'Is that logic?' 'No,' the scorpion replied, 'but I can't help it.' "

Vadim rose to his feet and smiled ironically. "It is, you see, my character."

George Sidney

What a craftsman George Sidney is! Few pictures have given me
more pleasure to watch than *The Harvey Girls, Scaramouche,
Jeanne Eagels,* and *Pal Joey.* He has a marvelous command of
movie rhythm. His pacing and timing are flawless. And he created
one of my favorite sequences in all movies: Tyrone Power and Kim
Novak walking through the rain in Central Park in *The Eddy Duchin
Story,* Novak in a red raincoat, carrying a red umbrella. It gave the
special shock of pleasure of a Hokusai. It was a moment out of
dreams.

———————★———————

1974

Comfortably puffing at a pipe, George Sidney sits in his large,
luxurious office in Beverly Hills surrounded by stacks of
goodwill mail and contributions and grosses of small transis-
tor radios. . . . he heads Radios for Israel and is in the process
of sending the radios as a morale booster to the wounded
soldiers in Israel. Everywhere are memorabilia: oil paintings,
his thousands of personally shot photographs, pipes, pipes,
pipes, and numerous awards . . . the most treasured a gold
medal from the Director's Guild of America for service as
president for sixteen years, as well as life membership as
director and assistant director. In a handsome tweed jacket

and with an outdoorsman's high color, he still looks very much the M-G-M classic director, a world removed from the shag cuts, bell-bottoms, and suede, nail-studded, casual jackets of the studio figures today. For years he has not wanted to make a picture. He has turned his talents to the financial aspects of filmmaking—interim financing, completion, bonding, postproduction, and distribution—dismayed by today's sheer lack of musical talent, both among composers and performers.

The heavyweights in composers and artists have disappeared, but at last strong contenders for the niches of Berlin, Kern, Gershwin, and Sinatra, Crosby, Garland, etc. are surfacing. He is beginning to plan a new musical—subject top secret. Amid Watergate and gas shortages, amid news of an increasing devastation to national resources, it was good to escape for a while into a discussion of Sidney's musicals, from *Anchors Aweigh* to *Bye Bye Birdie,* musicals which unpretentiously, brightly, and freshly lit up the period and for almost twenty years after World War II. Born in 1916, the son of Louis K. Sidney, pioneer showman, exhibitor, filmmaker, radio-stage producer, and vice-president of M-G-M. His mother, Hazel, one of the famed Mooney sisters of Winter Garden fame. Sidney had little or no interest in formal schooling and took off for Hollywood, joining M-G-M as a bright-eyed and bushy-tailed messenger boy of fourteen. With talking pictures still new in 1932, he managed to finagle a job in the M-G-M sound recording department under Norma Shearer's brother, Douglas. He was a boom jockey on *Dancing Lady* with Clark Gable, Joan Crawford, and a very young Fred Astaire. (He directed them all much later.)

"A singer called Gene Mallin was cast to do a spot in the picture," Sidney remembers, "but one night when Mallin was coming out of the Ship Cafe at the beach he accidentally put his car in reverse, went off the pier. The word went around: 'Find a boy who can fill Gene's wardrobe.' A nobody called Nelson Eddy was just large enough, so they threw him into Gene's clothes. And that's how Nelson got his first break." For years, Sidney labored on Nelson Eddy–Jeanette Mac-

Donald pictures, working in sound, music editing, orchestration, and choreography, later graduated at twenty-one to being a director of musical and straight screen tests. He played the piano, clarinet, violin, and saxophone and was a member of ASCAP. Between 1936 and 1942 he made over eighty-five short subjects (several won Academy Awards), directed musical numbers in other people's pictures, and acted as second-unit director on a wide variety of features. He even composed, conducted, and orchestrated. In 1943, he was given the chance to direct a full-scale musical, *As Thousands Cheer.* "Mr. Louis B. Mayer had been watching me and nursing me, and I guess he finally thought, Give the kid a break. A wonderful thing in those days—it has gone out of the industry—was 'continuity.' They would take someone (director, star, writer, producer) and watch him grow and grow and grow (I ended up at two hundred and eighty pounds), and then they'd figure he was ready for the big time. Mr. Mayer loved music. He had a great ear for a song, and a Midas touch on talent.

"*As Thousands Cheer* just growed like Topsy. It began as a little picture called *Private Miss Jones,* about a girl, played by Kathryn Grayson, who interrupted her singing career to join the WACs. It was going to be low budget, black and white, with just a few simple numbers. But when I got into it, I kept getting more ideas to expand it and expand it. With Joe Pasternak's approval, at the last minute we switched to color. Luckily, Mr. Mayer let me 'go.' I was like a kid in a candy store.

"I worked in free-form that was possible then. I improvised scenes, dialogue, whole musical numbers. It was creatively exciting; everything was spontaneous, exhilarating. Some scenes were shot before they were written. Stanley Donen was my dance assistant. Gene Kelly was just beginning his gigantic screen career. We had a hundred players in the orchestra under contract, and they were the best available. If you needed more, you sent for more. The music department was par excellence.

"I was involved with the arrangements. I remember we had a big number, conducted by José Iturbi, 'American Patrol,' that called for all brass. We had a feeling that the brass needed 'warming up,' so we had sixty strings play the clarinet parts. You couldn't see or hear the strings after we mixed them under brass, but it warmed and smoothed the sound of the brass.

"*Bathing Beauty* with Esther Williams was a challenge." Sidney, who had made Esther's first screen test, explained: "We shot underwater for weeks. It was necessary to devise equipment capable of playing music underwater for the bathing beauties to swim to. We developed cameras and lighting equipment that had mobility on top or underneath water, plus makeup, hairdress, and choreography. The music and rhythmic cuing had to be kept to a low volume, because water acts as a conductor and the sound could easily have shattered the swimmers' eardrums. The water had to be an exact temperature at all times, not too hot, not too cold. One morning we were shooting at Lakeside Pool on a bitterly cold January day. The boys and girls refused to go in the water; it was too cold. I took off my overcoat, two sweaters, long underwear. I stripped naked and dived in myself. I swam up and down— and I broke every Olympic record. When I hit that cold water —WOW! I came out purple! But I shamed them into action!"

In his later musicals, Sidney prepared photographic storyboards, personally taking a photograph of every possible position and every camera movement. He mounted them on huge boards, numbered the shots, playback starts, setup by setup. But in those earlier times, he and his dancer-stars simply evolved a sequence on the dance floor, tossing ideas to and fro. The most brilliant example of his improvisatory techniques was the big, brash, stunningly staged *Anchors Aweigh,* a story of sailors on shore leave, with Gene Kelly and Frank Sinatra.

The two high spots of the picture were Gene Kelly's dance with a very small Mexican girl played by Sharon McManus, and with Jerry, the M-G-M cartoon mouse. "Sharon McManus had no training as a dancer. She was just one of many little girls under contract. Her hair had to be dyed black, as she was Irish and fair, with dark makeup to look convincingly Mexican. She had to be trained meticulously to match Gene Kelly's steps. It took a lot of patience, but it paid off.

"Originally, the dance with the cartoon figure was to have been Gene Kelly and Donald Duck. Walt wanted to do it, but then I got a call from Roy Disney saying, 'You S.O.B., you've got Walt all steamed up and he's got four uncompleted pictures over here. He can't do your picture.' So we decided to use Jerry the mouse instead. Hanna-Barbera and I worked the sequence out with Gene and Stanley." (Years later, Sidney formed the Hanna-Barbera company and served as president.)

"Gene had only a few days before he went into the Navy, and we had to rush live photography through. We went by feel and touch. We cut a mouse out of a cardboard and put it on a long stick, then we lined up our shots and rehearsed with that stand-in mouse. We photographed the whole dance routine, then we added twenty thousand drawings of the mouse dancing, matching his every movement to Gene's. Finally we ran it. It was fine. There was only one thing we'd forgotten. The dance was on a shiny floor and Gene was reflected in it. The mouse wasn't. So we had to go back and draw twenty thousand mouse reflections that matched the mouse's movements and Gene's reflection as well." Did Sidney have to train Sinatra to dance? "Well, that was very interesting. One scene with him had to have ninety-eight takes. Dancing was never one of Frank's greatest loves; luckily he had the greatest sense of rhythm of anyone alive. But he didn't care about dancing. It was quite a struggle. Stanley Donen, Gene, and I kept pushing him until we achieved victory."

The Harvey Girls had been a pleasure to make, and Sidney adored Judy Garland from the day he made her first screen test. The highlight of the picture had been the Academy Award–winning "Atchison, Topeka and Santa Fe" number, co-starring Garland and a fabulous antique train. "Judy made the recording and then I went down and spent days lining up the number, which was shot in a nine-minute take. We had hundreds of dancers, cowboys, Indians, horses, God knows what. Judy saw a 'dance-in,' a dancing stand-in, do a run-through only once, then she said 'I'm ready,' and she went right through it, every movement matched to the subtle changes in her voice, every movement of the dance-in memorized at a glance. I never saw such concentration. It was incredible. That girl could do seventy lip-synch loops of a post-recording session in one hour.

"The major problem with her was that she was terrified of horses. Here we were, making a musical Western, and she wouldn't play a scene with a real horse. It had to be a dummy every time. Many stars have phobias. Lana Turner hated cats, Ava Gardner hated monkeys, Judy also hated guns, and she wouldn't handle a real one, even with blanks in it.

"*Annie Get Your Gun* had originally been scheduled for Judy Garland. She shot about a day, with Chuck Walters directing, and collapsed on the set. She was very sick. The picture was shut down and we had to find another Annie. Betty Garrett was seriously considered, but she had some differences with the studio, so we went with Betty Hutton."

Sidney had seen the Kern/Hammerstein *Showboat* both on the stage in the original production at the Ziegfeld Theatre and in the screen versions directed by Harry Pollard and James Whale. "Both versions lost money and Metro thought Arthur Freed and I were crazy to try again. I hadn't liked the other versions conceptually: the Whale was all whipped cream and spangles, the other nonmusical. But Metro finally let me do it. I was fiercely attacked by the press for using Ava Gardner as the half-caste Julie, the role Helen Morgan had made famous. I felt Ava had a kind of deep sense of insecurity, the second-best girl, very tragic. Perfect for Julie, who was a lost lady.

"The showboat itself was specially built on Lot Three. We had naval architects to help. I made a trip through the South with production designer, Jack Martin Smith. I took a great many photographs of old stern-wheelers, from which we built a boat to our liking. I decided against photographing the interiors with a wide-angle lens. I didn't want the little rooms to become huge. I used all long-focal-length lenses. It worked well."

In the 1950s, Sidney made *Kiss Me Kate,* both in 3-D and normal ratio; he still regrets that 3-D was killed off by get-rich-quick hustlers and sees a great future in holographic techniques. *Jupiter's Darling* was based on *The Road to Rome* by Robert Sherwood, an elaborate affair set in ancient Rome, with Esther Williams. Technically, it was his greatest challenge to date.

"We painted a troop of elephants for a scene. They were supposed to be painted with watercolors. We were horrified to discover that the paint shop, thinking they were helping, had used oils. We had a contract with the circus to paint only in watercolors. The paint stained them for months. The circus sued us, and we had to settle: There were some pretty gay pachyderms under the big top for a long time.

"Doing the underwater scenes was quite a job. We shot a hundred and twenty-five feet under water. We went to Catalina to start a shot, but the weather became too rough and we transferred to Silver Springs, Florida. I said, 'That's one hell of a swim.' We used Aqualungs and compressed oxygen for the deep-water shots. I went into training at the Navy Diving School at Long Beach to get full breath control. We put mirrors in the water and reflected arc light at a forty-five-degree angle to get needed exposure."

Sidney puffed his pipe, savoring the memory of licking another technical challenge. "I switched to Columbia for *The Eddy Duchin Story.* Eddy Duchin had given me piano lessons when I was a kid. I had seen his last appearance at the Empire Room of the Waldorf. I had discussed the picture with Ty Power years earlier. Ty studied the piano like a madman. He carried a dummy keyboard everywhere, practicing for hours each day. He matched his fingering to Carmen Cavallaro's recorded track. Ty's work was so perfect he actually believed he made the track himself!"

One particularly beautiful scene showed Duchin walking through Central Park in the rain with his first wife, Marjorie, played by Kim Novak. "There was a strike at the time, and we were left crewless. So Harry Stradling and I, with Harry's son, Harry, Junior, just went out and shot the scene ourselves. The other night I saw *The Way We Were* with all the scenes in Central Park—Harry, Junior, shot it. That brought back a happy memory.

"I built special pianos for the picture, with mirrors inside the strings. I altered the sounding board and harp. The entire insides of the pianos were reconstructed and made wild.

"*Pal Joey* was another problem. I went to Chicago, where John O'Hara had set his original story, and found it so depressingly tacky that I realized I just couldn't do an 'up' picture there. So I shifted the location to San Francisco. Rita Hayworth was hypersensitive to cold. We shot a number at Coit Tower and the weather changed to a bitterly cold, windy, and foggy day. She went purple! Actually! I told her she mustn't continue! She wanted to go on, but we finished the sequence in Hollywood. San Francisco is a heartbreaking city. You set up spectacularly wonderful things and then, boom, the fog rolls in. Three pictures in San Francisco were enough for me."

Making *Bye Bye Birdie* with Dick Van Dyke and Ann-Margret and *Viva Las Vegas* with Ann-Margret and Elvis had been a breeze. But *Half a Sixpence*, the first big musical to be made in England, with Tommy Steele was not. "One number, 'Flash, Bang, Wallop' was shot in a corrugated iron shed because we couldn't get proper stage space for the large set. The heat was so terrible that several of our dancers keeled over. We had to rip out a whole wall of the building to give them enough air. Then on the number 'If the Rain's Going to Fall,' we were caught in a River Thames flood. We were swamped in about eight feet of mud and ooze. We had to build a whole caravan and tent colony to feed and house the people. And then we had to bring rain machines so the rain would fall on cue when the real rain stopped."

Sixpence, although a smash in England, did not do well in the United States. "Too English," Sidney suspects.

"But it's good now to be planning another musical. The American breed of musical is an art form that belongs to the people of the world. I'm still in my fifties, still excited by pictures and talents. I can't wait to get back into harness."

Paul Schrader

Paul Schrader has had the wit to use the industry for his own ends: namely, to show the squalor, ugliness, and violence of the American urban environment. Aware of the nature of the community he is working in, he has found a way to play it against itself. That takes cunning and rigor.

I have encountered a barrage of criticism for writing admiringly of him. The Hollywood underbrush bristles with Schrader's enemies. It's easy to understand why. He is not a charmer and at thirty-two he has grown very rich, very fast.

He *is* an artist. He will go on to greater strengths.

1978

A hand is chopped off by a ceremonial Japanese sword. A cab driver goes berserk and shoots down several people in an outburst of rage. A hand is pushed down the garbage disposal unit of a sink and cut to pieces. These images of violence, vivid and horrifying, seen in, respectively, *The Yakuza, Taxi Driver,* and *Rolling Thunder,* are typical of the thirty-one-year-old screenwriter Paul Schrader. Naturally, Mr. Schrader has been accused of exploitation, and an audience at a San Francisco preview loudly booed the hand-shredding scene in *Rolling Thunder.* MCA-Universal will release his first film as writer-director, *Blue Collar,* a movie marked by violence not only in its plot line but also in its actual making.

Surprisingly, Mr. Schrader turns out to be—on the surface, at least—meek and soft-spoken, slurring his syllables in a Brandoesque near-whisper. Once chubby, he is now slim and pale, lying rather than sitting in a low chair in his surprisingly modest office located in a bungalow at the Burbank Studios. Reportedly suffering from emphysema, he sometimes appears to be dangerously short of energy; when speaking, it often seems a struggle for him to reach the end of the long, complicated sentences that he favors.

His subdued, melancholy air and rather drab, conservative clothes scarcely suggest the millionaire he has become from the earnings of his films. Yet he is considered one of the sharpest wheeler-dealers in the business today, fanatically watching out for his own interests by reading the finest points in his contracts and ensuring himself handsome percentages of everything he touches. His low-key air and murmuring voice evidently disappear in confrontations with actors, film crews, or recalcitrant business contacts. In boardrooms, he is said to be more tiger than pussycat.

He has had to be. His rise from Poverty Row has been startling in its velocity. The child of Calvinist parents in the Middle West, he hadn't seen a single movie until he was eighteen. Movies were "sinful," so it isn't surprising that once he shook off his family's influence and moved West, he gobbled up films like a child gobbling candy. He struggled along in Hollywood as a poorly paid film critic for the *Los Angeles Free Press* and as editor of the magazine *Cinema.* He wrote a scholarly book, *Transcendental Style in Film,* which flopped commercially. He wrote a script about Canadian pipe-laying crews *(Pipeliners)* but the financial backing fell through at the last minute. Filled with despair, he drove aimlessly through several states; he drank heavily, put on an enormous amount of weight, and entered into a brief and unhappy marriage.

As if all this were not enough, Mr. Schrader's first big picture, *The Yakuza,* a melodrama set in contemporary Japan that starred Robert Mitchum and was directed by Sydney Pollack, was a dismal disaster. With his expensive house in Brentwood heavily mortgaged and the future uncertain, Mr. Schrader again plunged into melancholia. He was rescued from his financial difficulties by his friend, Martin Scorsese, who decided to film Mr. Schrader's screenplay, *Taxi Driver.* Awash in the writer's own obsession with urban violence, this story of a homicidal New York cabby proved to be a smash hit, earning close to $1 million from his percentage of the film's profit.

His next movie, *Obsession,* an homage to Alfred Hitchcock's *Vertigo* and directed by Brian De Palma, was also a commercial success despite mixed reviews. In its portrait of a man (Cliff Robertson) obsessed with the memory of a dead woman, it had much the same consuming nightmarish quality as *Taxi Driver.*

Given his instinct for what will deliver at the box office, it is understandable that Mr. Schrader decided to direct as well as write his new movie, *Blue Collar.* Its story centers on three workers in a Detroit automobile plant who clash over union issues in an atmosphere of industrial repressiveness. There are fistfights in the film, but none of the bizarre violence that characterized earlier Schrader films. Richard Pryor and Yaphet Kotto are costarred with Harvy Keitel. None of these actors has a reputation for being particularly easy to handle; indeed, Mr. Schrader claims that he was turned into a referee of sorts for their many on-set battles.

"The stars lived out the script's antagonisms in our day-to-day work," Mr. Schrader said recently over coffee in his Burbank office. "Making *Blue Collar* was the most unrelentingly unpleasant experience I have ever had. Richard, Yaphet, and Harvey were like three young bulls locking horns every day. Each one was determined that every line of dialogue in every scene would belong to him and him only. The ego competition was constant. There were racial arguments which were really transferred ego arguments. Richard would say, 'You're making an antiblack movie.' What he really meant was that in the scene we were doing, I was giving Harvey more attention. When Harvey would say, 'You're making an antiwhite movie,' he meant that I was throwing the scene to Richard. It was hell working with these guys, but the tension ensured that they put real feeling into the racial conflict in the scenes. It was a life-or-death struggle between actors.

"They constantly rewrote lines. And they came to blows. There were fistfights. It seemed that every day we had to close down for an hour or two, or they battled it out. I tried to conciliate. If I'd really attacked one of these actors, he'd have walked off the picture and we'd have to close down."

Mr. Schrader looked bitter at the memory. "Did I see the guys after shooting? No, I didn't. I didn't want to. The picture almost didn't get made at all. We were frozen out of the auto factories in Detroit. The City Fathers refused to cooperate until they saw my script. Since the script attacks auto industry methods, I tried to hide it from them. Finally a member of the Council offered to help. He would read the script and concili- ate with his colleagues. He would tell us if there was anything dangerous, so we could fix it in advance. He reneged on his promises. He lied to us and cheated us. He was acting as a spy for the Council. He took the script to his people and we were locked out of Detroit.

"I was desperate. A week and a half to go before shooting and I had no auto plant to make a picture in. It was suicide time. Then I heard about the Checker Cab plant in Kalama- zoo. The man who owns it let us use it. He gave us a free hand. He didn't worry about loss of business because of the script's criticisms. People were going to use cabs no matter what we said. And finally we decided to shoot in the streets of Detroit anyway."

Mr. Schrader insists that the violence in the plot line of *Blue Collar* was not introduced for its own sake but rather for the sake of truth. One can almost hear his critics groaning at such protestations. But he certainly seems serious whem he says, "There is violence in our factories. It would be dishonest not to show it. The bosses like to have workers fight each other, especially black workers and white workers. It helps keep the competition going, makes the men work harder because they're trying to get ahead of each other. And the unions are no better. They've become part of the larger power structure.

They, too, want violence, because they're in league with the big bosses. It's vicious and corrupt from top to bottom."

When queried about the charges that he is essentially an exploitation filmmaker posing as an intellectual who looks at his themes from a purely sociological point of view, Mr. Schrader replied, "Not true. But you have to remember that both *The Yakuza* and *Rolling Thunder* were rewritten by other people. In the first drafts, I tried to use the techniques of the exploitation picture to analyze and criticize contemporary violence. But when they were finally presented, these movies stripped away my social arguments and left only the violence itself.

"In *Rolling Thunder,* I attacked the racist murderer who kills Mexicans in the picture. In the finished result, he came out as a kind of hero. An antiracist movie became a racist movie. I'm very angry about that."

What about Mr. Schrader's future plans and particularly *Hard Core,* a story about a Midwest Calvinist father whose runaway daughter becomes a pornography film actress? The movie was originally planned as a vehicle for Warren Beatty.

"I'll be making it very soon.* Warren listened to his friends who told him he would be miscast as a Calvinist. So George C. Scott will be playing it instead. It's in some ways autobiographical. The Scott character is suggested by my father—a remarkable man—and I hope to shoot part of the picture in my hometown of Grand Rapids, Michigan, using actual townspeople I've known and my own church. I'm tired of movies without moral heroes. The father in the story will be a heroic figure. I'm on his side. I'm on the side of all people who make moral decisions, whether I agree with their point of view or not. I like people who make decisions."

*The picture was completed in 1978.

William Wyler

Wyler has a reputation as a slow director who does dozens of takes and who is extremely hard on the actors. He is also one of the giants of the business. I have found him wry, modest, and retiring. He doesn't take himself seriously; in fact, he tends to underrate his work, picking holes in it more eagerly than any critic. But behind the self-criticism, there is the quiet pleasure of a craftsman in his craft. One feels that if he had not been a director, he might have been a lacemaker. The intricate mantilla worn by Bette Davis in the memorable last scene of *The Letter* seems to me symbolic of his work. He is a craftsman in filigree.

———————— ★ ————————

1973

William Wyler's house in Beverly Hills is large, sprawling, attractively informal, and comfortable. Scattered books, pink and beige settees, a pool table, a big open bar area, and upstairs a paper-strewn desk, unceremoniously situated in the annex to a bedroom. None of that familiar Los Angeles look in which every room seems to have been arranged like a shop window, to be admired rather than actually lived in. Even the bathroom is pleasantly lacking in the usually obligatory pyramids of multicolored perfumed soaps, baroque rugs, and complicated glass bottles.

It is the home of a man who lives by his own rules, who is modest, unassuming, unshowy. A house for children to play in without fear of knocking over some ostentatiously situated, self-important Sèvres vase. And his grandchildren are here: through the hot afternoon, their voices echo up through the floors or the windows from the garden—healthily raucous and harsh. Many of Wyler's films—among them *These Three, The Heiress, Carrie, The Little Foxes*—have dealt in family repressions, in secrets, in the muffled voice behind the velvet curtain. Here everything is open, free, spacious. And this great director has even abandoned the confines of the sound stages where he spent forty years of his life and more, for the space and light of the world itself. He and his wife have been traveling ever since his retirement two years ago, and have recently returned from an extraordinary trip which took them to the extreme tip of South America, and a journey to the Antarctic.

Wyler's retirement was entirely voluntary. He was preparing *Forty Carats* as part of a four-picture contract with Columbia when he decided, "I don't want to work anymore." He asked for and received a release from the contract. Since then, he continues to get scripts from producers who hope he will make a comeback. He hasn't—yet. "But it's nice to be asked," the director says.

If there is one sustained note in all of Wyler's films, it is a genial realism, a warm and compassionate truthfulness in approaching the tensions of business, family life, the struggles of the American middle class. A very high proportion of his films have dealt with Americans of comfortable means, both in the last and the present century, who have been faced with crises involving moral, financial, or emotional dilemmas. This fact has ensured the success of many of his pictures with a public which has barely heard of him. He is a great director because he has illuminated family life with piercing insights, taking established plays and novels and interpreting them with an extraordinary eye for detail, and with an inner ear that, despite encroaching deafness, has made his among the liveliest sound tracks in movie history. He has an unerring skill in the juxtaposition of sound and image. In *These Three* (1936) he orchestrated the voices of the cast like a musical arranger; in *Wuthering Heights* (1939), Cathy Earnshaw's declaration, "I am Heathcliff," was matched to a sudden flash of lightning which symbolized her realization of total emotional involvement; in *The Letter* (1940) the drip of rubber from a tree, coolies shifting in their hammocks, and a sudden shot from a veranda formed an opening sequence of extraordinary force; in *The Heiress* (1949), he deliberately exaggerated the snip of the ugly daughter's scissors on the last letter of an embroidered alphabet to illustrate the termination of her relationship with a wastrel. Only Cukor and Hitchcock have equaled him in the manipulation of the details of sound and image.

Wyler talks shyly and quietly, with the consideration and kindness one associates with his films. Born in Mulhouse, Alsace-Lorraine, in 1902, son of a haberdasher, he was brought to the New York office of Universal by Universal's boss, Carl Laemmle, in the mid-1920s. Laemmle was Wyler's uncle; he met the young man in Zurich, and he gave him a job. Wyler chafed at the confines of New York office life, and asked to be transferred to Hollywood. He began as prop boy, script boy, and third, second, and first assistant, then full director, on a series of Westerns, culminating in *Hell's Heroes* (1929) which won him a small reputation.

Promoted to domestic dramas, he got his first chance to make a major film with *Counsellor-at-Law* (1933), in which he had John Barrymore as his star. Cleverly directed, each effect calculated to a fault, the picture was a perfect realization of Elmer Rice's play about a New York attorney cracking up. "I was just a kid starting out and here was this big star, Barrymore. On the whole he behaved surprisingly well. But one day he misbehaved: he didn't know his lines, he was late, he had been drinking. I was determined not to let him think he could get away with it. I think it was in order to discipline him that I first got my reputation for making thirty takes. Ridiculous, of course, but I did take about fourteen takes of him, all day, so that he'd do what I wanted. After that he quit drinking and gave a good performance. Sometimes we'd have to put up a written cue, but not very often."

It was in this picture that Wyler learned to master the problem of making a film in a very confined area, in a set representing a group of offices in the newly completed Empire State Building. *Dodsworth* (1936), from Sinclair Lewis's novel, also involved much use of confined sets. "A problem in that picture was Ruth Chatterton as the wife. I wanted her to play like a well-rounded woman who is unhappy. She tried to make her an all-out villainess, a woman all on one note of shrewishness. I felt that was wrong, that she should be more human. I told her so."

For *These Three* (1936), Lillian Hellman altered her original play, which had dealt with the subject of lesbianism among schoolteachers in a small town. "I didn't feel that was important. She simply showed a young girl spying on a man and woman instead of on two women, and I thought it was just as effective. When I made the picture again as a lesbian story, as *The Children's Hour,* it was a disaster. Miss Hellman was busy at the time, and couldn't work on the second script, and I adhered too closely to the original play, which had dated badly. By the time I remade the story, so what if two lady schoolteachers had an affair? Who cared?"

He would have liked to have made *Dead End* (1937) in the actual setting of the play, in New York itself, but the producer, Samuel Goldwyn, insisted upon doing the whole thing on an elaborate Hollywood set. But *Wuthering Heights* (1939) was, Wyler felt, more comfortable to film in a simulated California Yorkshire.

"Somebody said to me recently—I shouldn't quote this in my own favor, but maybe it's interesting—that my version looked more real than the one recently made in Yorkshire itself. Our art director at the Goldwyn Studios, James Basevi, did an amazing job of creating a 'look' of Yorkshire, with long stone walls and heather. Well, the heather did give us a problem. The English critics kept saying it was too long. But the cast was extraordinary. I went to England to get the supporting players. I was very happy with Merle Oberon as Cathy. For her death scene, I closed the set. She thought out something on her own that was very effective: a kind of death rattle in the voice. It was very realistic. I think it was her best performance on the screen."

Wyler made three pictures with Bette Davis: *Jezebel* (1938), *The Letter* (1940), and *The Little Foxes* (1941). "With her it was a question of bringing her 'down', which was much better than having to bring 'up' a player. I liked *Jezebel,* except that the big house which was a central part of the action was entirely the wrong period. Luckily, it didn't matter, because when you put Bette Davis, Fay Bainter, and Henry Fonda in front of it, they looked so authentic it wasn't important if the house did not.

"*The Letter,* adapted from Somerset Maugham, had already been filmed with Jeanne Eagels in the early days of talkies. I felt my version suffered from too much emphasis on the moon, which seemed to suggest the murderess played by Bette Davis was moonstruck, or something. Also, the Chinese woman who has the telltale blackmail letter, though very well acted indeed by Gale Sondergaard, should have been played by a Chinese woman. But the only Chinese actress we had at the time was Anna May Wong, and she was much too young. The ending was a problem. The Breen office wanted it so that no murderess could go free. Not only was Bette Davis stabbed by the Chinese woman's servants in the last scene, but her killers had to be arrested as well. The police came out of nowhere. It was ridiculous.

"Another problem was that Bette wouldn't do the last scene the way I wanted, at first. She had to tell her husband that with all her heart she still loved the man she killed. Bette said no woman would say that to her husband's face. She wanted to look away as she spoke the line. I told her to say it to him. I won.

"I had reservations about *The Little Foxes* as well. Bette Davis was fine in *Jezebel* and *The Letter.* But I disagreed with her interpretation of Regina in *The Little Foxes.* I felt Regina should be amusing, womanly, worldly, very attractive, very appealing to an audience. Bette wanted her to be a cold, icy villainess. We argued a great deal. Generally, though, Bette and I got along well. I have to this day the highest regard for her."

Wyler said that he was not altogether happy with the casting of Olivia de Havilland as Catherine Sloper in *The Heiress* (1949), based by Ruth and Augustus Goetz on Henry James's *Washington Square,* a story of a frustrated spinster and her domineering father. "Here you have one of the most beautiful women in the world playing an ugly duckling. Today we would have someone more plain, someone frail and nervous and shy. We did everything in our power to make Olivia homely, but it didn't work. Ralph Richardson was great as the father, and I don't agree with the critics who said that Montgomery Clift was too nice and pleasant to play the fortune hunter Morris Townsend. In the play he was so obviously a villain there was no shock when he let the heiress down and failed to turn up for their elopement. In the film, because Clift was so sympathetic, people were horrified when he jilted her."

A companion piece, *Carrie* (1951), also written by the Goetzes, based with remarkable fidelity on the novel *Sister Carrie* by Theodore Dreiser about the disastrous love affair of a restaurant headwaiter and an actress, with Laurence Olivier and Jennifer Jones, was impressive, but a box-office disappointment. Its pessimism proved too much for audiences at the time. "It was cut in America," Wyler says. "We had a scene in a flophouse which, at the time of the Un-American Activities Committee, was said to show our country in an unfavorable light. That went and so did the suicide of Hurstwood, played by Olivier. The cuts didn't help. The picture died anyway."

Ben-Hur (1959) he had taken on as a challenge. When the producer, Sam Zimbalist, asked him to do it, "I told him it should be done by Cecil B. DeMille. But when Zimbalist accused me of being frightened of the subject, that was it. I had to do it. I told him I'd be happy just doing the chariot race, but he wouldn't hear of it. Of course *Cahiers du Cinéma* never forgave me for directing the picture. I was completely written off as a serious director by the avant-garde, which had considered me a favorite for years. I had prostituted myself. It was the most commercially successful picture I had ever made.

"The Desperate Hours, in which Humphrey Bogart was the head of a gang terrorizing a family, was supposed to have Spencer Tracy as the father of the household. But we could not resolve the billing situation. Neither would agree to let his name come in second place. As if the public cared. It was ridiculous."

Wyler had taken on *Funny Girl* (1968) as a challenge because he had never done a musical. "I kept hearing reports that Barbra Streisand quarreled with me on the picture, but I never had any evidence of it. It's true she quarreled with the producer, Ray Stark. She worked desperately hard with me on her part, she kept trying to improve herself, she worried about how she looked, she would come on in the morning and ask if we could do a scene over again, she was totally dedicated. She trusted me, and I trusted her."

Clearly, the realism and truthfulness that Wyler always aimed for in his pictures was largely dependent on a perfect rapport, an intimate understanding, built up between him and the players. "I could look into their eyes, read their thoughts, probe into their emotions. That was what always fascinated me most: personal relationships on the screen.

"Aside from miscasting, I was often handicapped by dealing with places, periods I knew nothing about. For instance, in *Mrs. Miniver* I had Greer Garson running out on an airfield in Britain to wave her son tearfully good-bye as he flew off in a Spitfire. Ridiculous. And we were rightly roasted for it in England. Recently I went back there—the criminal returning to the scene of the crime.

"But I really knew what I was filming in one picture at least: *The Best Years of Our Lives.* People kept saying to me and to Sam Goldwyn, 'You can't make a film about war veterans. Who wants to see that now? The war is over.' Well, we went ahead and made it anyway. I had been making pictures for the Air Force, I knew what it felt to be a returning serviceman coming home, I understood the men played by Fredric March and

Dana Andrews and Harold Russell. I achieved the realism I've always sought in that picture because for once I was an eyewitness of the facts. I wasn't guessing."

Wyler's films have ranged from the gentle *Friendly Persuasion* to the chilling *The Collector*. Today, this modest, unassuming realist is happily retired. "I enjoy my grandchildren, I travel, I read. I've been lucky." And so, too, one feels have been the actors and actresses who have worked with a committed craftsman who denies he has ever been an auteur.

"I am not the author of my films," Wyler says, "and there is no need to use a fancy French word—though I am one of the few directors who can pronounce it: *auteur.*

"It's like the music world: I am not the composer, but the conductor."

Roman Polanski

This interview was conducted before the famous child-molestation and statutory rape case in which Polanski was accused of having intercourse with a twelve-year-old girl in a whirlpool bath. In a town where vice and organized crime are rampant, the people suddenly behaved as though they were prim and proper Bostonians. Fingers were pointed and Polanski became everybody's scapegoat. Only Polanski could have written the scenario of manic farce and extravagant defiance that followed.

I found Polanski far too intelligent for his own good. Far too smart, far too rich, far too penetrating about life. He told a friend, "If they put me in jail for a long time, I will shoot myself." Instead, he went to jail for a short time, and has already announced he will make a film of the experience.

———————————★———————————

1974

It is Polanski weather: gray, threatening, with patches of fog, the weather of *Knife in the Water* and *Cul-de-Sac*, of *Repulsion* and *Macbeth*. The director is staying in a distinctly Raymond Chandlerish rented house in the hills above the Sunset Strip: a pretentious and run-down quasi-Moroccan folly, crowded with garish paintings and boasting a garden waterfall. It seems only appropriate that the house's owner is George

Montgomery, who played Philip Marlowe in a version of *The High Window (The Brasher Doubloon,* 1947), and that here Polanski has been completing with the writer Robert Towne the script for his new movie, a Chandlerish detective story of the thirties, *Chinatown.*

Hard to believe Polanski has just passed his fortieth birthday: his pointed, medieval page boy's face looks like that of a man at least fifteen years younger. Tiny, restless, and self-conscious, he paces about the patio, expressing a horror of Los Angeles, which is spread like a litter of gray boxes below the house. Gloomy one minute, he is sprightly the next, nimbly scaling a heap of stones and disappearing troll-like underground to turn on a complicated device which activates the waterfall. "You can dive from the waterfall into the pool!" he says, happily.

Back in the house, a phone call plunges him into despair again. "That was Sharon's sister," he says, memories of the horrific Manson case, in which his wife Sharon Tate was murdered, flooding his face with shadows. "She's somewhere I can't get to her, hemorrhaging. She's ill, alone, and frightened. Oh, God! What's the matter with these young people?"

Joy in physical action, whether in sport or sex, is always undercut in Polanski by the sense of the futility and pitiful absurdity of human existence which animates all of his work. "I stopped believing in God and the Devil," he says, "when I was twelve. I don't believe in the immortal soul, divine justice, or any kind of plan in existence. We are born; it means nothing; we die."

Giving interviews is clearly just another meaningless activity, like eating or fornicating, but not nearly as enjoyable. Polanski even records himself being interviewed, listens to the playback, convinced he is boring, and calls the interviewer the next day, agonizing over every word he uttered. To both mine and his own tape recorder he says, *"Chinatown* is a private-eye movie set in 1937. Jack Nicholson plays a sleeker version of Philip Marlowe, Chandler's detective, or Dashiell Hammett's Sam Spade. He specializes in divorce suits, acting as a highly successful snoop catching people in flagrante delicto.

"He accidentally becomes involved in a case of greater magnitude: a case in which certain local bigwigs are making money corruptly in the vital supply of the city's water. A girl he meets in the course of the case is called Chinatown, and she's played by Faye Dunaway. She is a rather sophisticated creature, who becomes involved with Nicholson. He is nouveau riche, charming, and witty and pushy; she gets on his nerves because she's so self-assured—she's always had money —and that gives him a need for her he rather resents. So in some ways that makes the film's story quite Chandlerish. It's all quite a departure for me.

"I have always loved Chandler. I didn't like Hammett so much—he was a little bit too poetic for my taste—Chandler is earthier. I'm trying to surround myself with people who knew the late thirties, among them Stanley Cortez, my cameraman on the picture, who emerged in that period and superbly photographed *The Magnificent Ambersons* and *Night of the Hunter* later on.* But the period isn't unfamiliar to me: I'm a movie buff, and I love pictures of that time, pictures I first saw when I was young. In a way, it's appropriate this picture should be made for Paramount because I always liked the Paramount crime pictures, like *This Gun for Hire* and *The Glass Key,* as well as the better known Warner/Bogart ones."

Chinatown, as he says, is something of a departure in Polanski's work, which from his earliest Polish films (including *Two Men and a Wardrobe* and *Knife in the Water*) has had a constant emphasis on the inconsequentialities, the non sequiturs, the essential absurdity, the madness of existence. His latest film, *What?,* made in Italy, is his most extreme absurdist work, except for *Cul-de-Sac* (1966). *What?* is the story of an Alice-in-Wonderland–like girl, played by Sydne Rome, who stumbles into a weird ménage which is headed by an eccentric old degenerate (Hugh Griffith) and includes Marcello Mastroianni and Polanski himself.

---

*Polanski fired Cortez the next day and replaced him with John Alonzo.

"I love Lewis Carroll," says Polanski. "I followed the irrational approach of his books, showing how in life today nobody listens to anyone else, nobody cares for anyone. Nobody even asks this girl's name. She's just 'that thing' there that happens to be around. And then all kinds of odd things happen to her. For instance, she sees a couple making love on the floor. I had them fornicating under a large bedcover of ostrich feathers, so that they looked like a strange bird rolling up and down the floor. She looks at this astounding apparition, and then she just blandly moves on. After all, that's the way young people are in a world in which any mad thing is probable. The whole film is made up of these bizarre, disconnected episodes."

Polanski had good reason to feel that life was insane from the beginning. He suffered extreme misery as a child under the German occupation of Poland. His mother died in a concentration camp. At sixteen in Warsaw he became overwhelmed by the literature of the absurd: Kafka, Bruno Schultz, Beckett. "These writers presented an approach utterly remote from the Stalinist social realism that dominated the arts in Poland. They had a tremendous impact on me. And then I discovered modern painters. When I went to art school, the Impressionists were supposed to be the end of art, and slightly sinful. I discovered Dali, Chirico, and Klee, and a new world opened to me.

"Later, when I saw *Waiting for Godot* on the stage, after the Khrushchev era opened the floodgates to Western theater, I saw how the hidden absurdity of life could be revealed in art without any loss of discipline. Then I saw *Citizen Kane*. This, too, influenced me, not only because of its pessimistic view of life—combined with a fantastic humor—but because of its studio-made surrealism of style." Together with *Odd Man Out* and Olivier's *Hamlet*—which he saw twenty-five times—it helped to form his visual approach, with its intense formalism, its emphasis on the nocturnal and the strange, and its concentration on interiors which reflect the souls of their inhabitants.

"I have always preferred 'indoor' films. They are intimate, they give you the feeling of total involvement with the characters. My favorite painting at art school was Jan van Eyck's painting of 'Arnolfini and His Wife,' done in 1434, a picture of a couple with a mirror at the back of the room, and under the mirror the words in Flemish, 'We were there with them.' On that piece of wood, the painter had created the illusion of actually being inside a room. That is the illusion I like to create in my films: that you are enveloped. Cinema should make you forget you are sitting in the theater."

Trained at the Lodz Film School in Warsaw, Polanski rejected Communist literature and film as too literal and humdrum, and embarked on a fantasy, *Two Men and a Wardrobe,* which made his reputation. His *Knife in the Water,* about the effect a young man has on a yachting husband and wife on a lake in Poland, introduced his recurrent theme of a stranger intruding upon a narrow world and sparking off tense and irrational behavior among those he comes in contact with.

In his first major effort, *Repulsion,* he showed the insanity lurking behind the bland front of a pretty young girl, an insanity disclosed when a young man erupts into the enclosed world of her apartment. In *Cul-de-Sac* he showed what happened when two eccentric thugs stumbled on a kinky married couple in a crumbling north of England castle. In *The Fearless Vampire Killers*—brutally cut by producer Martin Ransohoff in the United States—he depicted the odd, disconnected goings-on when an ancient professor specializing in vampire cults arrives in a vampire-haunted mountain region. In *Rosemary's Baby* we saw what happens when an innocent New York girl marries into a witches' coven and gives birth to the Devil. In all of these films, human beings are shown out of touch with each other, foolish or menacing or threatened, and tending toward extremes of irrationality in a world gone mad.

"When I made *Rosemary's Baby,* I was severely attacked by Catholic groups and individuals. Never by witches, as some people said. Witches told me they liked the film!"

What about the claim by William Castle, the producer of *Rosemary's Baby,* that during the shooting of the film, witchcraft caused him to become severely ill? And that while he was recuperating in the hospital, Christopher Komeda, the film's composer, was fatally injured in a fall just below Castle's hospital window, his death caused by devil worshipers?

"Ridiculous! If anything caused Bill Castle's illness, it was having too much success with the picture." Polanski gets up, paces impatiently around the living room.

"Just another example of irrationality. And then the critics claimed that I had based the murders of Macduff's family in *Macbeth* on the murder of my wife Sharon and her friends! But Shakespeare wrote the murders, and had the murder of one child on the stage! The *Time* critic attacked what he called 'the climactic battle with Duncan.' Didn't he know that Macbeth was fighting Macduff? You see, there's just a total lack of understanding everywhere: of one person for another, of critics for a given work."

Polanski shrugs, as if to say that this breakdown of communication is just another symptom of an Alice in Wonderland world. It is time to go. His date for the evening—a cool, slender blonde—has arrived and is playing pool by herself at a green baize table downstairs. Springing from his seat, Polanski walks me to my car. Although it is still afternoon, the sky is almost black, and a raven has perched on a bough nearby, looking at us. The director peers humorously through my car window, eyes twinkling with irony. "That headrest," he says, "seems to have been put on back to front. Not only won't it cushion your head if a car goes in your back, but it will probably decapitate you!"

He gives a charmingly macabre smile.

"Good-bye!"

Robert Wise

I run into Robert Wise often, in all kinds of places. I find him shy and owlish, on and off the set.

He made one of my favorite movies, *The Haunting*. With the magical Julie Harris and Claire Bloom in the starring roles, it is one of the few pictures which genuinely gave a feeling of the supernatural. Probably, this sprang from the fact that Wise began his directorial career working for Val Lewton, master of the horror film at RKO. I regret that at the time of the interview I felt asking him about *The Haunting* would have been too specialized. I've since found out it's one of his favorite pictures, too.

--------------- ★ ---------------

1968

He might be a genial bank manager, advancing a loan to a particularly well-favored client. Or a New York doctor, advising a businessman to take an immediate vacation in the Adirondacks. Nothing in Oscar-winning movie director Robert Wise's soft-spoken manner, except occasionally a tense narrowing of the eyes behind clerical glasses, suggests the nature of his career, the drive that took him from editing *Citizen Kane* and *The Magnificent Ambersons* to becoming one of the most successful box-office directors in Hollywood, creator of the blockbuster musicals, *The Sound of Music, West Side Story,* and the ill-fated but interesting *Star!*—the last with Julie Andrews as Gertrude Lawrence.

Wise's urgency and attack have given film after film considerable impact: the savage denunciation of boxing rackets in *The Set-Up* with Robert Ryan as a battered, punch-drunk heavyweight, overruled by a syndicate; the harshly accurate portrait of the Old West's bloodshed and violence in a brace of powerful Westerns; the realistic look at war in *The Desert Rats,* with James Mason as Rommel; the shockingly violent exploration of the lives of resurrectionists in his version of Robert Louis Stevenson's *The Body Snatcher.*

And in recent years, he has managed to give punch even to the marshmallow fudge of *The Sound of Music* and the improbable heroics of *The Sand Pebbles.* He has wrung the last drop of talent out of players like Julie Andrews, Richard Burton, William Holden, Natalie Wood, and Susan Hayward.

Susan Hayward's greatest performance was given in *I Want to Live,* Wise's film about the career and execution of the celebrated murderess, Barbara Graham. Wise wanted, characteristically, to spare the audience nothing, not even the last night before Barbara Graham died in the gas chamber at San Quentin.

"I went to see the priest who had administered her the last rites. He had left the prison because he couldn't stand the realization that a whole massive machinery was being put to work to take a human life.

"He suddenly, in speaking of this revulsion, gave me the idea of doing the execution sequence. I wanted to show in detail for the first time how that awful machinery worked. So I went back to the prison and they showed me everything they did, by the clock: how they'd bring the telephone in the morning and plug it in in a room near the death cell, to call the governor if need be to postpone the execution. How they'd come in with the cyanide pellets and the sulfuric acid, and how the warden would search the prisoner. How they'd use the stethoscope to check the heartbeat before she died. . . .

"I took still pictures of the death cell and the gas chamber, and they were reproduced thoroughly in the studio. I felt like a ghoul asking for this, but I finally decided I'd even now not got enough realism into it—I had to see exactly how a man died in the chamber. The warden knew I was right. I sat with him and the doctor and two witnesses and saw this Negro boy who had been convicted of murdering two white men killed before my eyes.

"That boy wasn't emotional about dying—he was stunned, rather knocked out; and I realized later, after talking to the doctor, that this was often the case: that people had some kind of safety valve at the back of the brain that worked in this kind of extreme situation and numbed them. So I decided I'd direct Barbara Graham's death without emotion, without hysterics. I didn't know how I'd react when I went to see the boy die. All I could say was, 'What good did it do?' And that made me feel capital punishment was pointless."

It was an ordeal for Susan Hayward to play the part, sitting in the death chair day after day, and the death cell and execution scenes, covering two and a half weeks of shooting, shattered Wise: he would come home every day utterly exhausted and drained.

Wise's boxing films were in many ways almost as tough to make. In The *Set-Up,* Robert Ryan, who played a battered and aging boxer in the grip of a crime syndicate, had really been an intercollegiate heavyweight champion, and the whole action of the central match was choreographed like a ballet. In *Somebody Up There Likes Me,* Wise was faced with the problem that the star, Paul Newman, couldn't box.

"We had a top professional boxer up against Paul, playing himself. Paul was scared. He was afraid that if he accidentally hit the boxer in a fake fight, the boxer would knock him out cold. So we had to replace the real boxer. . . ."

In *The Sand Pebbles,* a big spectacular color film with Steve McQueen about the Chinese-American hostilities of the 1920s, shot in Taiwan, Wise ran into a nightmare set of problems. Extras turned up with Beatle haircuts, interpreters for Mandarin, Fukien, and Canton dialects had to be hired to sort out a babel of actors' voices, female cast playing coolies wore permanent waves, and the gunboat which featured in the story, the *Pueblo,* ran into a typhoon.

An earthquake, the worst for fifteen years, disrupted shooting at Taipei; a fire swept through the unit's rented hotel. The *Pueblo* couldn't be sailed in the high seas, only on a river, so for a week the entire crew and cast had to do nothing while she was tugged from Taiwan to Hong Kong. Extras went on strike.

Beside that, *The Sound of Music* was a breeze. But Wise the realist had reservations about this, the most successful motion picture ever made.

"We tried to diminish the cuteness—kept cutting down on the saccharine. Julie Andrews said to me, 'What are you going to do about getting the sugar out of this thing?' And I tried."

In *Star,* Wise and Andrews aimed at complete honesty once again. "We talked to everyone who knew Gertie Lawrence, trying to find out what made her tick. We came up with a person with a tremendous hunger for approval and an inner unhappiness: she couldn't commit herself to a man, to a marriage, in the sense she committed herself to the stage.

"Finally she was over forty and she realized she'd missed out on life. She was more real onstage than offstage as a person, and that was her tragedy."

It is characteristic of Wise's modest honesty and decency as a director that he should now abandon road-show spectaculars for a small film, a documentary on the life of Martin Luther King, for a small cooperative called F.A.I.R. (Film Associates for Improvement and Reform) dealing with minorities. Among those involved are Brando, Poitier, Lemmon, and Streisand, and they will appear in these films to raise cash for reform.

What was Wise's most exciting moment? "I was on the *Pueblo* making *The Sand Pebbles* in Hong Kong. Suddenly news came that I'd won the Oscar for directing *The Sound of Music.* A courier speedboat carried the telephoned news to the suburb of Sai Kung. A whole team of dancers was hidden below decks, unbeknown to me, by our publicity man, and they came rushing out. Then a vast number of fireworks hidden in the mast above me went off all at once. Between the fireworks and the lion dancers leaping and shouting and the great roaring of the crowd it was an astonishing moment. Two o'clock in the afternoon in Hong Kong. And it was a moment I'll never forget as long as I live."

Maria Rasputin

I shan't forget the background to this story. It was 1970, and I had just arrived in Hollywood. I was contacted by a promoter named Guido Orlando. Orlando introduced me to the heiress Patricia Barham, who pronounced her own name, for some reason, Barnum. The day I saw her she had just been robbed at gunpoint by masked intruders who had stolen the original manuscript of "Rasputin." She told me she had been working for years with Maria Rasputin, daughter of the famous monk, and that she would like me to collaborate on Maria's memoirs. I declined.

She then proceeded to tell me a most peculiar story. She said that she and Maria had been searching for a decade for Grigori Rasputin's penis! I listened with astonishment while she unraveled a tale beside which *The Maltese Falcon* was uneventful. She described ransacking antique stores east and west of the Bosporus, plowing through cellars and attics the length and breadth of Europe, and even making inquiries in Russia. She announced that Prince Yussupov, who had assassinated Rasputin, had had a homosexual crush on him and took his male member as a souvenir. It was her bounden duty to recover it from wherever it had been hidden.

She described to me how, in a secret place in Paris, she had at last discovered a wooden box containing the treasure she sought. She opened it gingerly. As well she might. Inside, she saw something which she described as resembling an exceptionally large black banana. I was unable to elicit from her whether the missing part was presently to be found in her home in Los Angeles.

Guido Orlando promised me that I would be allowed a
one-second glimpse of Rasputin's penis if I embarked on the project.
This is the most peculiar bribe I have ever been offered. I was
forced to sacrifice the chance. And I couldn't help feeling that what
the box contained was nothing more nor less than—a very old
banana.

--------------------★--------------------

1970

The apartment is extremely simple, yet suggests a strong,
authoritative, remarkably disciplined personality. A single
icon, a portrait of Czar Nicholas of Russia, and a splendid
picture of a monk with penetrating, brilliant eyes dominate
the simple American furnishings of the living room.

Tea is poured from a fine samovar. And the woman who
lives there is extraordinary: dignified and striking, with eyes
that seem to change from palest turquoise to deep midnight
blue in the light. Her father's eyes.

Maria Rasputin. Remarkable, even in Los Angeles, which
houses more exotic exiles—from Stravinsky to Isherwood—
than any other city in the world, to realize that you are talking
to the daughter of Grigori Rasputin, holy and dissolute monk,
supreme power behind the throne of Russia, performer of
miraculous cures, and victim of one of the twentieth century's
most celebrated assassinations.

Today, interest in Rasputin is as great as ever, creating a
whole shelf of books on the subject in recent years. Latest of
these has the advantage over the others of being fully authorized and in fact coauthored by Maria Rasputin herself. This
is *Rasputin's Secret Diary,* by Patricia Barham, daughter of an
executive of the Hearst newspaper empire. Drawn from Rasputin's own notebooks and Maria's contemporary accounts, it
creates a unique picture of Rasputin's private life as seen from
his daughter's point of view.

In addition, Leigh Vance, author of a number of British film screenplays *(The Frightened City, Crippen)* is preparing the libretto of a musical version of Rasputin's family life.

And Guido Orlando, a famous publicist, is arranging a worldwide campaign to launch these two ventures, with Maria Rasputin going to London for television, press, and radio interviews.

Patricia Barham has needed courage and perseverance to write her book: she met Maria Rasputin in 1961 at a White Russian get-together in Los Angeles, and it took her seven years to persuade Maria to give the full story of her father's —and her own—life. Crabbed and complex manuscripts, fading after more than half a century, had to be copied and translated line by line with Maria's approval.

Emissaries had to be sent to Lebanon, Greece, and Russia to obtain documents covering Rasputin's never hitherto recorded travels to visit his disciples. Incredibly, Patricia Barham even succeeded in getting hold of the secret police files in Moscow which disclosed details of Rasputin's autopsy. Rare books and manuscripts came to light in such unlikely places as Honolulu, Hawaii—and still the immense search went on. Then in a recent robbery of her house in which she was held at gunpoint, Patricia Barham lost many original manuscripts. But she hasn't been fazed.

Rasputin's must be the most frequently filmed life story: no less than seven versions of it have been made. Born in 1872, he was first heard of in 1905, when he appeared in St. Petersburg salons: evil-smelling, filthy hair tumbling around his powerful shoulders, with blazing, hypnotically intense eyes, a cross hanging from his neck on an iron chain, he won the helpless adoration of elegant court women who fought with each other, abandoning their dignity in an attempt to attract his attention.

Introduced to the Imperial Palace by the Grand Duchess Militsa, he won a growing reputation as a saintly figure despite his dissolute habits. Czar Nicholas and his beautiful wife, Alexandra, succumbed totally to his influence when he claimed to have cured their young son of hemophilia.

His methods in arresting this tragic bleeding disease remain obscure, but the czarina unhesitatingly ascribed them to supernatural powers. He rose to immense, incalculable influence at the palace, so much so that he has been accused of placing the czarina herself under hypnotic influence.

He was destroyed by his effete rival, the late Prince Felix Yussupov, who in later years was involved in a number of libel cases when film and television versions of Rasputin's death were made depicting him as a cold-blooded murderer. Bisexual, a self-confessed transvestite, Yussupov detested Rasputin's hold over the czarina and his potential hold over Russia itself.

The official version of the story is that when he felt that the czar would abdicate and leave Russia to Rasputin and the empress, Yussupov decided to murder him. This, historians say, was done by feeding the monk poisoned cakes; when Rasputin still insisted on living, bullets were pumped into him, but he still seemed to resist death. Finally the body was wrapped in a curtain and thrust into a hole in the ice-covered River Neva.

I asked Maria Rasputin how she felt about the book on her life with her father: "Very happy," she told me, in a beautifully measured, modulated voice. "Patricia Barham is a close friend. I have told her, over the years, everything I know." Was her childhood a good one? "Perfectly. I attended a very good boarding school and had a French governess.

"My father was a very simple man at heart who at first could not read or write at all, though he learned to write by degrees and his diaries are very remarkable.

"He understood only the Bible, which he learned by ear, as it were 'thought by thought.' He would constantly tell us of the purity and goodness of Jesus' teaching.

"He loved music, especially Tchaikovsky. Opera he adored: *Eugene Onegin* was a special favorite, and *Faust.* Of course, we were never permitted to go to the cinema shows. We never heard jazz in Russia at that time.

"I was never in doubt for a single instant that my father had supernatural powers. Or that he cured the young Czarevich

Alexis of hemophilia by supernatural means. After all, my friends, they would not lie to me, who witnessed his miraculous curing of animals—horses, dogs, cattle.

"I have so many wonderful memories of my father. He has been portrayed as an inhuman monster, and I do not know how many books have appeared painting him in the blackest colors.

"But I never saw anything but a gentle and loving father. Let me give you an example of his wonderful powers. I remember once when I had diphtheria. He came to me and looked into my eyes and said a quiet prayer. Then he touched my throat. I fell into a deep, wonderful sleep at once. An overwhelming feeling of peace and warmth floated over me. When I woke, my throat was clear. My head was filled with bliss. I knew I could live now."

During the years when Rasputin lived a life of profligacy, of orgiastic self-indulgence, no detail of which will be shirked in the book, Maria was kept firmly sheltered, away from it all.

"My father was holy, but he was also human. At that time the whole court was profligate. It was a way of life. He lived his life with completeness, but historians have been wrong in calling him evil; I know he was not."

How did she learn of his death? "They brought me his boots. I shall never forget the pain, like a knife through the heart, when I saw them, huge, empty, and carried by the dreaded Secret Police.

"I hurried at once to the room where he lay. I was horrified to notice something that historians have completely neglected—that he had been castrated. I saw the bleeding flesh and I wept; they had not let him die a man. . . .

"Yussupov was so effeminate he bitterly envied my father's virility, and he believed that Rasputin's power over the Czarina Alexandra was sexual, when it was in fact spiritual.

"After all, she often entertained me and my sister at the Imperial Palace and was so charming and graceful; she could not have been having an illicit relationship with my father.

"Also, I have come to believe, after working with Patricia Barham on all the contemporary records, that there was a homosexual element in the murder. That Yussupov nourished a repressed desire for my father, who detested and abhorred homosexuality.

"I believe that Yussupov and his fellow officers did not originally intend to kill, but when they began to castrate my father, they panicked at the blood and had to get rid of him. I completely reject the story of the sweetmeats that were supposed to have poisoned him.

"My father detested sweetmeats of any kind. He would never have eaten them."

I asked Maria what happened to her and her family after the Revolution. "Many of them were killed. I managed to escape by ship. For many years, I lived in difficult circumstances. Then a very strange thing happened.

"A man from Barnum and Bailey's Circus came to see me in London. He wanted me to appear cracking a whip in a pony act, dressed in a Russian costume. They billed me as 'The Daughter of the Famous Mad Monk Whose Feats in Russia Astonished the World.' Later, they asked me to be a lion tamer. I needed the money, so . . .

"Then something terrible happened. I had needed courage, and now I needed more. A bear mauled me. Terribly. I had to leave the ring and retire here to Los Angeles.

"What has sustained me since has been the need to restore to the world the truth of my father's kindness, goodness, and decency at home, in his own domestic life, after all the cruel things that have been said of him.

"It is time a corrective came out—that the world sees not that terrible monster, but the man he really was."

Ralph Bakshi

Years ago, I interviewed Walt Disney. He sat in a suite of candy-colored offices in Burbank, surrounded by improbably pretty blond secretaries in carefully pleated skirts and starched white blouses, like waitresses in an M-G-M musical. I found him brooding and depressed, a somber genius who felt himself the victim of his public. He had longed to do *Winnie-the-Pooh* in the fastidious and delicate shades suggested by the original illustrator of the book, Ernest Shepard. Instead, his formidable brother Roy, who ran the business end of the Disney Studios, forced him to split the movie into two hideously garish shorts. He had hated *Alice's Adventures in Wonderland* since childhood, feeling it to be a paranoid view of a hostile universe, but had yielded to entreaties to make it. Now he longed to do George Macdonald's fairy tales, but feared they would be too specialized.

His opposite, Ralph Bakshi, the Kafka of cartoonists, has been more independent. He has poured the black vision Disney only rarely permitted himself freely over his audiences, and, in a nihilistic age, they have responded accordingly. Now he is completing *The Lord of the Rings*. Disney would never had dared do that picture.

———————★———————

1974

"The Ratings Board hates me. They give practically everything I do an X. They don't trust me. They don't *trust* this kid off the Brooklyn streets who dares to have a mind. He's a Brooklyn kid, so everything he does on the screen must be dirty. Well, they're out of their heads. And they call me erotic. I'm about as erotic as Adolf Hitler! My movies are antierotic; I hate sex. I always have. My films are filled with disgust of sex, life, everything."

Ralph Bakshi, creator of the very savage, very commercial, and very adult cartoons, *Fritz the Cat* and *Heavy Traffic,* as well as the soon-to-open, R-rated *Coonskin,* gives a high-pitched laugh as he contemplates what he regards as the idiocy of movie ratings and his own black vision. An ugly vision which has sickened some viewers, while pleasing most critics. Vincent Canby, for example, considered *Heavy Traffic* a "liberating, arrogant sort of movie, crude, tough, vulgar, full of insult and wit and an awareness of the impermanence of all things." He went on to say that the film was, at its best moments, "as nutty and bleak and beautiful as some scenes out of early Henry Miller, with whom Bakshi shares the inability to be entirely glum in the face of disaster."

Sitting in his drab office at Ralph Bakshi Productions, Bakshi doodles away impatiently on a pad. His large, pale, Russian-Jewish face—a cross between early Norman Mailer and the late John Garfield—tired dark brown eyes, heavy hirsute body in prison-blue demins, suggest a man exhausted by his own nightmares, and by the work of getting those nightmares across in animated or real-life images (live actors—including Charles Gordone, better known as the author of *No Place to Be Somebody*—are prominently featured in *Coonskin*).

But the insistent voice, the manic giggle, the imitation of the sound of machine-gun bullets as he describes a sequence, the thud of a fist on the desk evoke the destructive humor and violent assault on the emotions that are found in his work. Talking of his divorce from his first wife, he says, "Who'd want to be married to me? I draw all the time!" And it's easy to see how his obsessiveness must prove taxing to those around him.

Restlessly, he adds another ugly crooked face to his sketch pad, digging the pencil into the page like a stiletto, and launches into a description of *Coonskin.* "It's a jailbreak story. Three tired, very unhip blacks try to break a friend out of prison. Their contacts are waiting at night under the prison wall: an old guy and a young kid. The old guy is like Uncle Remus in Disney's *Song of the South.* He tells the young kid a story—the kind of thing an ex-con would remember. The world of *Superfly* in animation: the world of pimps, prostitutes, and gangsters: the whole, funky, black folktale world. And it's set against stock footage—actual film showing the history of the black people in this country. What we've done to them."

I ask Bakshi how he got started. "When I was a kid in Brownsville, I used to cut out Superman from the comic books and move him around a table, making up adventures for him. Brownsville was a very depressed area, with nothing to stimulate the mind. No Jewish theater even. Just a middle-class ghetto which moved to Levittown after World War Two. I would sit on the roof and look at the pigeons and dream. I would make up stories in my head out of the life of the street, rather then going onto the street and getting in another fight."

Heavy Traffic was a strongly autobiographical film: the story of a young cartoonist who goes through a series of harrowing experiences in the New York slums. "Everything in that movie is based on my life. There is a horrifying old publishing tycoon in the picture, being kept alive by blood transfusions. He's a composite of all the people who opposed me when I left the High School of Industrial Arts on Seventy-ninth Street and went to work as a cartoonist; I'll never forget the hell of working for Terrytoons in New York. I had married my first wife at eighteen and we had a baby. The guys at Terrytoons kept saying, 'Bastardize for money, that's the rule of the game, kid. You've got a wife and a child. Responsibilities!'

"I was surrounded by talented people being taught to draw junk—what they thought the public wanted. Ugly, terrible, schizophrenic cartoons. I got so nervous doing those cartoons I thought I'd die. When I saw this whole medium of cartoons being wasted, I thought I'd go crazy. I drew the two crows, Hekyll and Jekyll, and Mighty Mouse, for God's sake! Horrible! Terrytoons were terrified of giving me too much Hekyll and Jekyll to do because I might reveal in the dialogue that they were actually two blacks. They were afraid Middle America might stop their children from seeing Hekyll and Jekyll because Middle America hated niggers.''

Bakshi's first full-length animated feature, the outrageous *Fritz the Cat,* based on R. Crumb's underground comic books, was made in 1972, in association with a partner, Steve Krantz, from whom Bakshi has now split. (Krantz—but not Bakshi—also produced the disappointing *Nine Lives of Fritz the Cat.*) *Heavy Traffic* was a far more personal work, expressing Bakshi's one-man onslaught on New York.

Bakshi takes an imaginary gun from his pocket, fires it at the world at large, and lets out another fiendish laugh. "I work in a stream of consciousness, recalling events from my whole life. I go all out to express my hostilities. I was born in 1939, and a lot of *Heavy Traffic* is set in the 1940s. My parents were from Russia, and all except one of my mother's family died during the German invasion. When my father came here, he struggled to get work. That struggle and pain are in *Heavy Traffic.* No, my parents didn't quarrel like the ones in the film, but I did hear the quarreling of a Catholic father and a Jewish mother just like the ones in the picture.

"And there was a girl called Rosalind, just as I had it in the movie, who lay down on the roof and made love to all the boys on the block. I didn't accidentally push her off the roof—the way it was in the picture—but I would have liked that to have happened to Rosalind!''

Not only did Bakshi despise what he saw on rooftops and in the streets below, but he also hated much of what he saw in movie houses—for example, Hollywood movies combining real-life actors and cartoon figures, such as *Anchors Aweigh,* in which Gene Kelly danced with Jerry, the animated mouse, and *Three Caballeros,* in which Donald

Duck cavorted with Aurora Miranda and her dance troupe. "I hated those movies as a child because I had believed in Jerry and Donald Duck and when I saw them with live-action figures, it blew my dream. My reaction was violent. I felt instinctively that the filmmakers were saying, 'Look how cute we are, combining these two media.' But it was a tremendous put-down of both media to do those things the way they did. I got the idea even then there might be a way of combining the two more effectively."

Today, some critics feel that Bakshi has succeeded in creating cartoon figures which act as vivid personifications of ideas, that their frenetic movements actually match the rapid movements of thoughts. One wonders, though, how youngsters might respond to the scabrous, X-rated humor of *Fritz the Cat* and *Heavy Traffic*. How, for example did these films affect his own fourteen-year-old son, who saw them at private screenings? "The movies didn't frighten him or harm at all."

What about an image like that of the gang leader in *Heavy Traffic* eating people like spaghetti, or the image of his body being riddled with bullets and spurting blood, or Michael's head being blown off by a bullet? Couldn't such images prove harmful to tender minds? "No. Television has made kids used to that kind of thing. Cartoons are traditionally brutal. When children see *Heavy Traffic*, all they say is, 'Michael is stupid. Why does he get himself into a mess?' They actually understand him better than adults do. Adults think Michael is some kind of hero."

The picture Bakshi is working on now is called *Hey, Good Looking*. Set in 1955, it's a spoof of movies about black jackets, pegged pants, pistols, ducktail haircuts. "It's about a gorgeous guy who becomes the leader of the gang because he looks so handsome. It's anti-*American Graffiti*. That was so false, so sentimental. I'll spook it out of existence!"

Surprisingly, Bakshi—on the verge of becoming a household name—claims he wants to retire and devote more time to his second wife and to their two young children. And to his elder son, who is turning out to be a gifted artist. "I want to get out of this business. Los Angeles is a *nothing*. I miss New

York. I miss living for living's sake. I can't live this way forever. I will not spend the rest of my life making movies. I want to do nothing. Nothing means browsing in antique stores, collecting old books, wandering around museums. Daydreaming. I love to daydream. Nothing is Jones Beach in the winter, chasing my dogs with my kids. Nothing is traveling across the country in a car, like I did in 1956."

Bakshi gives a final, manic giggle. "I feel I'm living in a movie now. Maybe I *am* a movie! But if I am, there has to be an end title when I come back to life. Doesn't there?"

Raoul Walsh

I was delighted when Seymour Peck gave me the opportunity to meet Raoul Walsh. There's something irresistibly romantic in the idea of a grand old director of ninety in a ten-gallon hat and boots lording it over a property in a craggy mountain range.

Soon after the interview appeared, I was in New York where I accompanied Walsh, who is almost blind, from his hotel to a luncheon in his honor at the Museum of Modern Art. As we entered the room, even he, strikingly handsome figure though he was, found himself upstaged by a very small woman, entirely in white, with a floppy Garbo hat, her enormous eyes blazing out of her face. Nobody else in the room existed, though many other stars were present. Who was the woman? It was Gloria Swanson, who had starred in Walsh's *Miss Sadie Thompson* almost fifty years earlier.

1974

Raoul Walsh's white clapboard farmhouse stands high above sea level in the Santa Susanna Mountains some fifty miles northwest of Los Angeles. Outside the windows, orange trees are blanketed in late afternoon mist, horses whip flies with their tails, and ten cats and four dogs perform arabesques on the lawn.

As I arrive, Walsh's wife announces a dramatic little problem: a giant hawk has gotten caught in a bush and broken its wing. Walsh—a tall, grizzled, white-mustached man with a black patch over his right eye and wearing a green windbreaker, cream-colored chino pants sprinkled with cigarette ash, and cowboy boots—tells her how to tend the bird's wing and what fodder to give it ("bread 'n' scratch").

In view of his Hemingwayish appearance and evident Hemingwayish machismo knowledge of birds, animals, and the out-of-doors, it seems only appropriate that Walsh's wife's name should be Mary, and that she should call him "Papa." (Walsh has in fact been twice married before, to the actress Miriam Cooper from 1916 to 1927, and to Lorraine Welles.)

Walsh says that he really hasn't enjoyed making "indoor" pictures, that his passion for the out-of-doors has been the overriding inspiration of his life. Both his "indoor" and his "outdoor" films are the works of a man's man, and are pictures of men at their toughest.

Like John Ford, Walsh became celebrated as early as the 1920s for his vivid narrative style, the sweeping landscapes evoked by his camera, the deep love of his native soil, and the hard-bitten boisterousness of his humor. He denies having any philosophy about making motion pictures: like most filmmakers of his generation, he went home at the end of the day, hung up his Stetson, and forgot everything until the next morning's shooting.

Let others talk about art: Walsh simply poured his knowledge of riding and herding cattle into Westerns like *The Tall Men* and *Pursued,* his knowledge of the sea into such salty adventures as *The World in His Arms* and *Captain Horatio Hornblower,* and his knowledge of soldiers into *The Naked and the Dead* and *Battle Cry.* He is a celebrator of life. Considered by many critics one of the primitive artists of the screen, he has never seen himself as anything of the kind. "I just did my job," he says. "I let others make up their theories."

Walsh is, by his own cheerful confession, just turned eighty-seven years old. His one remaining eye is very nearly blind, and he has difficulty, as he lights one cigarette after another, seeing the flame of a match. But his hearing and his mind are in good shape, and he remembers events going back to the 1890s as though they had happened yesterday. Many of these —followed by details of a rich career as one of Hollywood's foremost action directors—will be recounted in his forthcoming autobiography, *Each Man in His Time.*

"Life was good when I was a boy. I was born in New York but raised in different cities. My father was a clothing designer, but when I was a young feller I hated the life of the city. I ran away to sea. My Uncle Matt owned a sailing vessel. We were broke up in a hurricane so I went ashore in Mexico and joined a cattle drive across the Texas panhandle. I learned breakin' horses, mendin' fences, and went on to Montana, where I broke in more horses for the wagons. They had tough boss fellas in those days. Toughest guys in the whole wide world, in Butte."

This early experience forged Walsh's vision as a maker of action pictures later on. "I could twirl a lariat, jump through the loop, rope a steer with it. Raised longhorns, dirty-tempered crossbreeds, nothin' fancy like Herefords. You could sell a cow and a calf for sixteen dollars. I tried to get into the Spanish-American War, but I was only eleven years old in 1898 and they wouldn't have me. My first taste of battle was in 1911, when I was twenty-two. I'd gotten a job with D. W. Griffith in New York and he sent me down with a camera to ride with Pancho Villa in Mexico."

From Griffith, Walsh learned the need for rapid cutting in the telling of a story. "He chose me because I was a real rider —I'd have ridden in the Rough Riders with Teddy Roosevelt if I'd been old enough." Mary Walsh brings in afternoon tea and home-baked cake, and a rooster crows loudly outside the window. "I rode alongside Pancho all the way from Juarez to Mexico City. We paid him five hundred dollars a month and gold to let us film him. I was in direct line of fire. I damn near got the bullets through my hat. When Pancho would line up the Federals along a wall to shoot them, I'd say, 'I haven't got enough lights to photograph them. Bring them back a couple of hours from now.' So they'd take those poor sons of bitches out and bring 'em back and I'd photograph 'em as they died. And then Pancho Villa's men would run over to see if they had any gold in their teeth.

"Griffith liked the stuff I shot—unfortunately, it's all been lost—and they put me on directin' shorts and actin'. I'd done some stage actin' in San Antonio, when I was breakin' horses, and later I played Paul Revere in a Pathé short. So Griffith decided I could play some parts and he let me do John Wilkes Booth in *Birth of a Nation.* In the scene where Booth kills Lincoln, I had to jump twenty-odd feet from the railing of Lincoln's stage box to the stage. I hurt a leg I'd smashed before under a rollin' horse in my buckaroo days. When I limped off the stage I wasn't actin'. I went into the hospital. An Indian cowhand—Crazy Wolf—brought me a bunch of flowers; I found out later he'd stolen the whole damned bunch from the hospital garden."

After his days with Griffith, Walsh went to work with William Fox in the old Fort Lee, New Jersey, Fox Studios, directing Theda Bara movies, among others. He made picture after picture, using his knowledge of horses, ships, and men, gradually becoming known as a major director of masculine subjects. Douglas Fairbanks, Sr., recognizing his genius for fast-moving narrative, hired him to direct his Oriental fantasy, *The Thief of Bagdad,* in 1924.

Exactly fifty years later, Walsh remembered every detail of the picture's making. "Doug was the greatest all-around athlete I ever knew. He and I used to run and box and go to the steam room every day. He did all of his own stunts. He could climb a rope, hand over hand, sixty feet up a wall. The toughest stunt was the flyin' carpet. Doug stood on it, flying over Baghdad or some goddamned place. I was up on a huge crane, and the carpet was suspended with airplane wire. We swung him around a hundred feet off the ground. There was no net, and if he'd fallen he'd have smashed hisself to bits right down there on the hard cement."

Walsh's next big hit was *What Price Glory* (1926), with Victor McLaglen and Edmund Lowe, from the play by Maxwell Anderson and Laurence Stallings. The stage play may have been pacifist, but Walsh changed all that for the screen, as well as opening up the action into characteristically sweeping battle scenes. "The Army loved it. I always stood good with the Army after that. They had more recruits after that picture than they'd had since World War One. It showed the boys having fun, getting broads. Young fellers saw it, they said, 'Jesus, the Army is great.'

"Years later, when I was making *Battle Cry* at a Marine base in the Caribbean, a general came over to me and said, 'Son of a bitch, you got me into this Army.' He'd seen *What Price Glory* almost thirty years earlier.

"The only trouble came from lip-readers. It was a silent movie. Victor McLaglen would say to Edmund Lowe, silent, 'You great big, fat, son of a bitch,' but the title would say, 'How are you today?' Well, the lip-readers picked it up, and there was a hell of an explosion over it. But the result was everyone went back a second time to see if they could read the lips—and that helped to make the picture one of the biggest hits Fox ever had."

Walsh enjoyed making *Miss Sadie Thompson* (1928), with Gloria Swanson playing the part Jeanne Eagels made famous on the stage, and he also played her lover, a boisterous marine sergeant. He changed the intense dramatic tone of the play, concentrating on knockabout comedy and building up the life of the soldiers in the South Seas. Instead of exuding the famous white heat of Jeanne Eagels, Swanson played the role much more lightly.

Shortly after that, Walsh directed the first talkie Western, the vigorous *In Old Arizona,* with Warner Baxter as the Cisco Kid—and lost his right eye. "I got a Fox Movietone News wagon and took it up to Utah, shovin' out on a Sunday. Winnie Sheehan, the studio boss, liked the two-reeler I did about the Cisco Kid and turned it into a five-reeler. I was comin' back home with a drunken cowboy at the wheel of the car. Well, Christ, he was missin' burros, horses 'n' deer, everythin', and finally a jackrabbit jumped up clean through the windshield and damn near cut my eye out. When they took me into the doctor's office in Cedar City, I swear the goddamn nurse fainted. I was all covered in blood. I asked for a shot of brandy when the doc went in without any chloroform, and he said, 'We don't have any liquor in Utah.' "

Walsh created a revolution in talkies by taking the talkie equipment out-of-doors. "We did some good things in *In Old Arizona.* I put microphones out in the cactus, and the rocks. The first scene I took was a man fryin' bacon. Audiences went crazy—they could hear it sizzle."

Walsh went on to make more Westerns, including *The Big Trail,* which gave John Wayne his first big screen opportunity, as well as vivid urban pictures like *The Bowery* (1933), and comedies, musicals, and melodramas. He switched from Fox to Paramount to Warners, getting bigger financial offers each time. One of his favorite Warner stars was Humphrey Bogart, whom he guided through such classic actioners as *The Roaring Twenties, They Drive by Night,* and *High Sierra. High Sierra* was offered to Paul Muni, who refused to play it; as a result of his refusal, Jack Warner terminated his contract. George Raft was offered the role, but turned it down because he was superstitious: the last scene called for him to die. So Bogart took it, and scored one of his major triumphs.

Walsh also made a number of vivid action pictures with Errol Flynn. The tough, hard-drinking Australian was a man after his own heart. One of his favorite pictures with Flynn was *Gentleman Jim.* Walsh had known James J. Corbett, the boxer Flynn played, in New York at the beginning of the century. "Flynn went in and boxed with real professional men. No doubles, no punches pulled. Flynn could box with the best of 'em. He'd fought with his fellow Aussies, and they're tough bastards."

Walsh's most famous movie of the forties was *White Heat,* a savage study of a psychotic gangster, Cody Jarrett, played by James Cagney. "We used actual prisons for the picture," Walsh says, "and shot all over California, much the way we did in *High Sierra.* Cagney was a hell of an actor. In the picture he suffered from these blinding headaches. When he moaned in agony, you wanted to help the poor guy, even though you knew he was playing a scene."

Walsh continued to make action pictures until the sixties when he finally retired after making *A Distant Trumpet* in 1964. His remaining eye severely afflicted, he has seen almost no films since.

In retirement, he is having difficulty hanging on to his frontier existence. When he first moved into the Santa Susannas ten years ago, he could hear nothing but birds and crickets and frogs. Deer used to come down from the mountain slopes and nibble the grass in his backyard. But now the area is very built up, freeway traffic roars away below the house. Soon the coyotes that howl at night and the mountain lions that prowl close by will disappear, and the vanishing of this wildlife is an agony for the old Westerner.

"We still raise Herefords—we at least do that," Walsh growls, sitting proud and erect at the dining room table in his ten-gallon hat. "But this isn't really a country life anymore. Even this far out, it's Los Angeles." He scowls, looking glum for a moment.

As evening falls, Walsh visibly grows tired. Before I drive home through the mountains, I ask him what was his favorite experience with an actor. "It was a joke I played on Errol Flynn when Jack Barrymore died. He and Jack were the best friends in the world. Jack always used to sit in the same position on a couch in Flynn's house. I went down to the morgue where Jack was lyin'. An ex-actor I knew used to work at the morgue and I arranged with him to borrow Jack's body. I took it up to Flynn's house and sat it down where Jack always used to sit. I tried to put a drink in his hand but his fingers were too stiff, so I stuck a cigarette between the fingers.

"Well, Flynn came in and saw the body. He went green and drove off down the hill like a madman. And you know what happened when I took Jack back to the morgue? My pal the attendant said, 'If I'd known you was takin' Jack up to Errol Flynn's house, I'd have given him a better suit.'"

François Truffaut

After I conducted this interview, François Truffaut made *The Story of Adele H,* a delicate and fastidious study of the daughter of Victor Hugo, which contains one of the most evocative moments I've ever seen in a movie: the heroine's exploration of the virginal white vellum pages of the first edition of *Les Misérables.* In that moment, a vanished world was evoked: a world in which it was possible to take pleasure in cutting uncut pages, in which the arrival of a volume by a beloved author could still stir the heart and senses, a world in which the book was still the main source of information . . . before newspapers and television had taken hold.

It was Truffaut's pleasure in the arts that made meeting him so rare and enjoyable an experience. We talked in the Beverly Hills Hotel, with its motifs of banana leaves on the walls suggesting the late Carmen Miranda's imminent arrival in the lobby, the carpets the approximate color of seaweed, and the room service, in my opinion, the worst on earth. The suave publicist Rupert Allan acted as interpreter, since Truffaut did not speak English at all, and my French had grown rusty over the years. And we talked, not about Truffaut's own work, but about American films he liked. I liked them, and I liked him, too.

─────────★─────────

1974

François Truffaut is small and wiry. Casually dressed, he has an air of informal, relaxed self-assurance, not at all aggressive or imposing. Humorous dark eyes illuminate a bony, slightly equine face devoid of excess flesh. This is a man spare, wry, cool, like his films, almost all of which are notable for their casual detachment.

He has been in town promoting his movie *Day for Night,* a very French act of homage to picture making itself. It is the film of a movie buff which Truffaut still unabashedly is. He is, in fact, an object lesson for picture makers who proudly announce to the interviewer that they never see anybody else's films. He still undertakes long and complicated journeys to see pictures by obscure or unfashionable picture makers. He adores movies known only to the hardest-core buffs (Edgar G. Ulmer's *The Naked Dawn,* Leonard Kastle's *The Honeymoon Killers,* Joseph H. Lewis's *Gun Crazy*) and has a French passion for Monogram B pictures, shared with his close friend, Jean-Luc Godard.

At the mention of his idols, Hitchcock, Hawks, Kazan, his face lit up and, despite the presence of an interpreter, he frequently addressed me directly and excitedly in French, without waiting for me to hear the translation. At his suite at the Beverly Hills Hotel, looking out on sprays of eucalyptus and the glittering traffic of Sunset Boulevard, he said, "As a small child before World War Two, I didn't see any American films at all. During the Occupation, of course, we saw nothing. Then, at the end of the war, I saw Cukor's *The Philadelphia Story* with subtitles. I was surprised to find I had to read when I went to a film! But I was delighted with the movie at the age of thirteen. I felt that it captured a completely foreign world of great allure.

"I liked its modernity. From the beginning I was not interested in seeing American 'costume pictures.' I did not like Westerns, pirate films, I only wanted to see love stories and detective stories, and psychological thrillers, of which there were many in the late 1940s. I could identify myself with

312 ☆ Celebrity Circus

these, not with men on horseback or carrying a cutlass."

Who was the first American director to stimulate his imagination? "W. S. Van Dyke. It was a film of his with Ingrid Bergman and Robert Montgomery." *Rage in Heaven?* *"Absolument.* That was the film in which Robert Montgomery fakes his own suicide as murder, to pin the rap on his wife, Ingrid Bergman, and her lover, George Sanders, by impaling himself on a knife in a door, after putting Sanders's fingerprints on the knife." Discovering that I know the film, Truffaut yells with delight, gets up, wild with excitement, rushes to the door of the suite, flings it open, and fits an imaginary knife above one of the hinges. He throws himself on it and falls. "Oh, I like that film," he says, happy as a child, in English.

Immediately we have established a rapport: *Rage in Heaven* was also my favorite picture as a child. Said Truffaut: "As soon as I left the cinema, I wrote down the name W. S. Van Dyke in a notebook. I also loved Gregory Ratoff's *Adam Had Four Sons,* with Ingrid Bergman, in which she played a governess, and Bette Davis and Claude Rains in *Mr. Skeffington,* directed so beautifully by Vincent Sherman. And Curtiz's *Mildred Pierce,* with Joan Crawford.

"I loved those forties movies from Hollywood, with everything recreated in the studio, including lakes and forests, seas and sands, a whole world that could be controlled by the director. As late as July 1946, I saw the great *Citizen Kane.* Suddenly, at the age of thirteen, I realized that a film could be written as one might write a book. Of course, so many directors of my generation felt they could become directors because of *Citizen Kane.* Kubrick, Resnais, Frankenheimer, Lumet. It was a film not only of a *cinéaste,* but of a *cinéphile.* Not only a film of a maker of films, but of a lover of films. A few months later I saw *The Magnificent Ambersons,* which in many ways I preferred. I felt it was more sincere, more moving.

"I liked all of his later films except *The Trial,* which should only have had Jewish actors. Welles would have been a greater director if he had not been an actor. I think that doing two jobs diffused his talents."

Truffaut began writing articles for *Cahiers du Cinéma* in 1952, strongly promoting the films of Hitchcock and Hawks. He kept a file of all American directors, building 250 complete dossiers over a period from Lloyd Bacon to Fred Zinnemann, which he later presented to Henri Langlois of the Cinémathèque Française, in return for a permanent free pass after he got out of military service.

The greatest of his excitements at the time were the films of Hitchcock. "I began with *Notorious*," he says, "*Shadow of a Doubt* and *Spellbound*. I loved that moment in *Spellbound* when Leo G. Carroll shot himself at the end and the whole screen went red. Hitchcock came to Paris for the opening of *Rope* and I met him for an instant. I first met Chabrol at that same screening. Years later, I sat down with Hitchcock for a week, working eight hours a day, and made a book of it, an immense interview. He found the experience of reliving his entire life, even then almost seventy years, in the space of a week, terribly disturbing. He said to me, 'Because of you, I'm not sleeping very well.'

"My main remembrance of those early experiences of seeing Hitchcock was a sense of fear. Not just a feeling that the characters on the screen were so often afraid, but because I was afraid when I saw them. I saw them in the afternoon instead of going to school. I played hookey. Often I sneaked in through the exits without paying. So I sat there, terrified of being discovered. Not only were the people in Hitchcock's films filled with anxiety and fear, not only, as I found later, was Hitchcock filled with anxiety and fear—he was raised by Jesuits in the Catholic faith—but I was filled with terror and guilt also and identified utterly with his world.

"The effect of this degree of empathy was overwhelming. He's the only director I've identified with completely. I liked certain films of Curtiz, Wilder, Preminger, but they moved through a wide range, whereas Hitchcock remained obsessively within one style of approach. His is an amazing unity.

"I like Hawks for a different reason. Not because of his unity, but because of his versatility. He made the very best film in each of the categories he worked in. He made the best gangster film, *Scarface,* the best detective film, *The Big Sleep,* the best aviation war picture, *Air Force,* the best aviation in peacetime picture, *Only Angels Have Wings,* and the two best Westerns, *Red River* and *The Big Sky.* Above all, the best comedy, *Bringing Up Baby.*

"The difference between him and Hitchcock is that Hitch only likes movies, that Hitch's films are about movies. Hitch's *Rope* simply exists for the ten-minute take. *Rear Window* is the perfect film about movies. James Stewart plays a photographer who looks at five little 'films' when he looks at what people are doing in apartments across the way from his own. In *Spellbound* there's the film of a dream. Now Hawks loves life. He makes a film about aviation not to make a film on the subject, but because he loves aviation. He makes *Hatari,* about big game hunting in Africa, because he loves hunting big game. He also loves women and has given us the most developed, mature, intelligent women we have ever seen in American films. They are like Hemingway women. They equal men."

Does Truffaut feel that Hitchcock's characters are equally interesting? "Chiefly the supporting characters. Hitchcock has no sympathy for his leading men. He finds them insensitive, and given an unfair amount of luck. His sympathy is usually with the villain. In *Notorious,* he clearly was more seriously concerned with the villain, played by Claude Rains, than with the hero, played by Cary Grant."

And Hitchcock's women? Why this emphasis on cool blondes—Grace Kelly, Tippi Hedren, Joan Fontaine, Vera Miles, Kim Novak, Eva Marie Saint, and others? "Well, because Hitchcock doesn't like obvious sex. He feels that a cool woman can often suggest sex much better than someone like Marilyn Monroe, Brigitte Bardot, Jane Russell, who throw sex at you.

"To me, Hitchcock's most fascinating film of recent years has been *Marnie,* the story of a kleptomaniac. I much prefer it to *Frenzy. Marnie* was quite a failure, critically, and, I think, commercially. But it's a fascinating picture, with a strange feeling that suggests Hitchcock may have been deeply troubled when he made it. Deeply agitated. I don't know what the problem was, but it makes the film intensely interesting for me. It's technically imperfect, strange, unsettling . . ."

What other directors have fascinated Truffaut? "None nearly as much. Raoul Walsh made so many Westerns and period films that I cannot claim to have seen much, but I admire his thriller *White Heat* with James Cagney, and his excellent *Gentleman Jim,* with Errol Flynn. I very much liked *Uncertain Glory,* also with Flynn.

"Walsh's great strength is his command of film rhythm. Wellman is very interesting, also Curtiz, and I like Samuel Fuller. Fuller is extraordinary for getting the maximum out of fifteen-day shooting schedules and tiny budgets. Kazan is wonderfully sensitive in his pictures about youth. But deeply as I admire all these men, and such unknowns as Lewis and Ulmer and Kastle, my most complete obsession is with Hitchcock, maybe Hawks, but chiefly Hitchcock at all times.

"And American films have influenced me. Ulmer's *The Naked Dawn* was a story of two nice men in love with the same woman, and I based much of the idea of *Jules et Jim* on that idea: the 'other man' in films had always been the villain, and Ulmer changed that. Also, my new picture *Day for Night,* was inspired by Stanley Donen's and Gene Kelly's musical about the early days of talkies, *Singin' in the Rain.* That was about the making of movies, and I like to make movies about movies.

"I hate to look into the future. Instead, I like to look always into the past, to go on learning from the great American directors that craft I have to tackle afresh every day. I renew myself at the fountain of the past. I go back, and see *Notorious* again, and I have courage and joy in going on. In going *forward.*"

Orson Welles

My feud with Orson Welles is still going on after eight years. He hated the idea of my writing a book* about him.

He is constantly telling interviewers that he offered to read the manuscript and that I could print his comments in the book itself. He made no such offer. Had he done so, I would certainly not have ruined the book by presenting his own doctored version of the facts.

It is significant that the "authorized biography" which he was planning with Peter Bogdanovich never appeared. It was supposed to sweep my book off the map. Bogdanovich went to the extent of circularizing every literary editor in England with a notice in advance of my British publication that my book was not to be taken seriously and in fact shouldn't be reviewed at all! The feud continued for years. In 1976, I decided to write an article on the making of *The Other Side of the Wind,* Welles's movie about an expatriate director who returns to Hollywood after a long exile. Bogdanovich got word of the piece from friends at *The Times* and immediately told Welles. One day before press day, Welles called my editor Bill Honen (who had succeeded Seymour Peck) and told him that he was terrified of the article being published and could it be withdrawn? Mr. Honen told him that it could not. Welles then said that his career was over, that I was destroying him, and hung up. He called back a few minutes later to ask if he could make a

* *The Films of Orson Welles* (Berkeley: University of California Press, 1970).

statement on the film which would be run in a special box next to mine. He was told the only way he could be heard was if it would seem that I had interviewed him, his comments to be incorporated in the body of my piece.

Welles said he would not be part of any article I wrote, and hung up again. Five minutes later, he called back, groaned, and said that if the only way he could be heard was by including his comments along with mine, he would have to agree. His comments were incorporated into the article. Thus, the article became the only one I have written which included an interview with someone I hadn't interviewed! And he's still grumbling!

——————★——————

1976

"It was an extraordinary experience being in the desert with Orson," recalls actress Susan Strasberg. "It was like being adrift with a Great White Whale. He would stand there, in a great flowing white caftan, roaring at everyone. Once, when the cameraman set up the lights and asked him what he wanted, he said, 'You idiot! Can't you see I haven't the vaguest idea of what I want?' "

For the past six and a half years, Orson Welles, the man who gave us *Citizen Kane*—arguably the greatest American movie—has been roaring, in the sands of Arizona and in some of the more remote regions of Hollywood, trying in his inimitable fashion to wind up a movie called *The Other Side of the Wind*. According to Welles himself, "the principal photography" is now completed and continued delay is brought about only because his investors are withholding the funds necessary to underwrite the cost of "a few retakes and the editing." But others have their doubts about that explanation.

What is this epic all about and why should it be so many years in the making? The first question is perhaps the easier one to answer. *The Other Side of the Wind*—financed by Iranian, French, and German money and shot in secrecy by a nonunion crew headed by cameraman Gary Graver, who had previously photographed mostly pornography—centers on an eccentric movie director named Jake Hannaford, a ferociously macho cross between Ernest Hemingway and John Ford. Hannaford, played by John Huston, returns from a lengthy European exile to make a Hollywood movie which will show that he can be as relentlessly hip as anyone else in town. Director Hannaford is himself gradually exposed as a repressed homosexual whose inability to express himself sexually, coupled with his failure to cope with contemporary Hollywood, drives him to a highly theatrical suicide.

Welles becomes somewhat evasive when asked to discuss the significance of this story or the theme of the picture, but says, "It is, we hope, a biggie. It's the result of many years of thinking about many things. It also has some superb performances in it. John Huston gives one of the best performances I've ever seen on the screen. When I get to the Heavenly Gates, if I'm allowed in, it will be because I cast the best part I ever could have played myself with John Huston. He's better than I would have been—and I would have been great!"

Huston, along with other members of the cast of *The Other Side of the Wind,* has been extraordinarily game, having spent weeks in such unlikely locations as Carefree, Arizona, going slowly but cheerfully mad under the pressure the director imposes on them. Mercedes McCambridge, remembered for her vivid performance as the sadistic leader of a band of motorcyclists in Welles's *Touch of Evil,* plays Hannaford's secretary.

Norman Foster, codirector with Welles of *Journey Into Fear* and the unfinished *My Friend Bonito,* plays Hannaford's stooge. Peter Bogdanovich, a Welles protégé in real life, plays a director who does imitations. Lilli Palmer, replacing Marlene Dietrich, is a society hostess and Susan Strasberg, replacing Jeanne Moreau, plays a character said to be patterned after critic Pauline Kael, and directors Paul Mazursky and Curtis Harrington appear as themselves.

Because of Welles's fanatical secrecy little has been written about *The Other Side of the Wind,* not even the fact that nightclub star Rich Little has been replaced in the cast by Peter Bogdanovich, who had originally essayed the part of a nosy reporter named Higgam. But the following account of Little's withdrawal has been furnished by a reliable source. During the shooting of one scene, Mr. Little, Mercedes McCambridge, and Norman Foster were told to teeter atop a tall building in Phoenix, Arizona. Little called down to Welles: "Orson, why are we swaying?"

"Because midgets have hold of your legs!" Welles yelled back.

"But there are no midgets up here!" Little replied.

"I'm going to shoot the midgets in Spain!" Welles screamed. Rich Little left the picture at once.

Some of the people with whom Welles has come into conflict over the years may suffer a twinge of recognition when they see *The Other Side of the Wind.* The film is said to contain something of a slap at Robert Evans, former head of Paramount, who refused to distribute Welles's earlier film, *F for Fake.* In a scene which takes place in a studio projection room, Hannaford's stooge is showing the director's film to a movie mogul (bearing a not very flattering resemblance to Evans) who flatly refuses to buy the film for distribution.

How does the real Robert Evans react to the idea of having an actor impersonate him? "I wish I had him playing me in my office," says Evans. "He could handle some of my problems."

As both the plot and dialogue have kept changing almost continually since 1970, some of the performers have had to cancel other assignments to rush to some distant spot to complete a sequence begun several years earlier. "Orson's like a painter," says Susan Strasberg. "He's creating on film. That's why he takes years. He can't create on somebody else's schedule."

She goes on: "There was a scene with a bus. At one point, the cameraman inside the moving bus could not avoid photographing a large red sign with a cross on it which loomed up. Somebody said, 'Let's cut that sign out, it doesn't fit into the story.' And Orson said, 'No, no, leave it in the shot. Pauline

Kael will write paragraphs about the symbolism of that red cross!'

"We were all in a cramped five-room house in Carefree for twelve hours and more at a stretch, with Orson yelling 'Quiet!' The people who drank turned to drink, and those of us who were compulsive talkers and were not allowed to talk turned to food. Bogdanovich was terrified of Orson. He brought an entire expensive wardrobe to play the part of the director and came out with one beautiful cashmere sweater after the other. Orson kept saying, 'My God! That's not what a successful young director would wear.' Peter said, 'But these are my own clothes!' And Orson said, 'That's just what I mean!' "

But, of course, the annals of moviemaking are filled with tales of extravagant temper tantrums and the stories one hears about Welles, even the unmistakably apocryphal ones, cannot explain six and a half years of delay. Accordingly, one looks for other explanations.

The actress Jeanne Moreau says she thinks Welles is inhibited by a "fear of completion." She believes he is compulsively postponing the day when he will have to face the verdict of critics. Miss Moreau has at least some basis for judgment since she acted opposite Welles in another of his unfinished films, *The Deep*. "Years ago," she says, "he promised to send me air tickets to come from Paris to Rome to dub it. He never did. He is obviously scared to let it out. I still haven't done the [sound] track!"

There are at least a couple of other films which Welles left unfinished. He ran out on *The Magnificent Ambersons* to fly to Rio to start shooting the carnival for *It's All True.* And then there's the case of *Don Quixote*, begun in 1955 with the Mexican star Francisco Reiguera as Don Quixote, Akim Tamiroff as Sancho Panza, and Patty Duke as an American girl of about twelve. Today, with the film still unfinished, the two male stars are dead and Miss Duke is well past her teens.

Welles has even admitted his hatred of finished movies in numerous interviews. He once hid his face on the Dick Cavett show when a scene from one of his films was projected on a screen. Years ago, he also told a reporter for *Sight and Sound* he could not face up to seeing any of his movies because there was so much he wanted to change.

Is the present delay with *The Other Side of the Wind* another illustration of a tragically self-destructive genius? Welles, himself, of course, heatedly—and eloquently—denounces the notion on the telephone from Los Angeles.

"Everywhere I go," he explains, "I have to pass an examination about the Welles legend. People—especially film producers—don't want to be associated with messy things. I tell them—and this is hard for people to understand—that the making of a motion picture is a very private affair until it is made public. Why should I have to answer all of these questions? I haven't committed a crime. I'm just a poor slob who's trying to make pictures.

"Nevertheless," he continues, "I can defend myself perfectly well. In the case of *The Magnificent Ambersons,* I didn't leave the film. I was asked. World War Two had broken out and I was entreated by Nelson Rockefeller, who was then head of the Office of the Coordinator of Inter-American Affairs, to make a documentary about the carnival in Rio, for no pay, because it would help in solidifying the unity of the Americans. *The Magnificent Ambersons* was completely shot at the time. And so I agreed to go to South America then on the condition that I would return if there should be any problem with the editing of the film. But RKO never lived up to the agreement. One bad preview of the film convinced RKO to ignore me.

"As for *The Deep,*" he continued, "well, I'd prefer to let everybody speculate about *The Deep.*" A few minutes later Welles added: "You have to understand this about *The Deep.* The picture has no date. There's no reason to release it. The holdup is entirely financial. The fact of the matter is the picture is five minutes short and so we need a prologue. And I need a hundred and fifty Gs or so to make that." A few minutes later Welles called back: "There are two things I should add about *The Deep.* First, the [investment] money was all mine, although there was a private investor who has been paid back by now. Second, *The Deep* has been delayed because it is really just a frivolous piece of light entertainment. I haven't had a film on the screen for a long while and did not want to return to the screen with a trivial little thing like that. I want to make my return with *The Other Side of the Wind.*"*

And what is really holding up his current film? "It's purely financial. There's no question of the creative process involved here. If I would consent to the producer system, I could have been working steadily all of these years. I only made a film that way once, and it wasn't all that unhappy an experience. But I learned that perfect independence is what lights a candle in me. When I was talked into going to South America, that was what started these difficulties. I couldn't get a job for five years. Then I began to earn some money as an actor and used that to finance my own pictures. About the time of *The Deep* the ax fell from Washington. They said I couldn't use the money I'd earned as an actor to produce my own films. I was effectively put out of business as a producer. And so, today I don't own *The Other Side of the Wind* and can't control it. At my time in life, I can no longer run my own store and am at the mercy of whatever credit I can raise. I need more money to finish this film. It's as simple as that.

"In the last couple of weeks, however, the light is breaking through. I can't discuss the details because that would rock the boat. But I feel confident that the film will be released. And then—ah, then!—I finally wrote a script for a small movie which I can make the minute this one is finished."

*As of 1978, he has not.